Investment Decision Making in the Private and Public Sectors

Investment Decision Making in the Private and Public Sectors

Henri L. Beenhakker

Q

QUORUM BOOKS
Westport, Connecticut • London

Library of Congress Cataloging-in-Publication Data

Beenhakker, Henri L.
    Investment decision making in the private and public sectors /
Henri L. Beenhakker.
        p. cm.
    Includes bibliographical references and index.
    ISBN 1–56720–028–1 (alk. paper)
    1. Capital investments—Decision making.   2. Investments—Decision
making.   3. Investment of public funds—Decision making.   I. Title.
HG4028.C4B415   1996
658.15'54—dc20   96–913

British Library Cataloguing in Publication Data is available.

Library of Congress Catalog Card Number: 96–913
ISBN: 1–56720–028–1

First published in 1996

Quorum Books, 88 Post Road West, Westport, CT 06881
An imprint of Greenwood Publishing Group, Inc.

Printed in the United States of America

The paper used in this book complies with the
Permanent Paper Standard issued by the National
Information Standards Organization (Z39.48–1984).

10 9 8 7 6 5 4 3 2 1

In Memory of George H. Brooks
Teacher, Colleague, and Friend

Contents

Tables and Figures

FIGURES

Preface

The modern analysis of investment decisions draws from a wide range of sources such as economics, finance, accounting, engineering economy, statistics, and operations research. This book comprehensively describes the multifaceted approach to investment planning which involves the interactions among various disciplines. It is self-contained since no prior knowledge of these disciplines is assumed.

An author who is writing in the area of investment analysis must make a decision about the use of mathematics. If the level of mathematical sophistication is too high, the text is likely to be inaccessible to many students and practitioners. If it is too low, some important issues will inevitably be treated in a rather superficial way. In this book, great care has been taken in the use of mathematics. Emphasizing the general nature and proper use of mathematics as decision-making tools, the text is written for use by business managers and investment analysts who lack a sophisticated mathematical background. For non-essential mathematical material, the reader is referred to end-of-chapter references. These references are also given for supplementary reading on specific topics rather than required reading.

The book should be of particular interest to professionals who have the responsibility for investing money in new ventures. Concepts that are likely to be new to many readers have been explained carefully, and many numerical examples have been included. The book can, therefore, also be used as a text in business schools and departments of economics or industrial engineering. It is particularly recommended for those educators who wish to bridge the gap between the worlds of practice and education, and enhance the connection between what a student learns in school and what he or she will need to solve problems experienced by real managers.

Each chapter is arranged so as to permit rapid review of an entire investment subject. Special attention has been given to the interrelationships of topics by means of suitable introductions and cross references. It is also worth noting that the chapters may be read in a different sequence from their order in the book since they are written in a modular, self-contained manner.

Unless otherwise specified, the discussions apply equally to private and public investment analyses. The development of a unified theory of investment decision making, which has been my major concern, calls for the identification of similarities and dissimilarities in the approaches followed by private and public investment planners. Both planners will enhance their understanding of fundamental relationships if they have an appreciation of each other's concept. The end result enables the business manager to deal intelligently with government contracts and public planners to incorporate to the maximum extent possible the views of private industry in their decision-making process. This approach is important in view of today's movement toward globalization of new ventures and financial markets and institutions. Even if a corporation operates only domestically, international events influence domestic interest rates and economic activity, so we are well advised to think globally about many decisions.

Special care has been taken to point out the assumptions underlying certain developments. Managers are continually faced with the tradeoff between elaborate models, on the one hand, and cursory approximations, based on implied assumptions, on the other. Whenever possible, the text presents both approaches and gives guidance for solving the dilemma. For instance, the heuristic procedure of Chapter 7 is relatively simple and sufficiently accurate for the many decision makers dealing with capital rationing and who say "give us a means of selecting projects which we can digest; it does not matter if small errors are entailed." Other techniques, such as integer programming and dynamic programming, are available for capital rationing; however, they are much more elaborate and mathematically complex, and are therefore not presented in this text. It is also noted that often there is a better method of handling the types of situations that give rise to capital rationing (that is, increasing the cost of capital).

Incomplete data pertinent to the evaluation of an investment proposal is no justification for abandoning a rational approach. Approximations and guesses of orders of magnitude frequently have to be made in real-world problems. It is important, however, to determine what is being approximated to so that errors of judgment are not compounded by subsequent errors of assessment.

The students in my course on private and public investment decision making at Johns Hopkins University have made many useful suggestions to improve the book from a student's perspective. I am also most grateful for the comments on an earlier version of this text that I received from teachers and private and public investment planners. In particular, I wish to thank Myrian Gardon and Britta Beenhakker for preparing the tables and improving the first draft of the text, and Jaroslava Miler for the graphics work. Last, but not least, I would like to thank my family. They have been unfailingly supportive and very understanding of the inevitable disruptions to family life caused by a project such as this. I hope and believe that this book will enable the reader to utilize the rich resources that are available in order to achieve optimal investment decisions.

Henri L. Beenhakker

CHAPTER 1

Financial Statements and Ratios

Read carefully anything that requires your signature. Remember the big print giveth and the small print taketh away.

—Jackson Brown

An understanding of basic accounting principles enhances the appraisal of investment. Such an understanding is particularly desirable for determining a company's cost of capital. This chapter summarizes the basic accounting principles. In addition, it explains financial ratios used to assess a firm's credit worthiness. Naturally, this chapter is not intended to replace a basic accounting textbook.

Accountants, like all other professionals, have developed a specialized vocabulary which is sometimes helpful, but sometimes also confusing. One example of this confusion is the labeling of the income account as a "Profit and Loss Statement," when it is bound to be one or the other. Therefore, we have to learn the basic technical terms.

In principle, accountants record systematically all the monetary transactions of business. Published accounting documents may be classified as a statement of assets and liabilities and a statement about net earnings.

1. ANNUAL REPORTS

Corporations issue annual reports to their shareholders. These reports give two types of information: that is, a verbal section and basic financial statements. The verbal section is often presented as a letter from the president and discusses the company's operating results during the last year. In addition, it describes the new developments which will affect future operations. The basic financial statements consist of the balance sheet, the income statement, the retained earnings statement, and the cash flow statement. These statements present an accounting picture of the corporation's operations and financial position.

Corporations often include in their annual reports balance sheets and income statements pertaining to the two most recent years. They also may provide quarterly reports; however, these reports are less comprehensive than the annual reports. In addition, large companies in the United States file even more detailed statements with the Securities and Exchange Commission (SEC). These reports are called 10-K reports, and give breakdowns for each major division or subsidiary. They are available to stockholders upon request to a firm's secretary. Finally, larger companies may also publish statistical supplements, which give financial data and key ratios for the last 10 to 20 years.

Investors use the information contained in an annual report to form expectations about future earnings and dividends and about the risks related to these expectations. Before making an investment decision, they should compare management's past statements to subsequent results.

When an annual report contains financial statements which have the stamp of approval from independent public accountants, you have a reasonable assurance that the figures presented in these statements can be relied upon as having been fairly presented. The certificate from the accountants which is printed in the annual report says: (1) the auditing steps taken in the process of verification of the accounts were in accordance with approved practice, and (2) the financial statements in the report have been prepared in conformity with generally accepted accounting principles. In the United States, the American Institute of Certified Public Accountants is responsible for adopting auditing procedures and broad policy concerning acceptable accounting principles.

The annual reports of many firms contain this statement: "The accompanying footnotes are an integral part of the financial statements." The reason is that the financial reports themselves are kept concise and condensed. Therefore, any explanatory matter which cannot readily be abbreviated is set out in greater detail in footnotes. Most people do not like to read footnotes because they may be complicated and they are almost always printed in small, hard-to-read type. Nevertheless, it is well worth the effort, because a careful reading of the footnotes in conjunction with the statements gives greater meaning to the financial story of the corporation.

2. BALANCE SHEETS

The statement of assets and liabilities is known as a balance sheet. Table 1.1 presents a skeleton balance sheet for a typical manufacturing establishment, which we call company *XYZ*. As shown in Table 1.1, the balance sheet represents the final picture of the company on December 31, 19__. It is divided into two sides—the assets on the left and the liabilities and stockholders' equity on the right. Both sides are always in balance. The assets column presents all the

Table 1.1
Abbreviated Balance Sheet of Company *XYZ* (December 31, 19___)

ASSETS		LIABILITIES AND STOCKHOLDERS' EQUITY	
Current Assets		Current Liabilities	
Total Current Assets	$7,000,000	Total Current Liabilities	$3,000,000
Investment in Unconsolidated		Long-Term Liabilities	3,500,000
Subsidiaries	400,000	Total Liabilities	$6,500,000
Property, Plant and			
Equipment		STOCKHOLDERS' EQUITY	
Net Property, Plant and		Capital Stock:	
Equipment	4,000,000	Preferred Stock	
Prepayments and Deferred		Common Stock	
Charges	100,000	Capital Surplus	
Good Will, Patents,		Accumulated Retained	
Trademarks	200,000	Earnings	
		Total Stockholders'	
		Equity	5,200,000
		Total Liabilities and	
Total Assets	$11,700,000	Stockholders' Equity	$11,700,000

goods and property owned together with claims against others yet to be collected. The liabilities and stockholders' equity column shows (under liabilities) all the debts due or the creditors' claims against the assets. The same column presents (under stockholders' equity) the amount of the stockholders' interest in the company or the amount for which the company is accountable to its stockholders. If company *XYZ* were to go out of business as of the date of the balance sheet of Table 1.1, and if, for instance, the assets when sold would bring dollar for dollar the amounts shown in this table, then the amount remaining for stockholders would be $11,700,000 − $6,500,000 = $5,200,000.

Table 1.2 is the balance sheet for the same company, but gives more detailed information. Let us examine each of the items of Table 1.2. The first one, current assets, represents cash and those assets which in the normal course of business will be turned into cash in the reasonable near future, say, one year from the date of the balance sheet.

Cash consists of bills, petty cash fund, and money on deposit in the bank. Marketable securities represent temporary investments of excess cash which are not needed immediately. Such funds may be needed on short notice; it is, therefore, important that these securities be readily marketable and be subject to a minimum of price fluctuations. The excess cash is normally invested in stocks, bonds, and government securities for the purpose of earning dividends and interest. The general practice is to show marketable securities at cost, with a parenthetic note of the market value.

Accounts receivable represent the amounts not yet collected from customers to whom goods were shipped prior to payment. Generally, some customers fail

Table 1.2
Balance Sheet of Company XYZ (December 31, 19___)

ASSETS			
Current Assets			
Cash			$ 990,000
Marketable Securities at Cost (Market Value 1,650,000)			1,610,000
Accounts Receivable		$2,100,000	
Less: Provision for Bad Debts		100,000	2,000,000
Inventories			2,400,000
TOTAL CURRENT ASSETS			$ 7,000,000
Investment in Unconsolidated Subsidiaries			400,000
Property, Plan and Equipment			
Land	$ 200,000		
Buildings	3,200,000		
Machinery	950,000		
Office Equipment	150,000		
	$4,500,000		
Less: Accumulated Depreciation	500,000		
NET PROPERTY, PLANT AND EQUIPMENT			4,000,000
Prepayments and Deferred Charges			100,000
Good Will, Patents, Trademarks			200,000
TOTAL ASSETS			$11,700,000

LIABILITIES AND STOCKHOLDERS' EQUITY		
Current Liabilities		
Accounts Payable	$1,500,000	
Notes Payable	840,000	
Accrued Expenses Payable	340,000	
Federal Income Tax Payable	320,000	
Total Current Liabilities		$3,000,000
Long-Term Liabilities		
Mortgage Bonds, 7% Interest Due 2005		3,500,000
TOTAL LIABILITIES		$6,500,000
STOCKHOLDERS' EQUITY		
Capital Stock		
Preferred Stock, 5% Cumulative $100 Par Value Each; Authorized, Issued, and Outstanding 9,000 Shares		$ 900,000
Common Stock, $5 Par Value Each; Authorized, Issued and Outstanding 300,000 Shares		1,500,000
Capital Surplus		800,000
Accumulated Retained Earnings		2,000,000
TOTAL STOCKHOLDERS' EQUITY		5,200,000
TOTAL LIABILITIES AND STOCKHOLDERS' EQUITY		$11,700,000

to pay their bills. The total of accounts receivable is reduced by a provision for bad debts in order to show the amount that most likely will be collected.

Inventories of a manufacturer normally comprise raw materials, partially finished goods in process of manufacture, and finished goods ready for shipment to customers. Cost for purposes on inventory valuation generally includes an allocation of production and other expenses as well as the cost of materials.

Total current assets comprise the aforementioned cash, marketable securities, accounts receivable, and inventories. Inventories, when sold, become accounts receivable; receivables, upon collection, become cash; cash is used to pay debts and running expenses.

Investment in unconsolidated subsidiaries represents the cost to our parent company, Company *XYZ*, of the capital stock of another company. The word "subsidiary" indicates that more than 50% of the subsidiary's outstanding capital stock is owned by the parent company.

Property, plant, and equipment, sometimes referred to as fixed assets, represent those assets not intended for sale but for the manufacture of products and their display, warehousing, and transportation. The generally accepted and approved method for valuation is cost less total depreciation written off to date.

Prepayments represent payments made in advance from which the company has not yet received the full benefits but for which it will receive benefits in the next accounting years (such as fire insurance premiums covering a three-year period). Deferred charges represent expenditures from which the benefits will be reaped over several years to come (such as research and development expenditures).

Good will, patents, trademarks, and licensing agreements are assets with no physical existence. However, they may represent a substantial value to the company.

The first item on the liability side of the balance sheet of Table 1.2 is current liabilities, which generally include all debts that fall due within the coming year.

Accounts payable represent the amounts that Company *XYZ* owes to its regular business creditors from whom it has bought goods on open account. If the money is owed to a bank or other lender, it appears on the balance sheet under notes payable, as evidence of the fact that a written promissory note has been given by the borrower.

Accrued expenses payable represent expenses such as interest on funds borrowed from banks and from bondholders, fees to attorneys, insurance premiums, pensions, salaries, and wages to its employees, which have not yet been paid at the date of the balance sheet. The debt due to the Internal Revenue Service is the same type of liability. However, it is generally stated separately as federal income tax payable.

Long-term liabilities represent debts due after one year from the date of the financial report (current liabilities generally include debts due within approximately one year from the date of the balance sheet). In Table 1.2, the 5% mortgage bonds represent the long-term liability. Another example of a long-term liability would be a loan due after one year from the date of the balance sheet.

Stockholders' equity, sometimes called net worth, is the total equity that the stockholders have in Company *XYZ*. Capital stock represents shares in the proprietary interest in the company. These shares are evidenced by stock certificates issued by the company to the shareholders.

Preferred stock means that these shares have some preference over other shares as regards dividends or in the distribution of assets in case of liquidation, or both. The specific provisions are described in the corporation's charter. The designation "5% cumulative, $100.00 per value each" means that each share is entitled to $5.00 dividends per year when declared by the board of directors before any dividends are paid to the common stockholders. The word "cumulative" means that if in any year the dividend is not paid, it accumulates in favor of the preferred stockholders and must be paid to them when available and declared before any dividends are distributed on the common stock. However, $5.00 per share may be all the holders of preferred stock will receive annually. Common stock, on the other hand, has no such limit on dividends payable each year.

Capital surplus is the amount paid in by shareholders over the par or legal value of each share. In the example of Table 1.2, Company *XYZ* sold 300,000 shares of common stock for a total of $2,300,000, although the common stock has a $5.00 par value for each share.

Accumulated retained earnings constitute the surplus which is accumulated from profits. Thus, these earnings are the profits accumulated over the years less the total of the dividends paid out during these years.

The balance sheet establishes the amount of the net current assets (sometimes called net working capital) or the difference between the total current assets and the total current liabilities. As mentioned earlier, current liabilities are the debts due within one year from the date of the balance sheet. Current assets constitute the source from which to pay these debts. Thus, net current assets represent the total amount that would be available if all current debts were paid off ($4,000,000 in the example of Table 1.2).

3. INCOME AND RETAINED EARNINGS STATEMENTS

The income statement shows the net earnings arising during a year and the manner in which it is divided up between the debenture holders and any other suppliers of long-term loans, different classes of shareholders, and the tax authorities. Some companies refer to this statement as the earnings report or the profit and loss statement.

While the balance sheet shows the fundamental soundness of a company by reflecting its financial position at a given date, the income statement shows the record of its operating activities for the entire year. Thus, the latter statement serves as a valuable guide in anticipating how a company may perform in the future. It records the changes in wealth during a year due to the interaction of costs and revenues. Consequently, it assists in the explanation of changes between balance sheets. However, the income statement does not explain changes in wealth which are of a capital nature. For instance, if a company uses its cash to buy machines or repay debts, or raises more capital, none of these items affects its costs or revenues; hence they would only be shown on the balance sheet. When cash is used to buy machines, then the amount of cash will decrease by the amount by which the value of the total fixed assets will increase. When cash is used to repay creditors, then both assets and liabilities are reduced by the same amount. If the company raises more capital, then the liabilities side of the balance sheet will increase, and will be counterbalanced by the same increase of cash on the asset side.

An example of an activity affecting the income statement is the writing off of fixed assets. Suppose an asset costing $2,000 is depreciated by 10% in a given year. This $200 of depreciation appears in the income statement as a cost and reduces the profit accordingly. This activity also affects the balance sheet— the values of fixed assets and retained earnings are both reduced by $200.

The upper and lower parts of Table 1.3 show the condensed and detailed income statements for Company *XYZ*, respectively. Both of these parts show that the statements match the amounts received from selling the goods and other items of income, on the one hand, against all the costs and outlays incurred in order to operate the company, on the other hand. The result is a net profit (or net loss) for the year.

The costs incurred usually consist of costs of the goods sold and supplies, wages, salaries, rent, depreciation, overhead expenses, interest on money borrowed, and taxes. The first item of the income statement is always the most important source of revenue. In our example, it is net sales, since Company *XYZ* is assumed to be a manufacturing company. If it were a utility or railroad, this item would be called operating revenues.

A secondary source of revenue, referred to as "other income" in Table 1.3 (sometimes called miscellaneous income), stems from dividends and interests received by the company from its interests in stocks and bonds (which are carried as assets in the balance sheet).

Cost of sales and operating expenses comprise cost of goods sold, depreciation, and selling and administrative expenses. Cost of goods sold include (in a manufacturing establishment) costs of raw materials, direct labor, overhead such as supervision, rent, electricity, supplies, maintenance, and repairs. Depreciation is the decline in useful value of an asset due to wear and tear. Each year's decline in value is a cost to be borne as an expense. Selling expenses include salespersons' salaries and commissions, advertising and promotion, travel, and entertainment. Administrative expenses comprise executive salaries, office payroll, office expenses, and the like.

The interest paid to bondholders for the use of their money (sometimes called fixed charge) differs from dividends on stocks in that the former item must be

Table 1.3
Income Statements of Company XYZ

Condensed Income Statement of Company XYZ, Year 19-

Plus Factors		
Net Sales	$7,150,000	
Other Income	150,000	
Total		$7,300,000
Minus Factors		
Costs of Sales and Operating Expenses	$6,395,000	
Interest on Bonds	245,000	
Provision for Federal Income Tax	310,000	6,950,000
Net Income		$ 350,000

Income Statement of Company XYZ, Year 19-

Net Sales		$7,150,000
Cost of Sales and Operating Expenses		
Cost of Goods Sold	$4,895,000	
Depreciation	900,000	
Selling and Administrative Expenses	600,000	6,395,000
Operating Profit		755,000
Other Income		
Dividends and Interest		150,000
Total Income		$ 905,000
Less: Interest on Bonds		245,000
Profit before Provision for Federal Income Tax		$ 660,000
Provision for Federal Income Tax		310,000
Net Profit for the Year		$ 350,000

paid year after year whether the company is making or losing money, while the latter item is payable only if the board of directors at a meeting declares the dividends to be paid. Company XYZ carries on the balance sheet mortgage bonds which bear 7% interest on $3,500,000 (see Table 1.2). Thus, the interest on bonds in the income statement is equal to $245,000.

Company XYZ's income before taxes is $660,000. Assuming tax rates of 22% on the first $25,000 of income and 48% on the income in excess of $25,000 results in a tax of $310,000 (rounded off). Therefore, the after-tax net income is $350,000.

The net profit or net income is the amount arrived at after we have taken into consideration all income or plus factors and deduct from these all costs and expenses or minus factors (see Table 1.3). Net profit is the amount available to pay dividends on the preferred and common stocks and to use in the business.

Table 1.4
Statement of Retained Earnings of Company _XYZ_, Year 1997

Balance of Retained Earnings, December 31, 1996		$2,000,000
Add: Net Profit for the Year 1997		350,000
Total		$2,350,000
Less: Dividends Paid		
On Preferred Stock	$ 30,000	
On Common Stock	120,000	150,000
Balance of Retained Earnings, December 31, 1997		$2,200,000

To the extent that dividends declared by the board of directors are less than the net profit, the excess is plowed back into the company and is reflected in the accumulated retained earnings.

In conclusion, the income statement indicates whether a company is earning money on its investment while the balance sheet reveals information about a company's stability and soundness of structure. Naturally, figures given for a single year are not sufficient; the historical record for a series of years should always be considered.

The retained earnings statement presents changes in the common equity accounts between two subsequent, most recent balance sheets. For purposes of presentation, assume that the accumulated retained earnings of Company _XYZ_ presented in Table 1.2 ($2,000,000) pertain to the year 1996, and that the net profit of Table 1.3 ($350,000) is the company's net profit for the year 1997. In addition, the company will pay $30,000 in dividends on preferred stock and $120,000 on common stock. The retained earnings for the year ending December 31, 1997 are given in Table 1.4.

4. CASH FLOW STATEMENTS

A company's net income as reported in the income statement is important; however, cash flows are even more important because cash is needed to purchase the assets required to continue operations and to pay dividends. In addition, the value of a company is determined by the cash flows it generates. A firm's cash flows are generally equal to cash from sales minus operating costs, interest charges, and taxes. A manager's goal should be to maximize cash flows in the long run in order to maximize the price of a share of stock of his or her firm.

As we mentioned before, depreciation is the decline in useful value of an asset due to wear and tear. It is an annual charge against income in the income statement and reflects the estimated cost of the capital equipment used up in the production process. However, depreciation is not a cash outlay such as labor or raw materials; it is a non-cash charge and, therefore, should be added back to

Table 1.5
Simplified Income Statement and Cash Flows

	Income Statement	Cash Flows	
Sales Revenues	$2,000	$2,000	
Costs Except Depreciation	1,400	1,400	
Depreciation	300	-	
Total Costs	$1,700	$1,400	(cash costs)
Earnings Before Taxes	$ 300	$ 600	(pretax cash flow)
Taxes (40%)	120	120	(from left column)
Net Income	$ 180		
Add Back Depreciation	300		
Net Cash Flow	$ 480	$ 480	(net income + depreciation)

net income to obtain an estimate of the cash flow from operations. The simplified income statement and cash flows (in thousands of dollars) of Table 1.5 show the impact of depreciation on cash flows. In the example, all sales revenues are received in cash, and all costs except depreciation are paid in cash during the year.

Cash flows are generally related to net income reported on the income statement. In general, a company with a high net income also has a high net cash flow; however, the relationship is not precise. Investors should, therefore, be concerned with both. The consideration of cash flows is also important since they are often the primary source of funds to make new investments.

Cash flows may be divided into two types: operating cash flows and non-operating cash flows. The former are those that arise from normal operations and are, in essence, the difference between sales revenues and cash expenses (including taxes paid). The latter arise from borrowing, from the issuance of stock, or from the sale of fixed assets. Although both types of cash flows deserve the investor's attention, it is particularly the operating cash flow which is crucial since a company's ability to pay dividends depends on its cash flows.

Operating cash flows can differ from net income (or profits) for two reasons. First, sales may be on credit and, therefore, not represent cash, and some of the expenses deducted from sales to determine net income may not be cash costs (e.g., depreciation). Second, all taxes reported on the income statement may not have to be paid in the current year, or actual taxes paid may exceed the tax deducted from sales to calculate net income. In other words, operating cash flows can be smaller or larger than net income during any given year.

A cash flow statement shows how a company's actions have affected its operations. More specifically, it enables us to determine whether a firm (1) has excess cash flows to repay debt or to invest in new products, and (2) is growing

Table 1.6
Cash Flow Statement of Company *XYZ*, Year 19__ (Millions of Dollars)

Operating Activities:	
Net Income	$500
Other Additions (Sources of Cash)	
Depreciation	187
Increase in Accounts Payable	50
Increase in Accruals	20
Substractions (Uses of Cash)	
Increase in Accounts Receivable	($ 60)
Increase in Inventories	(700)
Net Cash Flow from Operations	($ 3)
Long-Term Investing Activities:	
Acquisition of Fixed Assets	($300)
Financing Activities:	
Increase in Notes Payable	$ 60
Increase in Bonds	260
Payment of Common and	
Preferred Dividends	(60)
Net Cash Flow from Financing	$260
Net Reduction in Cash and	
Marketable Securities	($ 43)
Cash at Beginning of Year	55
Cash at End of Year	$ 12

so rapidly that external financing is required for maintaining operations or expansion. Table 1.6 presents an example of a cash flow statement. In the table and throughout the book, parentheses are used to denote negative numbers.

Note that the top part of Table 1.6 shows cash flows generated by and used in operations. The principal sources of operating cash flows in the example are net income and depreciation; the primary use is to increase inventories. The middle section of Table 1.6 shows long-term investing activities, while the lower section shows financing activities. The financing activities include borrowing from banks (notes payable), selling new bonds, and paying dividends on common and preferred stock. The total amount raised by borrowing amounts to $320 million, and the payment of dividends amounts to $60 million; hence, the inflow from financing activities amounts to $260 million. When all of the sources and uses of cash are totalled, we arrive at a cash shortfall of $43 million.

The cash flow statement of Table 1.6 should be of some concern to financial analysts because it shows a $3 million cash shortfall from operations, a $300 million cash outlay for the purchase of new fixed assets, and a payment of $60 million for dividends. These cash outlays are covered by borrowing heavily, by selling off marketable securities, and by drawing on the bank account.

5. FINANCIAL RATIOS

An analysis of a company's ratios is generally the first step in a financial analysis. The ratios show the relationships between financial statement accounts. In the following subsections, we will discuss the most commonly used ratios.

Liquidity Ratios

A company's liquidity position tells us whether it will be able to meet its current obligations. A "liquid" asset is one that can be converted to cash quickly at a reasonably well-known price. Two commonly used liquidity ratios are the current ratio and the quick ratio.

The current ratio is the ratio of current assets to current liabilities. Current assets normally include cash, marketable securities, accounts receivable, and inventories. Current liabilities consist of accounts payable, short-term notes payable, current maturities on long-term debt, accrued income taxes, and other accrued expenses (mainly wages). The current ratio for the example of Table 1.1 is 2.3:1. A current ratio of 1.5:1 is normally considered as the minimum acceptable, while a ratio of 2:1 is generally regarded as very good. It is noted, however, that current ratios vary among the various types of industry. Generally, companies that have a small inventory and easily collectible accounts receivable can operate safely with a lower current ratio than those companies having a greater proportion of their current assets in inventory and selling their products on credit.

The quick ratio is the ratio of current assets minus inventories to current liabilities. In other words, the difference between the current ratio and the quick ratio is that in the latter we deduct inventories from current assets in the numerator. This is done since inventories are typically the least liquid of a company's assets. They are the assets on which losses are most likely to occur in the event of liquidation. Hence, a measure of a company's ability to pay off short-term obligations without relying on the sale of inventories makes sense.

Quick ratios are sometimes called acid test ratios. The industry average quick ratio is 2.1:1. The quick ratio for the example of Table 1.1 is 1.5:1. Thus, for each $1.00 of current liabilities, there is $1.50 in quick assets available.

Asset Management Ratios

Asset management ratios measure how effectively a company is managing its assets. More specifically, they address the question of whether the total amount of each type of asset of the balance sheet seems reasonable, too high, or too low in view of current and projected operating levels. Companies must borrow or obtain capital from other sources to acquire assets. If assets are too low, profitable sales may be lost; however, if they are too high, a company will have too-high interest expenses and its profits will be depressed. The most commonly used asset management ratios are the inventory turnover ratio, the days sales outstanding ratio, the fixed assets turnover ratio, and the total assets turnover ratio.

The inventory turnover ratio is defined as sales divided by inventories. How large an inventory should a firm have? That depends on a combination of many factors. An inventory is large or small depending on the type of business and the time of the year. An automobile dealer, for example, with a large stock of autos at the height of the season is in a strong inventory position; yet that same inventory at the end of the season is a weakness in his or her financial condition.

There are dangers in a large inventory position. In the first place, a sharp drop in price may cause serious losses. Second, it may indicate that the company has accumulated a large supply of unsalable goods. The inventory turnover ratio is a measure of the adequacy and balance of inventories. Table 1.3 shows that Company *XYZ* has net sales of $7,150,000, while Table 1.2 indicates that its inventories amount to $2,400,000. Thus the inventory turnover ratio is 3:1. In other words, the turnover is three times, meaning that the goods are bought and sold out three times per year on the average.

It is noted that strict accounting would require the computation of the inventory turnover ratio by comparing costs of goods sold with average inventory. Such information is, however, in many cases not readily available in published statements; hence, an approved substitute is the ratio of sales to inventories. In addition, established compilers of financial ratio statistics, such as Dun and Bradstreet, use the ratio of sales to inventories so that we could not compare this ratio of a specific company to similar companies if we do not follow the same definition. The industry average of inventory turnover ratio is nine times.

The days sales outstanding (DSO) ratio is computed by dividing average daily sales into accounts receivable to find the number of days' sales tied up in receivables. It is also called the average collection period, and its main purpose is to appraise accounts receivable. In other words, the DSO ratio represents the average length of time that a company must wait after making a sale before receiving cash, or the average collection period. If a company observes a rising trend in the DSO ratio over the past few years and its credit policy has not been changed, it is time to take steps to expedite the collection of accounts receivable.

The fixed assets turnover (FAT) ratio is the ratio of sales to net fixed assets. It measures how effectively a company uses its plant and equipment. A problem arises when the FAT ratios of different firms are compared and the firms have a significantly different age. This is so since inflation can affect the value of fixed assets. Thus, if we are comparing a new firm which had acquired its fixed assets recently to an old firm which had acquired its fixed assets years ago at low prices, the FAT ratios are bound to be different unless the old company had re-evaluated its assets.

The FAT ratio pertaining to the example of tables 1.2 and 1.3 is 1.8:1. The average value of this ratio is about 3:1.

The total assets turnover (TAT) ratio is defined as the ratio of sales to total assets. It measures the turnover of all of the firm's assets. A company is not generating a sufficient volume of business for the size of its total asset investment if the TAT ratio is too low. If this is the case, some assets should be disposed of, sales should be increased, or a combination of these steps should be taken. A ratio of 1.5:1 is normally considered acceptable. In the example of tables 1.2 and 1.3, the TAT ratio is 0.6:1, which is low.

Debt Management Ratios

Financial analysts examine a company's debt by (1) reviewing balance sheet ratios to establish the extent to which borrowed funds have been used to finance assets, and (2) checking income statement ratios to determine the number of times fixed charges are covered by operating profits. Analysts use both types of ratios since they are complementary.

There are four important aspects to debt financing or financial leverage. First, if a company earns more on investments financed with borrowed funds than it pays in interest, the return on capital is increased (or "leveraged"), which makes the stockholders happy. Second, a company's owners can maintain control over it with a limited investment. Third, creditors are interested in equity, or owner-supplied funds, to provide a margin of safety. Fourth, the use of debt financing lowers the tax bill since interest is deductible and, therefore, debt financing leaves more of a company's operating income available to its stockholders.

Related to the above-mentioned first point is the fact that if the rate of return on assets, which is the ratio of earnings before interest and taxes (EBIT) to total assets, is higher than the interest rate on debt, as it generally is, then a firm can use debt to finance assets, pay interest, and have something left for its stockholders. However, if costs are higher and sales are lower than were expected, then the return on assets will be lower than was expected. In this case, the leveraged company's return on assets may decrease significantly, cash would be depleted, and losses would occur. Consequently, the company would be required to raise funds. This may be difficult since it is running a loss. Lenders would raise the interest rate, which would further aggravate the company's financial viability, and eventually the company may go bankrupt.

The most commonly used debt management ratios are the total debt to total assets ratio, the net worth ratio, the net tangible assets ratio, the times-interest-earned ratio, and the fixed charge coverage ratio. The ratio of total debt to total assets, often called the debt ratio, is defined as the ratio of total debt to total assets where total debt includes both current liabilities and long-term debt. Generally, owners prefer high debt ratios since they benefit from leverage which magnifies earnings. Creditors, however, prefer low debt ratios because the lower the ratio, the greater the cushion against creditors' losses in the event of liquidation. Most companies would find it difficult to borrow funds if their debt ratio is higher than 40%.

The net worth ratio is the ratio of long-term debt to net worth. Long-term debt is precisely what its name implies (that is, long-term loans). The net worth is defined as the net worth of the equity and preferred shareholders' interest in a firm at its book value. Thus, it is the common and preferred share capital plus the earned surplus and surplus reserves. In other words, the net worth is the total assets of a company less all third-party claims on those assets. A net worth ratio of approximately 1:3 to 1:2 is generally considered as normal.

The net tangible assets ratio is the ratio of long-term debt to the sum of net worth and long-term debt, where long-term debt and net worth are as defined above. Thus, the net worth and net tangible assets ratios are numerical variants of the same concept. Note that the ratio of long-term debt to net worth plus long-term debt equals the ratio of net worth ratio to 1 plus net worth ratio. A net worth ratio of 1/2 implies a net tangible assets ratio of 1/3.

The times-interest-earned (TIE) ratio is established by dividing earnings before interest and taxes (EBIT) by the interest charges. It measures the extent to which operating income can decrease before a company is unable to pay its annual interest costs, which may lead to legal action on the part of the company's creditors and, possibly, to bankruptcy. Note that the ability to pay interest is not affected by taxes since the numerator consists of EBIT rather than net income. Most firms would find it difficult to raise further long-term debt if the TIE ratio were less than 4. This benchmark, like the ones mentioned for the other ratios, is presented to give the reader a general idea of the order of magnitude. Naturally, these benchmarks do not apply if there is a significant element of risk associated with additional borrowing. In this case, further debt capital is difficult to obtain on any terms.

The fixed charge coverage ratio (FCCR) is defined as the ratio of (EBIT plus lease payments) to (interest charges plus lease payments plus sinking fund payments divided by [1 − tax rate]). Thus,

$$FCCR = [EBIT + LP]/[IC + LP + SFP/(1-TR)]$$

where

FCCR = fixed charge coverage ratio
EBIT = earnings before interest and taxes
　LP = lease payments
　IC = interest charges
　SFP = sinking fund payments
　TR = tax rate.

Note that since sinking fund payments are paid with after-tax dollars and interest and lease payments are paid with pre-tax dollars, the sinking fund payments must be divided by (1 − tax rate) to find the before-tax income required to pay taxes and still have enough left to make the sinking fund payment. It is evident that the FCCR is more comprehensive than the TIE ratio because it recognizes that many companies lease assets and also must make sinking fund payments. A sinking fund is a required payment designed to reduce the balance of a bond or preferred stock issue. It is noted that the fixed charge included in the FCCR is normally a rental payment under a one-year or longer lease. Thus, rent under a six-month lease would not be included in the FCCR. An FCCR of approximately 5 times is considered to be acceptable.

Profitability Ratios

As opposed to the ratios discussed above, which provide information about the way a company is operating, profitability ratios indicate the effects of liquidity, asset management, and debt management on operating results. In other words, these ratios give us general information about a firm and help us judge its prospects for the future. They have significance for the long term, since they tell us about the fundamental economic condition of a firm. The commonly used profitability ratios are the operating margin of profit (OMOP) ratio, the operating cost ratio, the net profit ratio, the basic earning power (BEP) ratio, the return on total assets (ROTA) ratio, and the return on common equity (ROCE) ratio.

The OMOP ratio is the operating profit divided by sales. For the example of Table 1.3, the ratio is $755,000/$7,150,000 (or 10.6%). This means that for each dollar of sales, there remains 10.6 cents as a gross profit from operations. By itself this figure is interesting, but it can be more meaningful in two ways. First, we can compare it to the margin of profit in previous years. Changes in profit margin can reflect changes in efficiency as well as changes in products manufactured or in types of customer served. Second, we can also compare a specific company to other companies that do a similar type of business. If the OMOP ratio of the specific company is low in comparison to other companies in the same field, it is an unhealthy sign. Naturally, if it is high, there are grounds for optimism.

The operating cost ratio is frequently used for the same purpose; it is the complement of the margin of profit. In the example of Table 1.3 we had an OMOP ratio of 10.6%. Thus, the operating cost ratio is 100% minus 10.6%, or 89.4%. It can also be found by dividing the total operating costs by net sales. Note that in the example of Table 1.3 we have $6,395,000/$7,150,000 (or 89.4%).

The net profit ratio is yet another guide to indicate how satisfactory the year's activities have been. It is defined as the ratio of net profit to sales. For the example of Table 1.3, its value is $350,000/$7,150,000 (or 5%). This means that for every dollar of goods sold, 5 cents in profit ultimately went to the company. By comparing the net profit ratio from year to year for the same firm, and to other firms in the same industry, we can best judge profit progress.

The BEP ratio is established by dividing earnings before interest and taxes (EBIT) by total assets. It shows the raw earning power of a company's assets—before the impact of taxes and leverage. Consequently, it is useful for comparing companies with different tax situations and different degrees of financial leverage. It is noted that EBIT is earned throughout the year, whereas the total assets figure is as of the end of the year. It could, therefore, be argued that it would be conceptually better to determine the BEP ratio as EBIT divided by average assets, where average assets equal (beginning assets + ending assets)/2. Normally one does not do this since published ratios used for comparative purposes do not include this adjustment. A similar adjustment would also be appropriate for the ROTA and ROCE ratios, but again, in practice, this is usually not done.

The ROTA and the ROCE ratios measure the rate of return on a company's assets and on the stockholders' investment, respectively. The ROTA ratio is net income available to common stockholders divided by total assets, while the ROCE ratio is net income available to common stockholders divided by common equity. Common equity, sometimes called net worth, is the aggregate of the three equity accounts (that is, retained earnings, common stock, and paid-in capital). The retained earnings account is built up over time as the company saves part of its earnings rather than paying all earnings out as dividends. The other two common equity accounts arise from the issuing of stock to raise capital. This breakdown of common equity accounts is important to potential stockholders and creditors. The stockholder normally wants to know whether the firm actually earned the funds reported in its equity accounts or whether it required the funds by selling stock. On the other hand, a potential creditor is more interested in the amount of money the firm puts up than in the form in which the money was put up.

Market Value Ratios

These ratios relate a company's stock price to its earnings and book value per share. If a company's liquidity, asset management, debt management, and profitability ratios are all satisfactory, then its market value ratios will be good and its stock price will probably be as high as can be expected. (There are exceptions, as explained in the next chapter.) In general, it can, however, be said that the market value ratios give management an indication of what investors think of a company's past performance and its future prospects. The two most commonly used market value ratios are the price/earnings (P/E) ratio and the market/book (M/B) ratio.

The P/E ratio is defined as the ratio of price per share to earnings per share. It is indicative of how much investors are willing to pay per dollar of reported profits. For instance, if a stock is selling at $30.00 and earning $2.00 per share, its P/E ratio is 15:1, usually shortened to 15. If the stock should rise to $40, the P/E ratio would be 20. Other things held constant, the P/E ratio is normally higher for firms with high growth potential, and lower for riskier firms.

The M/B ratio gives another indication of how investors regard the firm. It is arrived at by dividing the market price per share by the book value per share, where the book value per share is obtained by dividing common equity as defined above by the number of shares outstanding. Normally, firms with high rates of return on equity sell at higher multiples of book value than those with lower returns. For instance, successful firms such as computer software firms achieve high rates of return on their assets, and they have market values well in excess of their book values (9 or 10 times). On the other hand, a typical railroad company has a low rate of return on assets and an M/B ratio of less than 0.5.

The Use of Financial Ratios

As illustrated in the discussion of profitability ratios, it is important to analyze trends in ratios as well as their absolute levels, because trends give insight into whether the financial situation is improving or deteriorating. Thus, we can make a graph of a firm's ratios with their values indicated on the vertical axis and have the horizontal axis represent time in years (for example, the last five years). It is useful to also plot in the same graph the ratios of other firms with similar operations or services in order to examine how a particular company is doing in comparison to others. Comparative ratios are available from a number of sources such as those compiled by Dun and Bradstreet, the Annual Statements Studies published by the national association of bank loan officers, Robert Morris Associates, and the U.S. Commerce Department Quarterly Financial Report. In addition, financial statement information for thousands of publicly owned corporations are available on magnetic tapes and diskettes to which brokerage houses, banks, and other financial institutions have access. It is noted, however, that each of the data-supplying organizations uses a somewhat different set of ratios designed for its own purposes. In addition, there are sometimes differences in the definitions of ratios presented. We should, therefore, make sure that the definitions used by the different sources are the same as those we are applying to ensure consistency.

Finally, it is evident that where financial ratios are being applied, the manner in which the accounts are drawn up can affect the total borrowing open to a company. For instance, the extent to which assets are not written up to reflect their current value reduces the scope of borrowing cheaply. Also, a company's ability to raise money as cheaply as possible is likely to be reduced if fixed assets are written down as fast as possible in view of possible tax advantages. We will learn more about this in Chapter 4.

SUGGESTIONS FOR FURTHER READING

Altman, E. I. "Financial Ratios, Discriminant Analysis, and the Prediction of Corporate Bankruptcy." *Journal of Finance* (September 1968): 589–609.

Brigham, E. F., and L. C. Gapenski. *Intermediate Financial Management*. Hinsdale, Il: Dryden Press, 1990.

McCabe, R. K. *The Accountant's Guide to Peer and Quality Review*. Westport, CT: Quorum Books, 1993.

Most, K. S. *The Future of the Accounting Profession: A Global Perspective*. Westport, CT: Quorum Books, 1993.

CHAPTER 2

Valuation and Investment Problems when Shares are Under- or Overvalued

Evaluate yourself by your own standards, not someone else's.
—Jackson Brown

Every firm must pay its bondholders and shareholders for the amount of capital they provide, and for the period it is so provided. A bond is a long-term promissory note issued by a business or a government unit. Most of the corporate bonds are owned by and traded among the large financial institutions such as pensions funds, life insurance companies, and mutual funds. Common stock or share represents an ownership claim on the assets of a corporation. Equity holders (holders of common stock) have the inherent right to share in the profits of a firm. The words "share" and "stock" are used interchangeably.

A special class of ownership equity exists as preferred stock. Preferred stockholders, while legal owners, may have stock that denies them voting rights or any say in the management of the firm. They do, however, hold a preferred position in the case of liquidation or bankruptcy. As further consideration for limited ownership rights, preferred stockholders receive a fixed return based on adequate profits. The right to this return may be cumulative over periods of low profits, or it may apply only to years in which the company makes a profit of a specified magnitude. Preferred stocks are similar to bonds in some respects and to common stock in other respects. That is, preferred dividends are similar to interest payments on bonds since they are fixed in the amount and normally must be paid before common stock is paid. Like common dividends, preferred dividends can, however, be omitted without bankrupting the company.

This chapter starts with a brief discussion of bond and stock evaluation methods. Next, we discuss in detail that the application of the interest factors for discrete discounting of Appendix 1 to the cash flows on a proposed investment can give rise to other than optimal decisions even after allowing for the risk and uncertainty attached to cash flows as discussed in Chapter 5.

1. BOND EVALUATION METHOD

The value of a bond is based on the present value of the cash flows it is expected to produce. For a bond, the cash flows consist of interest payments during the life of the bond plus a return of the principal amount borrowed when the bond matures. The principal amount borrowed is called the par value. This amount must be paid off at maturity. The annual interest paid equals the coupon rate times the par value. Using two of the interest factors of Table A.1 of Appendix 1, we can state that the value of a bond is:

$$V_B = INT \text{ (given } A, i, n, \text{ find } P) + PV \text{ (given } F, i, n, \text{ find } P)$$

where

V_B = value of the bond
INT = dollars of interest paid each year (coupon rate $\times$ par value)
PV = par value
i = the appropriate interest rate on the bond
n = the number of years before the bond matures.

The (given A, i, n, find P) and (given F, i, n, find P) are the pwf and sppwf factors of Table A.1 of Appendix 1, respectively.

A newly issued bond is called a new issue, while a bond which has been on the market for a while (about one month according to the *Wall Street Journal*) is classified as an outstanding or a seasonal issue. Consider, for example, a new issue with a par value of $1,000.00, a coupon rate of 15%, and a maturity of 15 years. Using the above-mentioned V_B formula, we determine its value as follows:

$$
\begin{aligned}
V_B &= \$150.00 \text{ (pwf with } A = 150.00, i = 15\%, \text{ and } n = 15) \\
&+ \$1,000.00 \text{ (sppwf with } F = \$1,000.00, i = 15\%, \text{ and } n = 15) \\
&= \$150.00 \ (5.8474) + \$1,000.00 \ (0.1229) = \$877.10 + \$122.90 \\
&= \$1,000.00
\end{aligned}
$$

The pwf and sppwf values are obtained from Appendix 2 or with a financial calculator (see Appendix 1).

A bond which was sold at par when it was issued is likely to sell for more or less thereafter since interest rates in the economy can rise or fall. For instance, let us assume that, in the above example, the interest rate in the economy decreased from 15% to 10% at the end of the first year after the bond was sold.

Although the coupon rate (and, therefore, the coupon interest payments) and the maturity value remain the same, it would not be correct to use $i = 15\%$ in the pwf and sppwf factors. Since the interest rate in the economy is 10%, we should use $i = 10\%$. Thus, the value of the bond at the end of the first year is:

$$V_B = \$150.00 \text{ (pwf with } A = \$150.00, i = 10\%, \text{ and } n = 14)$$
$$+ \ \$1,000.00 \text{ (sppwf with } F = \$1,000.00, i = 10, \text{ and } n = 14)$$
$$= \$150.00 \ (7.3667) + \$1,000.00 \ (0.2633) = \$1,105.01 + \$263.30$$
$$+ \ \$1,368.31$$

Note that we use $n = 14$ since we determine the bond's value one year after it has been sold. In this example, the bond would sell above par, or at a premium. This is of no surprise since the decline in the interest rate means that if one had $1,000.00 to invest, one could buy a new bond which would pay $100.00 of interest every year rather than $150.00. Naturally, one would prefer $150.00 to $100.00, so one would be willing to pay more than $1,000.00 or $1,368.31 for the bond which sold for $1,000.00 a year ago.

If the interest rates rise from 15% to 20% during the first year after issue, the value of the bond in the above example would be:

$$V_B = \$150.00 \text{ (pwf with } A = \$150.00, i = 20\%, n = 14)$$
$$+ \ \$1,000.00 \text{ (sppwf with } F = \$1,000.00, i = 20\%, n = 14)$$
$$= \$150.00 \ (4.6106) + \$1,000.00 \ (0.0779) = \$691.59 + \$77.90$$
$$= \$769.49$$

Thus, the value of the bond has fallen, and in this case it would sell at a discount.

What would happen if, in the above example, interest rates would fall from 15% to 10% after the first year the bond was sold, but then remained 10% during the remaining 14 years before the bond matures? In this case, it would gradually decline in value from $1,368.31 at the end of the first year to $1,000.00 at maturity. For example, the value of the bond when it has 13 years remaining to maturity would be:

$$V_B = \$150.00 \text{ (pwf with } A = \$150.00, i = 10\%, n = 13)$$
$$+ \ \$1,000.00 \text{ (sppwf with } F = \$1,000.00, i = 10\%, n = 13)$$
$$= \$150.00 \ (7.1034) + \$1,000.00 \ (0.2897) = \$1,065.51 + \$289.70$$
$$= \$1,355.21$$

In other words, the value of the bond would have declined from $1,368.31 to $1,355.21, or the bond would have lost $13.10 in value. If you calculate the value of the bond at other future dates, you would observe a continuous decline in its value until the maturity date approaches.

If you bought the above-mentioned bond at a price of $1,368.31 one year after its issue and sold it one year later with interest rates still at 10%, you would have a capital loss of $13.10, or a total return of $150.00 of interest payment received minus $13.10 or $136.90. The percentage rate of return consists of (a) an interest yield (also called current yield) of $150.00/$1,368.31 = 10.96%, and (b) a capital gains yield of $- \ \$13.10/\$1,368.31 = -\ 0.96\%$. The total rate of return or yield would equal 10.96% minus 0.96%, or 10.00%.

2. STOCK EVALUATION METHOD

The value of a stock is determined in a manner similar to the way we established the value of a bond. In other words, we determine the present value of a stream of cash flows consisting of the annual dividends we expect the issuer of a stock to pay:

$$V_S = DIV \text{ (given } F, i, n = 1, \text{ find } P) + DIV \text{ (given } F, i, n = 2, \text{ find}$$
$$P) + DIV \text{ (given } F, i, n = 3, \text{ find } P) + \dots\dots\dots\dots\dots\dots\dots$$
$$+ DIV \text{ (given } F, i, n = \text{ last year, find } P)$$

where

V_S = present value of stock
DIV = dividend
   i = minimum acceptable, or required, rate of return on the stock, considering both its riskiness and the returns available on other investments
  n = the number of years after the stock has been issued.

The (given F, i, n, find P) is the sppwf factor of Table A.1 of Appendix 1. Note that we cannot apply the pwf factor as we did in the expression to determine the value of a bond since annual dividends are not likely to be constant over time. Instead, we use the sppwf factor repetitiously with n equal to 1, n equal to 2, and so on. Which year do we use for the last year in the above expression for V_S? If you were an investor who buys a stock with the intention of holding it forever in your family, the value of the stock to you and your heirs would be the present value of an infinite stream of dividends. Naturally, the present value of dividends after 40 or 50 years would be small due to the effect of discounting (the sppwf factor for $i = 10\%$ and $n = 50$ years is 0.0085!). Even in the more typical case where you expect to hold the stock for a finite number of years, you would use the above expression for V_S with an infinite stream of dividends since (1) your expected cash flows consist of expected dividends plus the expected sales price of the stock, and (2) the sales price you will receive depends on the dividends some future investor expects to get. Consequently, expected cash flows must be based on expected future dividends for all present and future investors in total. An exception would be the case where a company is likely to be liquidated or sold to another firm in the future (Chapter

4). With an infinite stream of dividends, we can rewrite the above expression for V_S as follows:

$$V_S = \sum_{t=1}^{t=\infty} D_t/(1 + i)^t \qquad (1)$$

where

V_S = as defined above
 t = term indicating year
D_t = dividend in year t
 i = as defined above
 ∞ = symbol indicating that the value of "t" is infinitely large.

Note that the term "i" in the above-mentioned expressions V_B for the value of a bond and V_S for the value of a stock has a different definition. In addition, in Appendix 1, we use the term "i" to designate the interest rate used in financial calculations. We could, therefore, have introduced terms different from "i" in the expressions for V_B and V_S; we did not do so since we make reference to the expressions "(given A, i, n, find P) and (given F, i, n, find P)" used in Table A.1 of Appendix 1. In other words, it may be difficult to follow the argument if we refer to Table A.1 of Appendix 1 and use an expression (given A, k, n, find P) since there is no term "k" in this table. However, we sometimes use the term "k_b" for the appropriate interest on a bond, and the term "k_s" for the minimum acceptable, or required, rate of return on a stock. Chapter 5 discusses the way in which we can determine the minimum acceptable, or required, rate of return on a stock.

The expression for V_S requires the analyst to make forecasts of an infinite stream of dividends, which is, of course, no easy task. As mentioned above, fortunately the dividends 40 or 50 years from now do not have to be that accurate due to the impact of discounting. An analysis of past dividends paid by a company together with an analysis of dividends paid by firms in the same type of business (competitors) is called for in order to determine the stream of future dividends of the company. Application of some of the financial ratios discussed in Chapter 1 may also be useful, since they provide insight into the way a company is operating and the effects of liquidity, asset management, and debt management on operating results.

To make the task of forecasting the stream of future dividends easier, they are often projected for the following types of stocks: a zero growth stock, a constant growth stock, and a non-constant growth stock.

A zero growth stock is a stock where dividends remain constant. We can, therefore, eliminate the subscript "t" on D and rewrite equation (1) as follows:

$$V_S = \sum_{t=1}^{t=\infty} D/(1 + i)^t \qquad (2)$$

where

D = the constant, annual dividend, and all other terms are defined as under equation (1).

Appendix 1 shows that equation (2) is the expression to establish the value of a perpetuity, and it can be rewritten as simply $V_S = D/i$. Thus, if the constant, annual dividends of a stock amount to, for instance, $12.00, and its minimum acceptable or required rate of return on the stock is 0.14, then its $V_S = \$12.00/0.14 = \$85.71$. The actual market value of the stock could be greater than, less than, or equal to $85.71 depending on other investors' perceptions of the dividend pattern and the riskiness of the stock.

Expected growth rates differ from company to company; however, dividend growth is often assumed to continue in the foreseeable future at about the same rate as that of the nominal gross national product (real GNP plus inflation). Thus, we may expect the dividend of an average company to grow at a rate of 6% to 8% per year. If we call the constant growth rate of a stock's dividend "g" and the stock's last dividend amounts to "D," then the value of its dividend in any future year "t," D_t, may be forecast as

$$D_t = D (1 + g)^t. \qquad (3)$$

Using equation (3) we can rewrite equation (1) as follows:

$$V_S = \sum_{t=1}^{t=\infty} D (1 + g)^t/(1 + i)^t \qquad (4)$$

or

$$V_S = D (1 + g)/(i - g) \qquad (5)$$

where all terms are as previously defined. The derivation of equation (5) from equation (4) is beyond the scope of this book.

For instance, if a stock's last dividend amounts to $1.20 and it is expected to grow at a constant rate of 8% and the minimum acceptable, or required, rate of return is 12%, then V_S or the value of the stock is $1.20 (1.08)/(0.12 − 0.08) = \$1.30/0.04 = \$32.50$. It is noted that stocks generally pay dividends quarterly; so, theoretically, we should evaluate them on a quarterly basis. However, most analysts work on an annual basis when evaluating stocks because the data are generally not accurate enough to warrant refinement to a quarterly model.

In order to deal with non-constant growth stocks or stocks with dividends growing (or declining) at a rate which is not constant, we note that companies typically go through life cycles. That is, during the early part of their lives, their growth is faster than that of the economy as a whole. Then they reach the economy's growth; and finally their growth is slower than that of the economy. Large companies can go through a similar cycle just after they have introduced a new product. In addition, a similar pattern can often be observed with companies just emerging from the depths of a recession.

With the above-mentioned observation of life cycles, we can think of a stock's dividend growing first at a non-constant rate, and next becoming a constant growth stock. To find the value of a non-constant stock, we proceed in the following three steps.

1. Find the present value of the dividends during the period of non-constant growth by applying equation (1) to a limited number of years in the beginning of the infinite time horizon (for instance, the term "t" on top of the summation sign equals 3, rather than ∞ if the period of non-constant growth is 3 years).

2. Find the price of the stock at the end of the non-constant growth period, at which point it has become a constant growth stock by using equation (5), and discount this price back to the present time.

3. Add these two components to find the value of the stock or V_S.

To illustrate the procedure for the evaluation of non-constant growth stocks, we assume the following facts exist.

—The minimum acceptable, or required, rate of return is 12%.

—The number of years of non-constant growth is 3.

—The rate of growth in both earnings and dividends during the non-constant growth period is 30%.

—The constant growth rate after the non-constant growth period is 7%.

—The last dividend the company paid is $1.20.

Following the above procedure, we first determine the dividends (D) in the first three years, and their present values (PV), as follows.

D in the first year is $1.20 (1.30) = $1.56.00, and its PV is $1.56.00 (0.8929) = $1.39, where (0.8929) is the factor (given F, find P, $i = 12\%$, $n = 1$) obtained from Appendix 2.

D in the second year is $1.56 (1.30) = $2.03, and its PV is $2.03 (0.7972) = $1.62.

D in the third year is $2.03 (1.30) = $2.64, and its PV is $2.64 (0.7118) = $1.88. Thus, the PV of the dividends during the first three years is $1.39 + $1.62 + $1.88 = $4.89.

Next, we determine the price of the stock at the end of the non-constant

growth period which is the PV of dividends from the fourth year to infinity. In
theory we could project all future dividends with growth at the constant rate of
7% used to calculate the fourth year dividend and all other dividends. However,
we know that after the dividend in the third year has been paid, the stock
becomes a constant growth stock, so we can use equation (5) or $V_s = D (1 + g)/(i - g)$. To do so, we first establish the dividend D in the fourth year or D
$= \$2.64\ (1.07) = \$2.82$. Thus, the price of the stock at the end of the non-
constant growth period is $\$2.82/(0.12 - 0.07) = \$56.40$. The $\$56.40$ is a third
year cash flow in the sense that the owner of the stock could sell it for this
amount at Year 3 and also in the sense that $\$56.40$ is equivalent to dividend
cash flows from Year 4 to infinity. The PV of $\$56.40$ is $\$56.40\ (0.7118) =$
$\$40.15$. Note that the total cash flow at Year 3 is $\$2.64 + \$56.40 = \$59.04$.
The value of the stock is $V_s = \$4.89 + \$40.15 = \$45.04$.

To enhance our understanding of this example, we illustrate the solution as
follows:

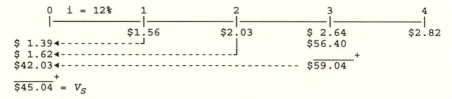

Note that in this illustration we have discounted $\$59.04$ rather than first dis-
counting $\$2.64$ and next $\$56.40$.

There is a number of interesting observations to be made about the above
given example. First, the growth rate could vary from year to year during the
period of non-constant growth. In addition, there could be several different non-
constant growth periods, such as 30% for three years, then 20% for four years,
and then a constant 7%. However, the basic approach to finding the value of a
stock with different non-constant growth periods is the same as discussed above.

Second, the above-mentioned value of the stock, $V_s = \$45.04$, is the expected
price of a stock today. It is the intrinsic, or theoretical, value of the stock today
as seen by a particular investor doing his/her analysis. It is his/her estimate of
the stock's expected dividend stream and the riskiness of that stream. This expected price could be above or below the actual market price (AMP) of the stock
today. The AMP is fixed and identical for all investors, while the V_s can differ
among investors depending on how optimistic they are about the company issuing the stock. Since there are many investors in the market, there can be many
values for V_s. However, we can think of an average, or marginal, investor whose
actions actually establish the market price. For this marginal investor, AMP must
be equal to V_s since, otherwise, a disequilibrium would exist, and buying and
selling in the market would change AMP until it equals V_s for the marginal
investor.

Third, the minimum acceptable, or required, rate of return in the above example was 12%. This is not the same as the expected total return which an investor who buys the stock actually expects to receive. The expected total return is the sum of the expected dividend yield and the expected capital gains yield. Naturally, the expected total return can differ from the minimum acceptable rate of return and the actual (after the fact) rate of return, while the minimum acceptable rate of return can be above or below the actual rate of return. Let us call the dividend a company is expected to pay during the coming year D_1, and the expected price of its stock at the end of Year 1 $V_{S,1}$. We can now define the following two terms which are often used by financial analysts:

D_1/AMP = the expected dividend yield on the stock during the coming year; and

$[V_{S,1}-AMP]/AMP$ = the expected capital gains yield on the stock during the coming year.

Assume that the analysis of the above example was done by a marginal investor, which, as we have seen, means that the $AMP = V_S$, where V_S is the expected price of the stock today. Also assume that the actual dividend the company will pay at the end of Year 1 will indeed be $1.56. The expected dividend yield on the stock during the coming year, D_1/AMP, will then amount to $1.56/$45.04 = 3%. The expected capital gains yield on the stock during the coming year, $[V_{S,1} - AMP]/AMP$, in this scenario is ($48.88 − $45.04)/$45.04 = 9%, where the $48.88 = $2.03 (0.8929) + $59.04 (0.7972). Hence, the expected total return is 3% + 9% = 12%. The actual rate of return is the actual dividend yield, which in our example is also 3%, plus the actual capital gains yield, which in our example is also 9%, or 12%. Thus, in this case, the minimum acceptable rate of return equals the expected rate of return which equals expected total return. This result should be of no surprise since we did the analysis from the point of view of the marginal investor.

3. INCORRECT CURRENT SHARE VALUES

Normally, a firm would only undertake a project if its net present value (NPV) is positive (Chapter 6). In a situation where investments are large relative to the firm involved (particularly in the case of takeovers), it may, however, not be enough to recommend investments which have satisfactorily high NPVs at the firm's cost of capital even after allowing for the risk and uncertainty related to the cash flows (Chapter 6). This situation can arise with a new project where the forecast benefits do not contribute significantly to the firm's profit over the next few years—years in which forecast benefits on existing business may seem to be too low already. In this case, the firm may conclude that the project, although attractive by normal standards, could depress the firm's share price unduly for some years to the detriment of the shareholders and, therefore, the project should not be undertaken. The firm may also conclude that the new project may make the firm vulnerable to takeover or even bankruptcy. In short, having a satisfactorily high NPV may not be a sufficient condition to implement a project. Reported profits over, for instance, the next five years are also relevant to investment decisions because the sensible goal of a firm is to have earnings increasing every year (if possible) and in as regular a way as possible. In other words, in a situation where a proposed investment is large relative to the firm and is forecast not to contribute significant profits over the next few years (a period in which profits on existing business are expected to be low), one should consider both long-term wealth maximization and short-term reported profits.

The same difficulty in using the cash flow approach to determine NPVs can arise when a firm's shares are significantly undervalued in relation to the shares of comparable companies. When shares are undervalued, and when share issues are involved, the expansion may be to the detriment of the existing shareholders. The new shareholders get cut in too cheaply on the firm's undervalued, existing income prospects. Thus, even if a project has an acceptable NPV using the firm's cost of capital standards as described in Chapter 5, a new project, financed by newly raised capital, can easily dilute the prospective income stream of existing shareholders when shares are significantly undervalued. Since management's duty is to safeguard existing shareholders' interest, the application of discounted cash flows may lead to wrong decisions. It is noted that our discussion of undervalued shares implies that we know the "correct" value of a share, which is, of course, not true. If we did, we would all be millionaires. Knowing the correct value of a company's share implies perfect knowledge of the future for the company and all other investments, which is impossible. In the absence of such knowledge, we define correct valuation as the best estimate of the company's management after taking into consideration expert informed stock market opinion. It is based on good knowledge of the company's future, the opportunities open to it, and the plans to exploit them. It is clear that the value of a share based on such correct value is not necessarily the same as its value given by the stock market.

We emphasize that the application of discounted cash flows only fails to give correct answers when the assumptions underlying the investment appraisal made by a company's management differ from the assumptions made by others such as shareholders, creditors, and investors generally. For instance, a firm's investment with a sufficiently high NPV, but with low earnings in the early years, is likely to be pessimistically evaluated by the stock market in general. This is so since the stock market, in general, judges the worth of a company mainly on existing data about past and current earnings and their trends (favoring regular and rising earnings), and so on. One could, in fact, argue that a firm's management should clearly reveal their investment methods and criteria. Why not? Shareholders are entitled to such basic information; however, most company managements would not share this point of view.

Are shares often undervalued? It is difficult to answer this question; however, the simple fact that takeover offers often exceed 30% for uncontested bids, and sometimes 50% or more on a contested bid, appears to indicate that shares may be more often undervalued than we would be inclined to think. Overvaluation appears to be more rare. The prime manifestation of overvaluation is probably the rapidly expanding fashionable growth companies which use their overvalued shares to acquire assets cheaply.

The approach of Sections 1 and 2 of this chapter gives us a first step to the valuation of shares. In principle, it sets out the equity cash flows of a company for the next five years or so in as much detail as possible, as well as the trend of cash flows for the next 10 to 15 years. This is discounted at the company's cost of capital; and the resulting present value, plus any surplus realizable assets, gives the current valuation of the company's shares. Ideally, this procedure should be carried out for a range of relevant assumptions of future costs, revenues, tax assumptions, and so on, and a probability distribution drawn up. From this we can calculate the mean valuation, and the upper and lower quartile valuations as an indication of variation around the mean (Chapter 5). We should then compare these three values to the current stock market valuation. The management of a company should consider taking action if the mean value is not within the band of plus or minus 15% of the current stock market valuation. The management should definitely take action if the stock market valuation is not within the upper and lower quartile valuations.

In case of undervaluation of a company's stock, the action would consist of concentration on projects with short-term profits. If a company's share is overvalued, the problem is a moral one rather than a commercial one. Shareholders selling out while a stock is overvalued receive a windfall profit at the expense of their successors, but it is an unjustified gain. It is, therefore, recommended that, if management believes its shares are significantly overvalued it should say so. Such a statement should suffice to bring the shares down. It could also be argued that, in the long run, this strategy is commercially correct since it is inevitable that under- or overvaluations are only temporary.

4. VALUATION OF A COMPANY'S SHARE

A company's management is usually the most capable group of people to assess their company's worth in isolation. However, it is seldom that their expertise extends to other similar companies, and still less to shares in general. It is, therefore, emphasized that the above-described valuation procedure be tempered by expert stock market advice which takes into account the current valuations of similar companies and shares in general. Without such advice, management could conclude that their own shares are overvalued at a time when all similar shares are overvalued, thus acting to the detriment of their own shareholders.

It is noted that many companies do not carry out systematic, regular internal valuations of shares (to the detriment of both themselves and shareholders). If such valuations are carried out regularly, future problems can be identified in time for remedial action. In addition, management may be able to turn under-utilized assets to better use, thus avoiding unnecessary risks of takeovers. In fact, since it is the primary duty of managers to look after the interests of their shareholders, they should discharge this responsibility adequately by regular, systematic internal valuations, tempered by expert stock market advice. An alert body of shareholders might reasonably require this procedure to be carried out regularly.

Management should try to correct wrong stock market valuations only in relation to similar shares, and not concern itself with the correctness or otherwise of share prices in general. In particular, our previous advice that overvaluation should be dealt with by a statement revealing the overvaluation, must be qualified. If management succeeded in forcing down only its own share price, it could end up being taken over by one of its competitors to the detriment of existing shareholders. The latter would probably be paid in shares which, in their turn, would eventually fall in value, and so the existing shareholders would suffer. In this situation, it is recommended that management content itself with a statement limited to claiming reasonable correct valuation in comparison to similar companies.

5. INVESTMENTS WHEN ENTIRE STOCK MARKET IS UNDER- OR OVERVALUED

Should management proceed with investing in a project with a satisfactory NPV if it has sufficient funds to do so, and if (a) the entire stock market is significantly undervalued and may well rise by 25 or 30% over the next year, or (b) the entire stock market is significantly overvalued and may well fall by 25 or 30% over the next year?

In case (a), it could be argued that management should postpone the investment for a year, and invest the cash in a general portfolio of shares, realize them after a year, then take up the postponed investment, and use the capital gain either for future investment or a special dividend payment to shareholders. However, most shareholders do not expect or want the company to use their money for speculative share investments since most companies are unlikely to possess the appropriate skills to do so. Imagine if the market went down instead of up! Thus, a speculative investment should be considered as inappropriate for all but specialist investment companies. Having removed this possibility, we should, however, consider whether there is any advantage in postponing the investment until shares have risen by the expected amount. Unless the postponement would result in a higher present NPV due to the actual rise in share prices, the company should not postpone the investment. It is noted that a higher NPV due to the rise in share prices is not likely to occur: it means that the rise would create a better market for the project's output.

In case (b), a similar conclusion should be reached. Unless postponement of the investment either results in a higher present NPV from the fall of share prices—an almost inconceivable possibility—or the fall in share prices would cause the company to regret the investment, the investment should not be postponed. A situation where a fall in share prices may cause the company to regret the investment could arise with projects whose products are particularly sensitive to share price falls (e.g., certain luxury products and services).

Let us now consider the above-mentioned cases (a) and (b) if a company contemplates a rights issue to finance the planned investment rather than using existing resources. To analyze these situations, we should ask ourselves what the shareholders would or could have done with the money if they had not subscribed to the rights issue (that is, an issue which grants a shareholder the right to subscribe at a comparatively favorable price to new issues of the company's stock in proportion to present holdings). It is reasonable to assume that any money shareholders would use to subscribe for the rights issue would be invested in other shares in the absence of the rights issue. Would they either have gained or lost in cases (a) and (b) from investing in other shares?

In case (a), the shareholders would have seen their money appreciate by the rise in the general stock price index, which seems to argue for a postponement. However, there is no reason to assume that the company's shares will not rise more or less in step with the general stock price index. Consequently, the existing shareholders would have suffered no loss, and proceeding with the rights issue is fully justified. In case (b), a similar conclusion is reached. Subject only to the qualifications given above, concerning the effect of postponing the investment on its NPV, we conclude that proceeding with the rights issue is in the interest of the existing shareholders.

Finally, we should consider the aforementioned cases (a) and (b) when a company is contemplating raising capital from new shareholders. In case (a), where the general price share is expected to rise, the existing shareholders would be better off if the new issue were postponed until after the increase in share prices, since the same money could then be raised by issuing significantly fewer shares. Thus, in this case, it is in the interests of the existing shareholders to postpone the investment except in the rare situation where the NPV now to the existing shareholders of postponement is lower. In case (b), where the general price share is expected to fall, there is a gain rather than a loss to the existing shareholders from proceeding with the new issue. Postponement until prices had fallen would mean giving up more shares to outsiders to raise the money to finance the investment. Thus, proceeding with the investment is in the interests of the existing shareholders except in the rare circumstances where its postponement results in a sufficiently increased NPV to the existing shareholders to more than compensate for the extra number of shares they would have to give up.

We conclude this section by stating that a company's management can ignore the likely future level of general share prices, and proceed with any investment with a satisfactory NPV, except in one instance. This exception is when the company contemplates raising capital from new shareholders, and the general level of share prices is expected to rise in the next year or so.

6. INVESTMENTS WHEN SHARES ARE UNDERVALUED RELATIVE TO SIMILAR SHARES

We now move on to the situation where a company has to decide on an investment when its shares are undervalued. We assume that the company is in the unfortunate position where no action is available to correct the undervaluation of its shares. It is noted that share undervaluation can only be temporary; when earnings and dividends materialize the undervaluation ceases to exist. If investments take a long time in coming to fruition, the period of undervaluation can be correspondingly long.

A company can justifiably consider existing and retained funds as being available for reinvestment if its shares are undervalued, as long as they can earn a return equal to or in excess of that which its shareholders can obtain elsewhere, for this must always be to their benefit. In other words, the cost of capital to the firm for the existing and retained funds is equal to the shareholders' cost of capital. In the case of newly raised equity, the cost of capital to the company can, however, exceed the shareholders' cost of capital. The reason is that to the extent that newly raised funds come from new shareholders, such new shareholders are enabled to participate in the undervalued income prospects of the existing shareholders. If the existing shareholders are not to be worse off as a result, it is necessary that the newly raised funds be invested to earn a return sufficiently above the existing shareholders' cost of capital to compensate them for the dilution of their existing undervalued income prospects.

Since undervaluation is a temporary state, the investment problem is to determine whether it is in the interest of the existing shareholders to proceed with raising capital from new shareholders now, or to postpone the investment involved. Postponement should be the earlier of (1) when the firm has sufficient internal resources for the investment thus obviating the need to raise capital from new shareholders, and (2) when the shares are correctly valued on the stock market. We consider two situations; that is, case (a) new capital now versus internal resources later, and (b) new capital now versus later.

In case (a) we must establish the company's NPV of the future equity cash flow to the existing shareholders in the two situations—"new capital now" and "internal resources later." To do this, we consider the following example. Assume a company with one million stocks has the prospect of the following equity cash flows on its existing projects:

Years:	1	2	3 and subsequent years
Cash flow ($000s):	100	100	150

Suppose the company's cost of capital is 10%. With the help of Appendix 2, we determine the present value of this series of cash flows to be $1,413,200.00 or $1.413 per share. The market capitalizes the firm on the basis of its current earnings, $100,000.00, and does not consider the likely increase in earnings; thus the market value is only $1,000,000.00 or $1.00 per stock. Now let us assume that the company contemplates a $100,000.00 investment which is expected to result in a $18,000.00 per annum cash flow for ten years. Hence, the investment's NPV is $10,600.00. Suppose that the investment can be postponed three years with no reduction in either cash flows or economic life. All of the next two years' cash flows are, however, required for dividends if the company is not to become even more undervalued. The company feels that in Year 3 the dividends can be reduced to $50,000.00 to pay for the investment by pointing out its increased level of earnings to the shareholders. Thus the choice is either to raise $100,000.00 from new shareholders now, or to postpone the investment for three years. Let us assume that the $100,000.00 can be raised from new shareholders at a 10% discount on the current market price of $1.00 per stock, that is, an issue of 111,111 new shares will bring in $100,000.00. This issue will result in the existing shareholders owning only 90% of the company, and the new shareholders 10%.

Let us first consider the net cash flows from postponement:

Years:	1	2	3	4–13	14 onwards
Cash flow ($000s):	100	100	50	168	150

At 10%, this cash flow has an NPV of $1,421,200.00. All of this cash flow belongs to the existing shareholders, and increases their stock value from $1.413 to $1.421.

The aggregate cash flow to both existing and new shareholders from raising the $100,000.00 of new capital now and realizing the investment is:

Years:	1	2	3–10	11 onwards
Cash flow ($000s):	118	118	168	150

At 10%, this cash flow has an NPV of $1,523,800.00. Only 90% of this NPV accrues to the existing shareholders, while the remaining 10% accrues to the new shareholders. Consequently, the existing shareholders receive $1,371,420, or $1.371 per share. Thus, they are worse off from raising capital from new shareholders rather than postponing the investment. If the investment could not be postponed, the existing shareholders would be better off passing it up altogether, and not having their existing undervalued income prospects diluted from the new issue.

It is noted that by raising the $100,000.00 cost of the new project from 111,111 shares, the company's worth increased by $110,600.00, to

$1,523,800.00 (prior to contemplating the new investment, the company's worth was $1,413,200.00); however, the price that the existing shareholders paid for this, was to give up 10% of the company's future income, including 10% of the existing undervalued prospects. Hence, the existing shareholders gave up 10% of $1,413,200.00 or $141,320.00, in return for 90% of the present value of the new project ($110,600.00), that is, only $99,540.00. The difference is $41,780.00, which is a loss to existing shareholders, but a windfall gain to the new shareholders, who participated in both the profitable investment and the much larger, significantly undervalued income prospects on the company's existing investments.

Let us now move on to the above-mentioned case (b), that is, new capital now versus later. Heretofore, we have considered the situation where the new investment can be financed eventually from internal resources, even though the shares may still be undervalued at that time. Now we consider the case where the choice is between raising capital from new shareholders now, or at a later date when the shares are no longer undervalued. We assume the same facts as in the above example, except that the company's shares will become correctly valued at the end of Year 3, when the increased earnings are seen to materialize. Thus, the comparison is between raising the $100,000.00 now, when the shares are significantly undervalued, and raising the $100,000.00 in three years' time when the shares are correctly valued. In three years time, the existing one million shares will be worth the present value of a $150,000.00 perpetuity discounted at 10%, that is, $1,500,000.00 or $1.50 per stock (Appendix 1). We saw already that a new issue now is not in the existing shareholders' interest since it decreases the value of the existing shareholders' income stream from $1,413,200.00 to $1,371,410.00. But what is the position if the raising of new capital is postponed three years? Again assuming that the shares are issued at a 10% discount on the then-current market price of $1.50 per stock, the company will have to issue $100,000.00 : $1.35 = 74,000 stocks. The new shareholders would have a 74,000/1,074,000 or approximately 7% interest in the company.

If $100,000.00 is raised in three years' time to finance the investment, the cash flow to the company will be:

Years:	1	2	3	4–13	14 onwards
Cash flow ($000s):	100	100	150	168	150

The cash flow to the existing shareholders will be the same as for the company over the first three years, and 93% of the cash flows from Year 4 onwards. At 10%, this cash flow has an NPV of $1,411,500.00 or $1.412 per stock. Consequently, the existing shareholders are better off from postponement, which is to be expected; however, they are even better off by not taking up the investment at all. It is left to the reader to carry out the exact arithmetic by replacing the $18,000.00 per annum cash flow during ten years by $24,000.00 per annum during ten years (and keeping the cost of investment, $100,000.00, the same). In this case, you will find an NPV to existing shareholders which is higher than $1,421,200.00. Thus, with the investment of $100,000.00 resulting in an $18,000.00 per annum cash flow for ten years, the best course of action is to postpone the investment for three years and not to issue new shares; if this investment results in an $24,000.00 per annum cash flow over ten years, the best course of action is raising capital from new shareholders when the shares are no longer undervalued.

It is noted that to simplify the computations, we have assumed in the above example that the last benefit streams of the cash flows considered (Years 4 onwards, 11 onwards, and 14 onwards) are a perpetuity; it is clear that our arguments would have been the same if these benefit streams would have been during a given period of time. It is also obvious that the larger the undervaluation, the larger the "new" capital to be raised, since this results in increasing dilution.

From the discussion in Section 5 of this chapter, it will be apparent that a problem arises only when a company's shares are undervalued, because current reported profits and past trends, and so on, plus any other information available to the stock market, fail to convey adequately the company's future income prospects. This condition can arise when relatively large amounts of capital are currently being invested in projects which are not yet in production, or when the method of accounting employed gives a conservative presentation of profits in the early years of a project's life. This latter condition is found in any accounting system which results in accelerated depreciation in the early years of a project's life (e.g., "sum of digits" method).

Finally, it is noted that the analysis of this chapter can apply equally to deciding when to raise loans. When interest rates are temporarily high, and can be fairly confidently expected to fall in a year or two, it is a matter of straightforward calculation to determine whether or not to raise, say, a 20-year debenture now, or later. However, since the net of tax, net of inflation burden of interest rates is generally small, it will seldom pay to postpone most projects which could be mainly or entirely financed from loan capital. But it is always worth investigating.

SUGGESTIONS FOR FURTHER READING

Grant, K. J. *Securities Arbitration for Brokers, Attorneys, and Investors*. Westport, CT: Quorum Books, 1994.

Lerner, E. M., and A. Rappaport. "Limit DCF in Capital Budgeting." *Harvard Business Review* (September-October 1968).

Linke, C. M., and J. K. Zumwalt. "Estimation Biases in Discounted Cash Flow Analysis of Equity Capital Cost in Rate Regulation." *Financial Management* (Autumn 1984): 15–21.

CHAPTER 3

Derivative Securities

Prudence is the knowledge of things to be sought, and of those to be avoided.
—Cicero

A derivative security is a security whose value depends on the values of other more basic underlying variables. Expressed in a simple manner, a derivative product is a contract. Basically, there are two types of derivatives: the over-the-counter (OTC) derivatives, which are contracts between two parties: and those in organized and centralized trading or exchanges. The most important ones among the first group are forward contracts and swaps; futures contracts and options are actively traded on different exchanges. Over the last decade, the growth of derivatives has been explosive. In terms of dollar value of outstanding (existing) positions in derivative securities, the market for exchange-traded instruments grew from $583 billion in 1986 to $7,839 billion in 1993, which is more than a tenfold increase. The OTC market is similar in size to the exchange markets.

In derivative securities we are frequently comparing two or more pecuniary values at different points in time. Consequently, we have to use interest factors for either discrete or continuous compounding which are briefly discussed in Appendix 1. This chapter uses continuous compounding (Appendix 3). When writing about derivative securities, we cannot exclude the use of mathematics. Great care has been taken in the level of mathematical sophistication since it is realized that if the level is too high, the material is likely to be inaccessible to many practitioners. If it is too low, some important issues will inevitably be treated in a rather superficial way. Nonessential mathematical material has, therefore, been eliminated. As the reader will become aware, the mathematics employed is primarily based on the application of two of the formulas of Table A.2 of Appendix 1.

People dealing with derivative securities have developed their own vocabulary. For instance, to "long" an asset means to buy an asset for a certain specified price at a certain specified future date. To "short" an asset means to sell it on the same specified date for the same specified price. In options, the underlying assets include stocks, stock indices, foreign currencies, debt instruments, commodities, and futures contracts. A "call" option gives the holder the right to buy the underlying asset by a certain date for a certain price. A "put" option gives the holder the right to sell the underlying asset by a certain date for a certain price. Don't let this special language discourage you from understanding derivative securities. Their underlying logic is straightforward.

Derivative securities can be used to hedge or to speculate. Since this book deals with investment decisions, we will only consider the hedging aspect. To hedge is defined as to safeguard oneself from loss on a risk by making compensatory arrangements on the other side. Thus, the economic functions of derivative securities are (1) risk management tools, and (2) price discovery for both those who are and are not involved in the derivative markets. These functions will become clear once the various types of derivative securities have been introduced. It is noted that the possibilities of designing new interesting derivative securities seem to be limitless. For instance, ski slope operators could issue bonds where the payoff depends on the total annual snowfall at a certain resort!

1. FORWARD CONTRACTS, FUTURES CONTRACTS, AND OPTIONS

A forward contract is a private contract or agreement to buy or sell an asset at a fixed price (called the delivery price) at a specific date in the future. The party who will buy the asset takes the long position, while the one who will sell takes the short position. The delivery price is set at a forward rate F, such that the value of the forward contract is initially (before it is carried out) zero. Consider, for example, a U.S. exporter who will receive DM1,000,000.00 six months from now when he or she delivers his or her merchandise to a German customer. Since the exporter is in the business to produce a product, he or she is not willing to have a loss (or profit!) due to changes in the exchange rate between the U.S. dollar and the German mark (DM).

The exporter wishes to hedge or eliminate the risk of foreign exchange losses. He or she contacts, therefore, a bank today and signs an agreement stipulating that when he or she will receive the DM1,000,000.00 in Germany, the bank will give him or her a specific amount of dollars (e.g., $666,000.00) in the United States in exchange for the German marks. Rather than paying a commission to the bank, banks normally give their exchange rates as ask quotes and bid quotes depending on whether one wishes to obtain dollars for foreign currency or the other way around. They receive their compensation by having ask quotes larger than bid quotes. There is no need to put up funds when signing the above-mentioned agreement. When the exporter receives DM1,000,000.00, he or she delivers them to the bank and gets $666,000.00. In other words, the German marks are sold forward. Another example may pertain to a farmer who sells a given number of bushels of wheat forward when he plants the wheat since he does not want to take the risk of not knowing how much he will get per bushel at harvest time.

Futures contracts are similar to forward contracts; the difference is that they are standardized. That is, the size of the contract is standardized (for instance, in the above example, the bank may only agree in the exchange of German marks for U.S. dollars in specified multiples of DM125,000.00), the expiration date is fixed (e.g., March 15, June 15, September 15, or December 15), and the credit risk is standardized. By a standardized credit risk we mean that each of the two parties of the futures contract is not exposed to each other's risk of default but rather to the risk of a clearing house. A clearing house is an adjunct of the exchange and acts as an intermediary or middleman in futures transactions. It guarantees the performance of the parties to each transaction. The clearing house has a number of members, all of which have offices close to the clearing house. Brokers who are not clearing house members themselves must channel their business through a member. Unlike forward contracts, futures contracts are normally traded on an exchange such as the Chicago Board of Trade (CBOT) and the Chicago Mercantile Exchange (CME). As the two parties to the contract do not necessarily know each other, the exchange provides the above-mentioned mechanism of the clearing house to guarantee that the contract will be honored. Futures contracts are fungible since they are standardized; this means that they can be sold or liquidated before the expiration date, which is not possible with forward contracts. It is estimated that about 90% of the futures contracts in the United States are sold before the expiration date.

Futures contracts call for: (a) the investor to deposit funds, referred to as the initial margin, in what is called the margin account at the time the contract is first entered into (the initial margin is like a performance bond in the construction industry); (b) the broker to adjust the margin account at the end of each trading day, which is known as marking to market the account; (c) the broker to give the investor a "margin" call if the investor's equity determined by the initial margin and the market value of the contract falls below the maintenance level; and (d) the investor to pay an amount to re-establish the initial margin. The following example elucidates this procedure. Suppose an investor contacts his or her broker on June 1, 1997 to buy three December 1997 gold futures contracts, and that the current futures price is $355.00 per ounce. Since the contract size is standardized in 100 ounces, the investor has contracted to buy a total of 300 ounces at this price. The broker requires the investor to deposit an initial margin equal to $2,000.00 per contract, or $6,000.00 in total on June 1, 1997; this initial margin is determined by the broker. The broker also requires the investor to maintain a maintenance level of $4,000.00. Now suppose that by the end of June 1, June 2, and June 3, the futures prices for gold are $360.00, $350.00, and $338.00 per ounce, respectively. Thus, at the end of each of these days, the margin account has to be adjusted to reflect the investor's gain or loss. By the end of June 1, the investor's equity increases to $6,000.00 plus the investor's gain of 300 × $5.00 or $7,500.00, which means that he or she can withdraw $1,500.00 from the margin account. By the end of June 2, the investor's equity drops to $6,000.00 minus a loss of 300 × $5.00 or $4,500.00, which is still above the maintenance level of $4,000.00. However, by the end of June 3, his or her equity drops to $6,000.00 minus a loss of 300 × $17.00 or to $900.00, which is below the maintenance level. The broker gives the investor a margin call requesting him or her to deposit $6,000.00 minus $900.00 (or $5,100.00) in the margin account. If the investor is unable to receive the call because he or she is vacationing in some exotic location without telephone connections, or if he or she is unable to deposit the $5,100.00, the broker will liquidate the long position in order to minimize the risk to the clearing house. This process is repeated at the end of each day until the futures contract is executed on its expiration date. It ensures that there will always be enough funds available to cover losses. It is noted that the investor normally receives interest on the amount deposited in the margin account.

An option is a private contract between two parties where one holder either has the right to buy an underlying asset at a fixed price "K" by a certain date "T" or the right to sell the underlying asset at a fixed price "K" by a certain date "T." The option with a right to buy is called a call option, and the option with a right to sell is called a put option. The price in the option is called the exercise or strike price; the date in the contract is referred to as the exercise or expiration date or maturity. American options can be exercised at any time up to the expiration date, while European options can only be exercised on the expiration date itself. It is noted that the terms *American* and *European* do not refer to the location of the option or the exchange; some options trading on North American exchanges are European and vice versa. There are four basic positions possible: a long position in a call position, a long position in a put position, a short position in a call option, and a short position in a put position. We have already denoted the strike price by K; let us denote the final price of the underlying asset by S_T. Consequently, the pay-off from a long position in a European call option, not including the initial cost of the option, is:

$$\max [S_T - K, 0]. \tag{1}$$

Expression (1) reflects the fact that the option will be exercised if S_T is larger than K, and will not be exercised if S_T is equal to or smaller than K. The payoff to the holder of a short position in the European call option is:

Figure 3.1
Payoff from Forward Contracts

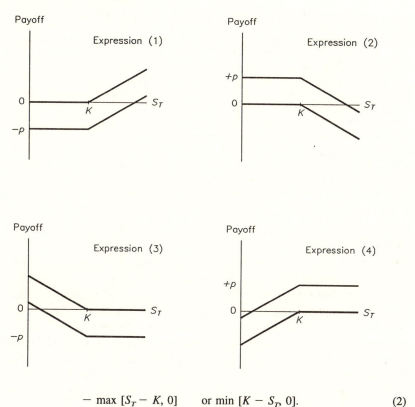

$$- \max [S_T - K, 0] \qquad \text{or } \min [K - S_T, 0]. \tag{2}$$

The payoff to the holder of a long position in a European put option is:

$$\max [K - S_T, 0]. \tag{3}$$

Finally, the payoff from a short position in a European put option is:

$$- \max [K - S_T, 0] \qquad \text{or } \min [S_T - K, 0]. \tag{4}$$

To enhance our understanding of expressions (1)–(4), we graph them in Figure 3.1. In each of the drawings in this figure, we have two lines: one which partly overlaps with the horizontal axis, which corresponds to one of the above four expressions where we ignored the initial cost of the option; and one which starts at the vertical axis at $-p$ or $+p$, where p is the present value of the premium one has to pay when one buys or sells an option. This premium reflects the amount of money one is willing to pay in order to hedge a risk.

2. VALUATION OF FORWARD CONTRACTS

To carry out this evaluation, we introduce the following notation:

T = time when forward contract matures (years)
t = current time (years)
S = price of asset underlying forward contract at time t
S_T = price of asset underlying forward contract at time T; this price is unknown at the current time, t
K = delivery price in forward contract
f = value of a long forward contract at time t
F = forward price at time t.
r = risk-free rate of interest per annum at time t, with continuous compounding, for an investment maturing at time t.

The term "risk-free rate" means the nominal risk-free rate, which includes an inflation premium equal to the average expected inflation rate over the life of a security. In general, we use the T-bill rate to approximate the short-term risk-free rate, and the T-bond rate to approximate the long-term risk-free rate. T-bills (or Treasury bills) are short-term securities issued by the United States government, with respective maturities of 13, 26, and 52 weeks. T-bonds (or Treasury bonds) are long-term securities issued by the United States government with a fixed maturity of more than 10 years. It is noted that the forward price, F, at any given time is the delivery price that would make the contract have a zero value. When a contract is initiated, the delivery price is normally set equal to the forward price so that $F = K$ and $f = 0$. As time passes, both f and F change.

In what follows, we will assume that (a) the market participants can borrow money at the same risk-free rate of interest as they can lend money, (b) the market participants take advantage of arbitrage opportunities as they occur, (c) there are no transactions costs, and (d) all trading profits are subject to the same tax rate. An arbitrage opportunity is a profit one could obtain in the securities market without any risk; naturally, such a situation does not exist.

We first consider the valuation of a forward contract that provides the holder with no income such as non-dividend-paying stocks and discount bonds. Using the concept of continuous discounting, the relationships between F and S and f, S and K are given by equations (5) and (6):

$$F = S \cdot e^{r(T - t)} \tag{5}$$

$$f = S - K \cdot e^{-r(T - t)}. \tag{6}$$

The centered "dot" in the above expressions is interpreted as "multiplied by." The following examples explain why these relationships must hold.

Consider a forward contract on a non-paying stock that matures in 3 months. Assume that the stock price is $50.00, and the 3-month risk-free rate of interest is 5% per annum. Thus, $T - t = 0.25$, $r = 0.05$, and $S = \$50.00$. Consequently,

$$F = \$50 \cdot e^{0.05 \times 0.25} = \$50.63$$

The amount of $50.63 represents the delivery price if a contract would be negotiated today. If the actual forward price would be greater than $50.63, an arbitrageur could borrow money, buy the stock, and short the forward contract for a net profit. If, on the other hand, the forward price would be less than $50.63, an arbitrageur could short the stock, invest the proceeds, and take a long forward position. Again, a net profit would be realized. Since we assumed that there are no arbitrage opportunities, which is the right thing to do in the real world, we conclude that equation (5) must hold.

Now consider a long 6-month forward contract on a 1-year discount bond when the delivery price is $975.00. The 6-month risk-free rate of interest is 6% per annum and the current bond price is $950.00. Thus, $T - t = 0.50$, $r = 0.06$, $K = \$975.00$, and $S = \$950.00$. We compute the value, f, of the long forward contract with equation (6):

$$f = \$950 - \$975 \cdot e^{-0.50 \times 0.06} = \$3.86$$

An arbitrage argument similar to the one given for the previous example leads us to conclude that equation (6) must hold.

The above value of the long forward contract is $3.86. Similarly, the value of a short forward is −$3.86. This means that if you had bought the long 6-month forward contract on the 1-year discount bond six months ago at $K = \$975.00$ and would liquidate (sell) it today, you would lose $3.86. Naturally, this is a hypothetical situation, since the definition of a forward contract refers to buying or selling at a fixed price, K, at a specific date in the future, T. It is necessary to explain the meaning of the value of a long (or short) forward contract. Also recall that when a forward contract is initiated, the forward price equals the delivery price specified in the contract and is chosen so that the value of the contract is zero. In equation (6), we can verify that when $T = t$, the e exponential factor becomes one; and since the value of S at $t = T$ is equal to K, the value of f is indeed zero.

Let us now consider a forward contract on a security that provides a predictable cash income to the holder such as a stock paying known dividends or a coupon bearing bond. Following the above arbitrage argument, we conclude that in this situation the equations (5) and (6) become equations (7) and (8), respectively;

$$F = (S - I) \, e^{r(T - t)} \tag{7}$$

$$f = S - I - K \cdot e^{-r(T-t)} \tag{8}$$

where

I = the present value (using the risk-free discount rate) of income to be received during the life of the forward contract, and all other symbols are as defined earlier.

Consider, for example, a 5-year bond with a price of $900.00. Assume a forward contract on the bond with a delivery price of $910.00 has a maturity of one year. After six and twelve months, coupon payments of $50.00 are expected. The second coupon payment is immediately prior to the delivery date in the forward contract. The risk-free rates of interest are 9% per annum for six months and 10% per annum for one year. So, S = $900.00 and K = $910.00. Consequently,

$$I = \$50 \cdot e^{-0.09 \times 0.50} + \$50 \cdot e^{-0.10} = \$93.04$$

and the value, f, of a long position in the forward contract is obtained by using equation (8):

$$f = \$900.00 - \$93.04 - \$910.00 \cdot e^{-0.10} = -\$16.41$$

The value of the short position is +$16.41.

3. VALUATION OF FUTURES CONTRACTS

In this section, we will use the same notation as the one introduced in the previous section. In addition, we will also assume that (a) the market participants can borrow money at the same risk-free rate of interest as they can lend money, (b) the market participants take advantage of arbitrage opportunities as they occur, (c) there are no transactions costs, and (d) all trading profits are subject to the same tax rate.

Through an arbitrage argument, we can arrive at the following two relationships between prices of forward and futures contracts.

—When the risk-free interest rate is constant and the same for all maturities, the forward price for a contract with a certain delivery date is the same as the futures price for a contract with the same delivery date.

—When risk-free interest rates vary (as they do in the real world), forward and futures prices are no longer the same; if the price of the underlying asset is strongly positively correlated with interest rates, futures prices tend to be higher than forward prices; however, if the price of the underlying asset is strongly negatively correlated with interest rates, forward prices tend to be higher than futures prices.

The above first relationship is intuitively obvious. The second one has to do with the daily settlement procedure described in the above Section 1. That is, if the price of an underlying asset is strongly positively correlated with interest rates, and if this price increases, an investor who holds a long futures position makes an immediate gain because of this procedure. This gain will tend to be invested at a higher-than-average interest rate since increases in the price of the underlying asset tend to occur at the same time as increases in interest rates. Similarly, if the price of the underlying asset decreases, the investor will make an immediate loss. This loss will tend to be financed at a lower-than-average interest rate. An investor holding a forward contract is not affected in this way by interest movements because the daily settlement procedure does not apply. A similar argument can be given to demonstrate that forward prices tend to be higher than futures prices if the price of the underlying asset is strongly negatively correlated with interest rates.

It is noted, however, that the above-mentioned differences between forward and futures prices are sufficiently small to be ignored for contracts which last a few months. It is, therefore, not unreasonable to assume that forward and futures prices are the same. We will make this assumption in this chapter and use the symbol F to represent both the forward price and the futures price of an asset. The valuation of futures contracts will be discussed for the following categories: (a) stock index futures, (b) foreign currency contracts, (c) commodities held for investment (e.g., gold or silver), (d) commodities held for consumption, and (e) interest rate futures.

Stock Index Futures

A stock index tracks the changes in the value of a hypothetical portfolio of stocks. The weight of a stock in the portfolio is equal to the proportion of the portfolio invested in the stock. The percentage increase in the value of a stock index over a small interval of time is usually defined so that it equals the percentage increase in the total value of the stocks comprising the portfolio at that time. A stock index is normally not adjusted for cash dividends. Thus, any cash dividends received on the portfolio are ignored when percentage changes in most indices are being calculated.

The following are the most common stock indices.

a. The Standard & Poor's 500 (S&P 500) Index, which trades on the Chicago Mercantile Exchange (CME) and is based on a portfolio of 500 different stocks.

b. The New York Stock Exchange (NYSE) Composite Index, which is based on a portfolio of all the stocks listed on the New York Stock Exchange.

c. The Major Market Index (MMI), which is based on a portfolio of 20 blue-chip stocks listed on the New York Stock Exchange.

d. The Nikkei 225 Stock Average, which is based on a portfolio of 225 of the largest stocks trading on the Tokyo Stock Exchange.

It is noted that the MMI is closely related to the widely quoted Dow Jones Industrial Average, which is also based on relatively few stocks.

Stock index futures can be used to hedge the risk in a well-diversified portfolio of stocks. As explained in Section 5 of Chapter 5, the relationship between the return on a portfolio of stocks and the return on the market is described by a parameter β (= beta). When $\beta = 1.0$, the return on the portfolio tends to mirror the return on the market; when $\beta = 2.0$, the excess return on the portfolio tends to be twice as great as the excess return on the market; when $\beta = 0.5$, it tends to be half as great; and so on. In other words, the market "beta" is a measure of the exposure to market movements. A hedge using index futures separates the market risk from the portfolio risk.

Suppose an investor holds a portfolio of stocks worth V and he or she wishes to hedge against changes in this value during a period of time, $T - t$. The investor has expertise in these particular stocks, which he or she expects to outperform the market, but is worried of market movements. These can be hedged using stock index futures because movements in the portfolio can be decomposed into a portion due to the market (subject to risk related to the market, sometimes referred to as systematic risk), and an idiosyncratic portion (subject to unsystematic risk). We define:

ΔV = change in the value of \$1.00 during time $T - t$ if it is invested in the portfolio
ΔM = change in the value of \$1.00 during time $T - t$ if it is invested in the market
ΔF = change in the value of \$1.00 during time $T - t$ if it is invested in the market index
V = current value of the portfolio
M = current value of the market
F = current value of one futures contract
N = optimal number of contracts to short when hedging the portfolio.

The value of one futures contract, F, is the futures price multiplied by the contract size. In the case of the S&P 500, one contract is on 500 times the index. If the futures price of the S&P 500 is \$300, then $\$300 \times 500 = \$150,000.00$ is the value of one contract.

From the definition of β, it is approximately true that

$$\Delta V = \alpha + \beta \cdot \Delta M$$

where α is a constant. A futures contract on the S&P 500, defined as the market in our example, essentially behaves as:

$$\Delta F = \Delta M.$$

We can, therefore, construct a new portfolio consisting of the original one plus a short position in N futures contracts, whose value will fluctuate as:

$$V \cdot \Delta V - N \cdot F \cdot \Delta F = V \cdot \beta \cdot \Delta M - N \cdot F \cdot \Delta M = (V \cdot \beta - N \cdot F) \Delta M = \text{exposure} \times \Delta M \quad (9)$$

where the exposure is the exposure due to the systematic risk or the risk related to market fluctuations. The portfolio will be immunized against the systematic risk by setting the exposure or $(V \cdot \beta - N \cdot F)$ equal to zero, or choosing:

$$N = \beta \cdot V/F. \quad (10)$$

As demonstrated in the following example, equation (10) can be used to determine the number of contracts to sell short.

A company wishes to hedge a $2,000,000.00 portfolio using S&P 500 futures. The futures price is $300, with a multiplier of 500.00. The portfolio's β is 1.5. The number of contracts to sell short is $N = 1.5 \ (\$2,000,000.00)/(500 \times \$300) = 20$.

A stock index hedge, if effective, should result in the hedger's position growing at approximately the risk-free interest rate. If the hedger's goal is to earn the risk-free interest rate, why should he or she go through the trouble of using futures contracts rather than simply sell the portfolio and invest the proceeds in Treasury bills? One reason is that the hedger is planning to hold a portfolio for a long period of time and requires short-term protection in an uncertain market situation. The alternative strategy of selling the portfolio and buying it back later might involve unacceptable high transaction costs. Another possibility is that the hedger feels that the stocks in the portfolio are undervalued (Chapter 2), and is uncertain about the market's performance as a whole; however, he or she is confident that the stocks in the portfolio will outperform the market. Using index futures as a hedge removes the risk arising from market moves and leaves the hedger exposed only to the performance of the portfolio relative to the market.

Beta coefficients for thousands of companies are calculated and published by Merrill Lynch, Value Line, and numerous other organizations. They are based on a stock's historical values. Most stocks have betas in the range of 0.50 to 1.50, and the average for all stocks is 1.00 by definition.

Foreign Currency Contracts

A foreign currency has the characteristic that the owner of the currency can earn interest at the risk-free interest rate prevailing in the foreign country by, for instance, investing the currency in a foreign denominated bond. We introduce the following notation:

$S =$ the current price in dollars of one unit of the foreign currency
$K =$ the delivery price agreed to in the futures contract

r = domestic risk-free interest rate per annum with continuous compounding
R = foreign risk-free interest rate per annum, with continuous compounding
f = value of a long futures contract at time t
t = current time (years)
T = time when contract matures (years).

To compute the price of a contract on a foreign currency, we compare one long futures contract plus an amount of cash equal to $K \cdot e^{-r(T-t)}$ to an amount $e^{-R(T-t)}$ of the foreign currency. These two situations can be considered as two portfolios. Both of them will become worth the same at time T. They must, therefore, be equally valuable at time t. Consequently,

$$f + K \cdot e^{-r(T-t)} = S \cdot e^{-R(T-t)}$$

or

$$f = S \cdot e^{-R(T-t)} - K \cdot e^{-r(T-t)}. \tag{11}$$

The futures price (or futures exchange rate), F, is the value of K that makes $f = 0$ in equation (11). Hence,

$$F = S \cdot e^{(r-R)(T-t)}. \tag{12}$$

Expression (12) is the interest rate parity relationship from the field of international finance.

The *Wall Street Journal* publishes futures prices for contracts trading on the major currencies in the International Money Market of the Chicago Mercantile Exchange. The futures exchange rate is quoted as the value of the foreign currency in U.S. dollars; in the case of yen, the value of the foreign currency is in U.S. cents.

Equation (12) shows that when the foreign interest rate is greater than the domestic interest rate, F is always less than S and F decreases as the maturity of the contract, T, increases. The foreign currency sells at a discount. When the domestic interest rate is greater than the foreign interest rate, F is always greater than S or the foreign currency sells at a premium.

Commodities Held for Investment

A significant number of investors hold gold or silver solely for investment. They can be considered as being analogous to securities paying no income if storage costs are zero. Using the notation introduced in the beginning of Section 2 of this chapter, S is the current spot price of gold. Equation (5) shows that the futures price, F, is given by:

$$F = S \cdot e^{r(T-t)}. \tag{13}$$

Storage costs can be considered as negative income. It follows from equation (7) that if storage costs are incurred, the value of F is given by:

$$F = (S + U)e^{r(T-t)} \tag{14}$$

where

U = the present value of all the storage costs which will be incurred during the life of a futures contract.

The value of F is given by equation (15) if the storage costs incurred at any time are proportional to the price of the commodity, in which case they can be considered as a negative dividend yield:

$$F = S \cdot e^{(r+u)(T-t)} \tag{15}$$

where

u = the storage costs per annum as a proportion of the spot price.

Consider, for example, a 1-year futures contract on gold, and suppose that it costs \$3.00 per ounce per year to store gold, with the payment made at the end of each year. Assume that the spot price is \$450.00 and the risk-free interest rate is 7% per year for all maturities. Hence, $r = 0.07$, $S = 450$, $T - t = 1$, and $U = \$3 \cdot e^{-0.07} = \$2.80$. With the help of equation (14), we compute the futures price, F, as follows:

$$F = (\$450.00 + \$2.80)\, e^{0.07} = \$485.63$$

Commodities Held for Consumption

Companies and individuals who keep a commodity in inventory do so because of its consumption value, not because of its value as an investment. They would, therefore, be reluctant to sell the commodity and buy futures contracts which they cannot consume. Since from the investment point of view there is an insignificant benefit from holding the commodity, we conclude that in equations (14) and (15) the "equal" sign has to be replaced by a "smaller than" sign.

When F is smaller than $S \cdot e^{(r+u)(T-t)}$, the users of the commodity must feel that there is a benefit from its ownership. The benefit may be the ability to keep a production process running smoothly or to profit from a temporary local shortage. This type of benefit is sometimes referred to as the convenience yield provided by the commodity. It reflects the market's expectations about the future availability of the commodity. If users of a commodity have high inventories, there is little chance of shortages in the near future and the convenience yield tends to be low. On the other hand, low inventories tend to lead to high convenience yields. In terms of our notation, the convenience yield, y, is defined so that

$$F \cdot e^{y(T-t)} = (S + U)e^{r(T-t)} \tag{16}$$

where

$$U = \text{the present value of the storage costs.}$$

If the storage costs per unit are a constant proportion, u, of the spot price, equation (16) becomes:

$$F \cdot e^{y(T-t)} = S \cdot e^{(r+u)(T-t)}$$

or

$$F = S \cdot e^{(r+u-y)(T-t)}. \tag{17}$$

It is clear that for investment commodities, the convenience yield is equal to zero since, otherwise, there are arbitrage opportunities.

Interest Rate Futures

An interest rate futures contract is a futures contract on an asset whose price is dependent solely on the level of interest rates. Treasury bond futures contracts traded on the Chicago Board of Trade (CBOT) are the most popular long-term interest rate futures contracts. In these contracts, any government bond with more than 15 years to maturity on the first day of the delivery month, and not callable within 15 years from that day, can be delivered.

Treasury (T)-bond prices and T-bond futures prices are quoted in dollars and thirty-two seconds of a dollar. A T-bond normally has a face value of $100,000.00. Thus, a quote of 90-05 means that the price for a bond with a face value of $100,000.00 is $90,156.25, where 156.25 = 5(1/32) (1,000). The quoted price is not the same as the cash price which is paid by the purchaser because the accrued interest since the last coupon date is added to the quoted price in order to arrive at the cash price.

In the T-bond futures contract, there is a provision for the party with the short position to choose to deliver any bond with a maturity over 15 years and not callable within 15 years. When a bond is delivered, a parameter known as its conversion factor defines its price received by the party with the short position. The quoted price applicable to the delivery is the product of the conversion factor and the quoted futures price. Taking accrued interest into account, the cash received by the party with the short position equals the quoted futures price times the conversion factor for the bond delivered plus the accrued interest on the bond delivered. Suppose, for instance, that the quoted futures price is 90-05, the conversion factor for the bond delivered is 1.5705, and the accrued interest on this bond at the time of delivery is \$3.50 per \$100.00 face value. The cash received by the party with the short position when it delivers the bond is (\$90,156.25 $\times$ 1.5705) + \$3,500.00 = \$145,090.39.

The conversion factor for a bond is equal to the value of the bond on the first day of the delivery month on the assumption that the interest rate for all maturities equals 8% per year (with semiannual compounding). In order to enable CBOT to produce comprehensive tables, the bond maturity and the times to the coupon payment dates are rounded down to the nearest 3 months for the purposes of calculation. If, after rounding, the bond lasts for an exact number of half years, the first coupon is assumed to be paid in 6 months. If, after rounding, the bond does not last for an exact number of 6 months (that is, there is an extra 3 months), the first coupon is assumed to be paid after 3 months and accrued interest is subtracted. The following example elucidates the procedure.

Let us calculate the conversion factor of a 14% coupon bond with 18 years and 4 months to maturity. To simplify the calculation, it is first carried out for each \$100.00 face value of the bond. In view of the above rounding procedure, the bond is assumed to have exactly 18 years and 3 months to maturity. Discounting all the payments back to a point in time 3 months from today gives a value of

$$\sum_{n=0}^{36} 7 / (1.04)^n + 100 / (1.04)^{36} = 163.74$$

The interest rate for a 3-month period is 1.98%. Discounting back to the present gives the bond's value as $163.74/1.0198 = 160.56$ and, after subtracting the accrued interest of 3.5, this becomes 157.06. Since the calculation was carried out for each \$100.00 face value of the bond, we divide by 100 to arrive at a conversion factor of 1.5706. Note that the 1.04 in the denominator of the above expression is based on half of the 8% mentioned in the definition of the conversion factor, and that the accrued interest of 3.5 is equal to $(3/12) \cdot (14)$.

At any time, there are about 30 bonds that can be delivered in the CBOT T-bond futures contract. These vary as far as coupon and maturity are concerned. The party with the short position can choose which of the available bonds is "cheapest" to deliver. For example, a party with a short position has decided to deliver and is trying to choose between the three bonds with the quoted prices, conversion factors, and the current quoted futures price (93-08 or 93.25) as given in the second, third, and fourth columns of Table 3.1. To compute which of the three bonds is the cheapest to deliver, the party computes the cost of delivering

Table 3.1
Example of Deliverable Bonds

Bond	Quoted Price	Conversion Factor	Quoted Futures Prices	Cost of Delivering
1	98.50	1.0380	93.25	1.71
2	142.50	1.5177	93.25	0.97
3	117.75	1.2515	93.25	1.05

each of the bonds. This is done by first multiplying the current quoted futures price by the conversion factor of each bond. Next, the party computes the cost of delivering each bond as the difference between the quoted price and the result of the aforementioned multiplication. The results of these computations as shown in the last column of Table 3.1 indicate that the cheapest-to-deliver bond is bond #2. Note that the 1.71 in the last column of Table 3.1 is the result of 98.50 − (1.0380 × 93.25). The other amounts in the last column are obtained in a similar manner.

An important concept in the use of interest rate futures is "duration." The duration of a bond is a measure of how long, on average, the holder of the bond has to wait before receiving cash payments. A zero-coupon bond that matures in n years has a duration of n years; however, a coupon-bearing bond maturing in n years has a duration of less than n years since some of the cash payments will be received prior to year n. The duration, D, of a bond is defined as:

$$D = (\sum_{i=1}^{n} t_i \cdot c_i \cdot e^{-y t_i}) \, / \, B \qquad (18)$$

where

t_i = the time at which a bond provides the holder with a payment c_i; during the duration there can be one or more payments
y = yield of the bond, continuously compounding (years)
B = price of the bond.

The relation between the price, B, and the yield, y, is given by equation (19):

$$B = \sum_{i=1}^{n} c_i \cdot e^{-y t_i}. \qquad (19)$$

Taking the first derivative with respect to y of B, or equation (19), and using equation (18), yields:

$$\frac{dB}{dy} = -B \cdot D$$

or

$$\frac{\Delta B}{B} = -D \cdot \Delta y. \qquad (20)$$

Equation (20) shows that the percentage change in a bond price equals its duration multiplied by the size of the parallel shift in the yield curve.

The duration of a bond portfolio is defined as a weighted average of the durations of the individual bonds in the portfolio with the weights being proportional to the bond prices. As we will see in the following, duration measures the exposure to movements in interest rates.

We define the following notation:

F = contract price for the interest rate futures contract
V = value of asset being hedged
D_F = duration of asset underlying futures contract
D_V = duration of asset being hedged
ΔV = change in value of asset being hedged
Δy = change in yield
N = optimal number of contracts to short when hedging the asset (portfolio).

The movement in prices can be described as:

$$\Delta V/V = -D_V \cdot \Delta y. \qquad (21)$$

For a futures contract,

$$\Delta F/F = -D_F \cdot \Delta y.$$

Similar to the derivation of equation (10), we can construct a portfolio consisting of the original asset plus a short position in N futures contracts, whose value will fluctuate as:

$$\Delta V - N \cdot \Delta F = -D_v \cdot V \cdot \Delta y - N\,(-D_F \cdot F)\,\cdot \Delta y = (N \cdot D_F \cdot F - D_V \cdot V)\,\Delta y$$
$$= \text{exposure } x\ \Delta y.$$

The portfolio will be immunized against interest rate risks by setting the exposure equal to zero, or choosing

$$N = V \cdot D_V / F \cdot D_F. \qquad (22)$$

Expression (22) is the duration-based hedge ratio. It is sometimes also called the price sensitivity ratio.

It is noted that, strictly speaking, equation (21) is only valid if (a) small yield changes are considered, and (b) all interest rates change by the same amount. When large yield changes are considered, a factor known as convexity is sometimes important. Some financial institutions, when managing portfolios of assets and liabilities, try to match both duration and convexity. The effect of the aforementioned item (b) can be minimized by hedging a portfolio with primarily long-term bonds with futures contracts with primarily long-term bonds, or hedging a portfolio with primarily short-term bonds with futures contracts with primarily short-term bonds.

To enhance our understanding of equation (22), we consider the following example. A company wishes to hedge a $10,000,000.00 portfolio invested in U.S. government bonds using T-bond futures. The current futures price is 93-04 or 93.13, with a face value of $100,000.00. The duration of the cheapest-to-deliver bond in the T-bond contract is 9.1 years. The portfolio duration is 6.7 years. Thus, $V = \$10,000,000.00$, $F = \$93,130.00$, $D_F = 9.1$, and $D_V = 6.7$. The value of N is obtained with equation (22):

$$N = \$10,000,000 \ (6.7)/\$93,130 \ (9.1) = 79.06$$

Consequently, the number of contracts to sell short is 79.

Before we move on, we make the following observations about this example.

a. The company would hedge the value of its portfolio if it is concerned about interest rates to be highly volatile over, for instance, the next three months. If this were in the beginning of August, the company would use a December T-bond futures contract to hedge the value of its portfolio.

b. If interest rates decrease, a loss will be made on the short position, but there will be a gain on the bond portfolio. If interest rates increase, a gain will be made on the short futures position and a loss will be made on the bond portfolio.

c. The duration of the bond portfolio, 6.7 years, is obtained with equation (18), where D is the above-defined duration of a portfolio.

d. The company determines the cheapest-to-deliver bond in a manner similar to the above given example pertaining to Table 3.1. Its duration is again determined with the help of equation (18).

4. MORE ABOUT HEDGING USING FUTURES

As we have seen, hedging is used to eliminate risks. These risks can be price risks or cost risks. For instance, a farmer who is going to sell his crop at harvest time, that is, at a particular time in the future, can hedge by taking a short futures position. In this case, he hedges to eliminate the risk related to future price fluctuations. It is noted that hedging to eliminate price risks is normally done for short-term price fluctuations; if it were long-term, the farmer is likely to go out of business! An example of using hedging to eliminate cost risks is an airline taking a long futures position for buying fuel. A futures hedge reduces risk by making the outcome more certain. It does not, however, necessarily improve the overall financial outcome. In fact, we can expect a futures hedge to make the outcome better about 50% of the time, but also worse about 50% of the time.

In general, we cannot hedge against a quantity risk. For instance, in the above example of the farmer, the farmer normally does not hedge the risk that, due to bad weather, his total crop may be less than expected in average weather conditions. As a rule of thumb, he takes a short futures position on two-thirds of his expected production. Although normally not done, the farmer could take a put option on one-third of his expected production for which he does not take a short futures position, if he uses the rule of thumb.

In practice, the use of futures contracts may work less than perfectly since (a) the hedge may require the futures contract to be closed out before its expiration date, (b) the asset whose price is to be hedged may not be exactly the same as the asset underlying the futures contract, and (c) the hedger may be uncertain as to the exact date when the asset will be bought or sold. Situation (a) can arise since futures contracts are, as we have discussed, standardized. An example of situation (b) would be airlines who sometimes use the NYMEX heating oil futures contracts to hedge their exposure to the price of jet fuel since suitable jet fuel futures contracts are not available. Situation (c) may arise with a company with recent labor troubles or strikes and, therefore, uncertain about the delivery date of a product to be sold. Any of the above problems (a)–(c) give rise to what is called "basis risk." The basis in a hedging situation is defined as the spot price of the asset to be hedged minus the futures price of the contract used. If the asset to be hedged and the asset underlying the futures contract are the same, the basis should be zero at the expiration of the futures contract. Prior to expiration, the basis may be positive or negative.

From the above definition of the basis, it is clear that when the spot price increases by more than the futures price, the basis increases. This is called a strengthening of the basis. Alternatively, when the futures price increases by more than the spot price, the basis declines. This is called a weakening of the basis.

We introduce the following notation to analyze the nature of basis risk:

S_1 = spot price at time t_1
S_2 = spot price at time t_2
F_1 = futures price at time t_1
F_2 = futures price at time t_2
b_1 = basis at time t_1
b_2 = basis at time t_2.

It is assumed that a hedge is put in place at time t_1, and closed at time t_2.

Consider, for example, a situation where the spot and futures prices at the time that the hedge is initiated are \$2.40 and \$2.10, respectively, and that at the time the hedge is closed out they are \$1.90 and \$1.80, respectively. Thus, $S_1 =$ \$2.40, $F_1 =$ \$2.10, $S_2 =$ \$1.90, and $F_2 =$ 1.80. Consequently, $b_1 = S_1 - F_1 =$ \$0.30, and $b_2 = S_2 - F_2 =$ \$0.10. Assume a hedger takes a short futures position at time t_1 on an asset which will be sold at time t_2. The price realized for the asset is S_2 and the profit on the futures position is $F_1 - F_2$. The effective price which is obtained for the asset with hedging is, therefore, $S_2 + F_1 - F_2 = F_1 + b_2$ or \$2.20 in our example. The problem is that unlike the value of F_1, the value of b_2 at time t_1 is not known; if it were known, a perfect hedge, or one eliminating all uncertainty about the price obtained, would result. The hedging risk is the uncertainty associated with b_2. Consider now a company interested in buying an asset at time t_2 and initiating a long futures position at time t_1. The price paid for the asset is S_2 and the loss on the hedge is $F_1 - F_2$. The effective price paid with hedging is, therefore, $S_2 + F_1 - F_2 = F_1 + b_2$, or \$2.20 in our example. Here, again, the value of F_1 is known at time t_1, and the term b_2 is the basis risk.

As we have seen in the previous section, arbitrage arguments lead to a well-defined relationship between the futures price and the spot price of an investment asset such as foreign currencies, commodities for investment (e.g., gold or silver), and stock indices. The basis risk for these investments tends, therefore, to be fairly small. The basis risk for an investment asset arises mainly from uncertainty as to the level of the risk-free interest rate in the future. In case of commodities such as copper, oil, or soy beans, imbalances between supply and demand as well as difficulties associated with storing the commodity can lead to large variations in the basis.

An important factor affecting basis risk is the choice of the delivery month, which is likely to be affected by several factors. It might be assumed that, when the expiration date of the hedge corresponds to a delivery month, the contract with that delivery month is chosen; however, in these circumstances, a contract with a later delivery month is often chosen. This is so since futures prices are in some circumstances quite erratic during the delivery month. In addition, a long hedger runs the risk of having to take delivery of the physical asset if he or she holds the contract during the delivery month. This can be expensive and inconvenient. In general, basis risk increases as the time between the hedge expiration and the delivery month increases. To choose a delivery month that is as close as possible to, but later than, the expiration of the hedge is, therefore, a good rule of thumb.

Consider, for example, a U.S. company which expects to receive 100 million yen at the end of July. On March 1, 1997, the company wishes to short yen futures contracts. Yen futures contracts on the International Monetary Exchange have delivery months of March, June, September, and December. One contract is for the delivery of 12.5 million yen. The company therefore shorts eight

September yen futures contracts. When the yen are received at the end of July, the company closes out its position. Suppose that the futures price on March 1, 1997 in cents per yen is 0.7700, and that the spot and futures prices when the contract is closed out are 0.7100 and 0.7150, respectively. Thus, the basis is −0.0050 when the contract is closed out. The effective price obtained in cents per yen is 0.7700 − 0.0050 = 0.7650. The company receives a total of 100 × 0.007650 million dollars (or $765,000.00).

The hedge ratio is defined as the ratio of the size of the position taken in futures contracts to the size of the exposure. Heretofore, we have always assumed a hedge ratio of 1.0. We now demonstrate that a hedge ratio of 1.0 is not necessarily optimal if the objective of the hedger is to minimize risk. To do so, we introduce the following notation:

ΔS = change in the spot price, S, during a period of time equal to the life of the hedge
ΔF = change in the futures price, F, during a period of time equal to the life of the hedge
σ_S = standard deviation of ΔS
σ_F = standard deviation of ΔF
ρ = coefficient of correlation between ΔS and ΔF
h = hedge ratio.

The change in the value of the hedger's position during the life of the hedge when the hedger longs the asset and shorts futures is $\Delta S - h \cdot \Delta F$; for a long hedge, it is $h \cdot \Delta F - \Delta S$. In either case, the variance, v, of the change in value of the hedged position is given by:

$$v = \sigma_S^2 + h^2 \cdot \sigma_F^2 - 2h \cdot \rho \cdot \sigma_S \cdot \sigma_F$$

so that

$$\frac{dv}{dh} = 2h \cdot \sigma_F^2 - 2\rho \cdot \sigma_S \cdot \sigma_F.$$

Setting this equal to zero, and noting that the second derivative of v with respect to h is positive, we obtain the value of h that minimizes the variance:

$$h = \rho \cdot \sigma_S / \sigma_F. \tag{23}$$

In other words, the optimal hedge ratio is the product of the coefficient of correlation between ΔS and ΔF and the ratio of the standard deviation of ΔS to the standard deviation of ΔF.

A high correlation coefficient means that the variance of the hedged position will be very small in relation to the original variance. If it is unity, the hedge is perfect. If it is zero, the hedge is useless. When a company has a choice of futures contracts to hedge a particular exposure, it should take the contract that has the highest correlation with the spot price. Let us consider the following example to elucidate the use of the hedge ratio.

An airline wishes to hedge a future payment for one million gallons of jet fuel in three months using heating oil futures. One heating oil futures contract is on 45,000 gallons. The standard deviation of jet fuel is 0.034 over a 3-month period, that of heating oil futures is 0.042 over a 3-month period, and the correlation coefficient is 0.8. The hedge ratio is $h = (0.8) (0.034)/(0.042) = 0.65$. Since one futures bears on 45,000 gallons, the company should buy 0.65 $(1,000,000)/(45,000) = 14.4$ contracts or, rounding to the nearest whole number, 14 contracts.

The expiration date of the hedge is sometimes later than the delivery dates of all the futures contracts used. In this case, the hedger can roll the hedge forward. This involves closing out one futures contract and taking the same position in a futures contract with a later delivery date. Hedges can be rolled forward many times. If this is done and if, for instance, there are five futures contracts with progressively later delivery dates, then there are five basis risks or sources of uncertainty.

5. SWAPS

Swaps are private agreements between two companies to exchange cash flows in the future according to a prearranged formula. They are extensions of forward contracts. The most commonly used swaps are interest rate swaps and currency swaps. The International Bank for Reconstruction and Development (IBRD), also known as the World Bank, entered the first currency swap in 1981. IBRD wanted to raise the equivalent of $200 million in Swiss francs. By directly raising funds in Switzerland, its funding cost would have been 8.38%. Because the World Bank (with its headquarters in Washington, DC) has a comparative advantage in U.S. markets, it issued a dollar-denominated bond, then entered a currency swap agreement to pay francs and receive dollars. As a result, the dollar cost was transformed into a franc cost of 8.10%. This derivative contract lowered the annual funding cost by $560,000.00, which was passed along to the borrowing countries. Since 1981, swaps have saved the World Bank over $900 million. It is, therefore, worth our time to examine how swaps work.

In an interest rate swap, Party A agrees to pay Party B cash flows equal to interest at a predetermined floating rate on a notional principal for a number of years (normally two to fifteen years). At the same time, Party B agrees to pay Party A cash flows equal to interest at a fixed rate on the same notional principal for the same period of time. The currencies of the two sets of interest cash flows are the same. The swap has the effect of transforming a fixed rate loan into a floating rate loan or vice versa. The reason why two parties enter into a swap is that one has a comparative advantage in floating rate markets, and the other one has a comparative advantage in fixed rate markets. Naturally, it makes sense for a party to go to the market where it has a comparative advantage when obtaining a loan. By doing this, however, the party ends up borrowing fixed when it wants floating or vice versa.

In many interest rate swaps, the floating rate is the London Inter-Bank Offered Rate (LIBOR), which is the rate of interest offered by banks on deposits from other banks in Euro currency markets. Similar to the prime rate being often the reference rate of interest for floating rate loans in the United States, LIBOR is frequently a reference rate of interest in international markets. One-month LIBOR is the rate offered on 1-month deposits, 3-month LIBOR is the rate offered on 3-month deposits, and so on. To enhance our understanding of how LIBOR is used, consider a loan where the interest rate is specified as 3-month LIBOR plus 0.5% per year. The life of the loan is divided into 3-month time periods. For each period, the interest rate is set at 0.5% per annum above the 3-month LIBOR rate at the beginning of the period. Interest is paid at the end of the period.

The simplest way of explaining how a swap works is by giving an example. Suppose that two companies, A and B, both want to borrow $15 million for a period of ten years and have been offered the following rates:

	Fixed Rate	*Floating Rate*
Company A	10.00%	6-month LIBOR + 0.35%
Company B	11.25%	6-month LIBOR + 1.00%

Assume that A wants to borrow floating funds at a rate linked to 6-month LIBOR, and B wants to borrow at a fixed interest rate. The above fixed and floating rates show that B has a lower credit rating than A since it pays a higher interest rate in both markets. Company A appears to have a comparative advantage in fixed rate markets, while company B appears to have a comparative advantage in floating rate markets since the extra amount that B pays over the amount paid by A is less in this market than in the fixed rate markets. The fact that the difference between the two fixed rates is greater than the difference between the two floating rates (B pays 1.25% more than A in fixed rate markets and only 0.65% more than A in floating rate markets) allows a profitable swap to be negotiated. Company A borrows fixed rate funds at 10% per annum and company B borrows floating rate funds at LIBOR plus 1% per annum. Next, they enter into a swap to ensure that A ends up with floating rate funds and B with fixed rate funds.

Typically, a swap is carried out through the intermediary of a bank. To enhance our understanding of how a swap works, we first assume that A and B get in touch directly. The sort of swap that they might negotiate is as follows:

Company A agrees to pay company B interest at 6-month LIBOR on $15 million and company B agrees to pay company A interest at a fixed rate of 9.95% per year on $15 million. Company A has three sets of interest rate cash flows: (1) it pays 10% per annum to outside lenders, (2) it receives 9.95% per annum from B, and (3) it pays LIBOR to B. The first and second cash flows cost A 0.05% per annum. Thus, the net effect of the three cash flows is that A pays LIBOR plus 0.05% per annum or 0.30% per annum less than it would pay if it went directly to floating rate markets. Company B also has three sets of cash flows: (1) it pays LIBOR + 1% per annum to outside lenders, (2) it receives LIBOR from A, and (3) it pays 9.95% per annum to A. The first two cash flows taken together cost B 1% per annum. Consequently, the net effect of the three cash flows is that B pays 10.95% per annum or 0.30% per annum less than it would if it went directly to fixed rate markets.

From the above discussion, it is clear that the swap arrangement improves the position of both companies A and B by 0.30% or 30 basis points (a basis point is 0.01%) per annum. The total gain is, therefore, 60 basis points per annum. The total gain from an interest rate swap is always $x - y$, where x is the difference between the interest rates facing the two parties in fixed rate markets, and y is the difference between the interest rates facing the two parties in floating rate markets. In our example, $x = 1.25\%$ and $y = 0.65\%$.

Let us now consider the financial intermediary or the bank. Thus, the total gain of 60 basis points per annum has to be split three ways, that is, between A, B, and the bank. A possible arrangement is as follows:

```
                      9.9%              10.0%
      10.0%         <--------         <--------        LIBOR + 1.0%
  <-----------  | A |  LIBOR  | Bank |  LIBOR  | B | ----------->
                      -------->          -------->
```

Now A has the following three sets of interest rate cash flows: (1) it pays 10% per year to outside lenders, (2) it receives 9.9% per year from the bank, and (3) it pays LIBOR to the bank. The net effect of these three cash flows is that A pays LIBOR plus 0.10% per annum, which is a 0.25% per annum improvement over the rate it could get by going directly to floating rate markets. The interest rate cash flows of B are: (1) it pays LIBOR + 1% per year to outside lenders, (2) it receives LIBOR from the bank, and (3) it pays 10% per year to the bank. The net effect of these three cash flows is that B pays 11% per year, which is a 0.25% per year improvement over the rate if it went directly to fixed rate markets. The bank's net gain is 0.10% per annum, since the fixed rate it receives is 0.10% higher than the fixed rate it pays and the floating rate it receives is the same as the floating rate it pays. The total gain to all parties is again 60 basis points.

Let us now examine currency swaps. Such a swap involves exchanging principal and fixed rate interest payments on a loan in one currency for the principal and fixed interest payments on an approximately equivalent loan in another currency. As in the case of interest rate swaps, currency swaps come into being due to comparative advantage. Suppose that companies A and B are offered the following fixed interest rates in dollars and sterling:

	Dollars	Sterling
Company A	7.0%	11.0%
Company B	6.2%	10.6%

Company B is clearly more credit worthy than company A since it is offered a more favorable interest rate in both currencies. Company A wishes to borrow dollars and company B sterling. Since A has a comparative advantage in the sterling market (the difference between the sterling rates is smaller than the difference in the dollar rates), it borrows in the sterling rate. For B it is advantageous to borrow in the dollar market. They then use a currency swap to transform A's loan into a dollar loan and B's loan into a sterling loan.

There are many ways in which the swap can be arranged. One way is as follows:

```
                     11.00% £              10.45% £
    11.00% £       ◄- - - - - - - -      ◄- - - - - - - -      6.20% $
    ◄- - - - - - -│ A │  6.85% $  │Bank│  6.20% $  │ B │- - - - - - -►
                  └───┘- - - - - - -►└────┘- - - - - - -►└───┘
```

The swap's effect is to transform the sterling rate of 11% per year to a dollar rate of 6.85% per year for company A. Note that the advantage of the swap to A is $(7.00\% - 6.85\%) = 0.15\%$ per annum, and to B $(10.60\% - 10.45\%) = 0.15\%$ per annum. The bank gains 0.65% per annum on its dollar cash flows and loses 0.55% per annum on its sterling cash flows. Ignoring the difference between the two currencies, the bank comes out ahead with 0.10% per annum. The total gain to all parties is 0.40% per annum, which is equal to the difference between the dollar rates minus the difference between the sterling rates.

Assume, for instance, that the principal amounts are 15 million dollars and 10 million sterling. At the beginning of the swap of our example, A pays 10 million sterling and receives 15 million dollars. Each year during the life of the swap, A receives 11% of 10 million sterling and pays 6.85% of 15 million dollars. At the end of the swap's life, A pays a principal of 15 million dollars and receives a principal of 10 million sterling. It is noted that, in our example, the bank is exposed to foreign exchange risk. Each year it makes a gain of 0.65% of 15 million dollars (or 97,500 dollars) and a loss of 0.55% of 10 million sterling (or 55,000 sterling). The bank can avoid the foreign exchange risk by buying 55,000 sterling per annum in the forward market during each year of the swap's life. By doing so, the bank locks in a net gain in U.S. dollars.

SUGGESTIONS FOR FURTHER READING

Black, F., and M. Scholes. "The Behavior of Stock Prices." *Journal of Business* 38 (January 1965): 34–105.

Chicago Board of Trade. *Commodity Trading Manual*. Chicago, 1989.

Duffie, D. *Futures Markets*. Englewood Cliffs, NJ: Prentice-Hall, 1989.

International Swap Dealer's Association. *Code of Standard Working, Assumptions and Provisions for Swaps*. New York, 1986.

Kolb, R. W. *Understanding Futures Markets*. Miami, FL: Kolb Publishing Company, 1994.

McMillan, L. G. *Options as a Strategic Investment*. New York: New York Institute of Finance, 1986.

CHAPTER 4

Diversification

Every noble acquisition is attended with its risks; he who fears to encounter the one must not expect to obtain the other.

—Pietro Metastasio

We define diversification as the production of a commodity which differs from a company's existing line, and which is sold in a different market. There are four important reasons for devoting a separate chapter to diversification, although the criteria and grounds which justify it are the same as those applicable to any other investment open to a firm.

First, for many companies, the need to diversify is not a continuous one. Consequently, it is desirable to be able to add or eliminate diversification planning without disrupting other planning procedures. Second, diversification planning is more complex than other capital investment planning, since it involves people to a much greater extent. Third, diversification often sets in motion currents of adverse reaction during the adjustment of the existing business to the new activity. Fourth, the evaluation of company acquisitions calls for a scrutiny of generally accepted accounting principles.

Two forms of diversification can be distinguished—internal expansion and external expansion. Internal expansion feeds on research and development, while external expansion feeds on acquisitions. When a corporation acquires the stock or assets of another company, legal, tax, and financial factors determine whether the form of bringing together the two companies is a consolidation, a purchase of assets, a merger, a stock purchase, or a stock exchange. This chapter does not treat these legal forms separately, since we are interested primarily in the evaluation of a potential form of diversification and the necessary steps to be taken to make it work after a decision has been made.

It is of interest to note that negotiating executives of an acquiring company frequently use the word "merger" in discussions with the management of the company to be acquired; but the word "acquisition" is used in discussions with their board of directors. In other words, there seems to be an inoffensive quality in "merge." The management of a company to be acquired prefers to merge mutual interests rather than to be acquired.

The following types of diversification alternatives are common in business literature: market-related, production-related, technology-related, closely related, and unrelated. The first four types are related to an existing capability of a firm, while the last type is unrelated to a company's capability. A market-related diversification is one where a company's existing knowledge of retail facilities, channels of distribution, customers, or general marketing and selling techniques provide the key link to a diversification venture. A diversification is considered production-related when the techniques of fabrication, assembly, or processing provide a valuable capability in the new field. The technology-related move is one where a firm's research and development capability or general knowledge about the practices, methods, or procedures for developing or understanding the technical aspects of a new product area are the link. A closely related diversification is one where both the market and either the production or technology capability provide the key link to a diversification venture. Closely related moves may not be called "diversification" by some because they often involve more of an extension of existing activities (for instance, from aircraft to spaceships) rather than a movement into a wholly new field.

1. REASONS FOR DIVERSIFICATION

The main reasons for diversification are the following.

a. Expansion constraints existing in a firm's product-market scope. These constraints may be caused by market saturation, competitive pressures, general decline in demand, or product obsolescence.

b. Excess equity. A firm may diversify because its retained cash exceeds the expansion needs in its own line of products. Naturally, a firm could also adjust its pattern of dividends or invest its excess equity into liquid resources (such as bank deposits and bonds). The rate of return available on liquid resources is, however, generally lower than that from operations.

c. Promising diversification opportunities. That is, diversification opportunities open to a firm may promise greater return on investment than opportunities of expansion in its own line of products. For instance, a diversification program may contribute to fuller utilization of plant capacity and some staff capabilities.

External growth or acquisitions can fulfill one or more of the following additional business goals: strengthening a company's financial position; stabilizing cyclical or seasonal types of business; securing sales outlets for products; safeguarding raw materials; procuring the services of one or more key personnel or new executive talent; obtaining land, buildings, and equipment for expansion; acquiring the technical skills of highly trained scientists; avoiding litigation; gaining a patent position; and other critical elements in business which determine success. As opposed to these reasons for a company's interest in acquiring others, we have the following reasons why some companies conclude that there is merit in selling to another owner: lack of capital for expansion, greater financial backing to improve operations, lack of management succession, management dissension, unbalanced product line, preparation for valuation and liquidity for estate taxes, and expected declining demand in the concerned segment of industry.

2. INTERNAL VERSUS EXTERNAL EXPANSION

In the United States and Great Britain, there is statistical evidence that the rate of failure for external expansions is higher than that for internal expansions. In addition, experience shows the following.

a. In production- or technology-related diversification, acquisition seems more effective for improving company profit than internal expansion.

b. In market-related diversification, internal expansion seems to meet overall company needs and objectives more frequently than external expansion.

c. Low-profit firms are particularly apt to be successful via the acquisition route when they lack marketing skills for diversification.

d. For both internal and external expansions, the profit experience during the second to fourth years of operation is strongly indicative of the profits a company should expect to be receiving from the venture five to ten years later.

One disadvantage of acquisition is that it is often difficult to find for purchase a company that has precisely the assets desired. Consequently, a necessary but often involuntary expansion into diverse activities results. In addition, acquisition often results in ambiguous supervisory relationships. On the other hand, acquisition may provide a means by which the underutilized resources of the acquiring and, possibly, the acquired company, can be more fully employed. Moreover, the technical and administrative demands of a major internal expansion may make the desired internal growth unfeasible.

Potential problems of internal expansion include interference of control procedures and standards designed for existing work with the needs of the new venture, adaptability of tooling and work methods to a different unit volume and unit value, and entry into a new market. An important objective of internal expansion should, therefore, be the establishment of a viable new line of products with maximum effective use of existing facilities and organization resources. The main potential problem of external expansion is that of orientation, since an acquisition often results in policy changes and management reorganization for the acquired company. The orientation is frequently difficult since the process of finding and concluding an acquisition is one which cannot be delegated very far below the president of a company. Important objectives of an acquiring company should, therefore, be the establishment of budget controls and reports that provide relevant information and clarify mutual responsibilities, and a reorganization to bring together related functions and separate unrelated ones.

In the above paragraphs, we have concentrated on differences between internal and external expansions. It is important that management be familiar with these. Naturally, the two forms of expansion have common features. For instance, the successive determination of effective relationships among the business units of any diversified company depends on management's ability to discern their essential similarities and differences. In brief, the principal management problem of diversification is the development of appropriate new standards of business judgement.

3. DIVERSIFICATION PLANNING

In principle, diversification planning consists of the following elements:

a. establishing the need for diversification
b. finding opportunities
c. projecting their consequences in combination with current operations and other planned developments
d. selecting the appropriate action or actions.

Diversification, the least familiar means of achieving corporate development, should be attempted only after the full potentials of development of the existing product-market position have been considered. The determination of the need for diversification is, therefore, a very important element of diversification planning.

Need for Diversification

The first step in the establishment of the need for diversifying a firm is a review of current objectives in the light of past performance and, concurrently, the preparation of a tentative forecast of future performance. Extrapolation of historical data of performance into the future should be adjusted for expected new developments.

A comparison between the objectives and the tentative forecast of future performance may result in a gap indicative of the discrepancy between aspirations and anticipations. We should examine whether the firm cannot improve its operations if the gap is zero or negative (expectations exceed aspirations). More often we will find a positive gap. If the gap is too great in view of existing market constraints and/or limitations of the firm, we should revise our objectives.

The extent to which the objectives should be revised can be established first by analyzing the prospects of the industry as a whole. This analysis consists of the projection of trends in growth, profitability, market shares, and costs of entry and exit from the industry. If possible, the potential impact of new technological developments is also examined. These trends form the basis for the projections of performance of a fully competitive firm with objectives similar to those of the firm in question.

Before revising its objectives, the firm should compare its strengths and weaknesses to those of the fully competitive firm. This comparison calls for an examination of the management and organizational capabilities, personnel skills, and status of facilities and equipment related to each of the following activities: general management and financing, operations, marketing, and research and development. The more detailed this examination, the better it will be. For instance, the status of facilities and equipment of marketing may include warehouses, retail outlets, sales and service offices, and transportation equipment. The organizational capabilities of marketing could include distributor chain, retail chain, direct sales, industrial and consumer service organizations, and inventory distribution and control. Such a detailed comparison of the firm's strengths and weaknesses to those of the fully competitive firm may, for example, reveal that an unfortunate distribution of warehouses results in high costs of transportation which may contribute to a lag in profitability.

The results of the analyses of the prospects of the industry as a whole, and of the strengths and weaknesses of the firm, together with the tentative forecast of future performance, form the basis for revising the objectives as well as the projections of future performance. These revisions may result in closing the aforementioned gap. On the other hand, they may narrow the gap, but not close it if, for example, the industry maximum cannot be attained without costly relocations. A comparison between the revised objectives and forecast of future performance determines the "diversification gap."

The establishment of a diversification gap is not sufficient to justify the need for diversification since the intent is to realize fully the potentials of the existing product-market position. Thus, we have to estimate the requirements in terms of dollars, manpower, and other resources to achieve this full realization. These requirements, together with existing requirements, are to be compared to the resources available to our firm and estimated on the basis of the revised projections of future performance. Upon completion of this comparison, we can decide whether present and future resources are adequate to attempt a diversification move.

Finding Opportunities

Consideration of certain economic and technical factors is useful to start the search for a venture in a new industry. The economic factors include size, cost structure, price changes, profitability, growth rate, and type of customers; the technical factors are stages of the process, scale of equipment, and specifications and technology. Data pertaining to these factors may be obtained from the *Thomas' Register of American Manufacturers*, the U.S. Department of Commerce *Statistical Abstracts of the United States*, and other government publications.

The size of the industry, its annual sales, value added and profits, number of employees, as well as the size range and number of companies and manufacturing plant units in the industry, and the role of large and small companies, provide a basis for comparison to the size of our firm's operations. The cost structure of an industry reveals information about the importance of raw materials, direct labor, overhead, capital equipment, and selling expenses in relation to those of our firm. Such information helps to assess the potential impact on the management, organization, work methods, and control procedures of our firm.

Information about price changes in materials, wages, capital equipment, and products provide insight about major trends and whether improved efficiency is keeping pace with prices. Profitability can be assessed on the basis of inputs and prices. In addition, we may determine the effect of unit volume on profitability. An examination of the growth rate of the industry during the last ten years may give an idea of changes in market requirements, assets, technology, product value, and so on.

Information about the type of customers served can help to examine to what extent warehouses, retail outlets, sales offices, and transport equipment of our firm can be used for the new venture. In addition, it reveals whether mail-order services can be used, whether the industry depends primarily on one customer, and whether knowledge of bidding practices and cost allocation systems as required by military contracting is required.

Facts about the stages of the process are helpful in determining whether production should be carried out at one location, at separate locations, or by separate companies. The scale of equipment is determined by industry size. It is useful to know whether the equipment can be easily scaled up or down, and what the costs of additional units are in case production levels change. Information about the specifications and technology of the industry involved gives us insight about the necessary technical skills and production capabilities.

A careful examination of such economic and technical factors discloses whether the desired economic and technological potentials exist within an industry as a whole. It does not reveal much about an individual participant in an industry since the data used are not specific enough. The examination serves, however, to establish a preliminary list of candidate industries. Some industries will be eliminated from further consideration because factors such as cost structure and type of customers are found to be incompatible with current objectives and/or operations.

The next step is to collect additional data for the candidate industries. This should be done according to clearly established criteria, such as criteria related to economics, costs of entry and exit, and synergy. Economic criteria include rate of return, growth, stability, and competitive pressures. The costs of entry and exit are significant because firms in some industries may be priced out of proportion to their real values, and great mobility of firms in and out can be expected if the minimum investment required to enter is small. This mobility is often attractive to small firms but not to large ones since they lack the flexibility and desired quick response. Price-earnings ratios and price-book values are indications of the cost of entry.

Synergy (or the "2 + 2 = 5" effect) refers to a firm's desire to find a product-market posture with a combined performance which is greater than the sum of its parts. We distinguish the following types: investment, operating, sales, and management synergy. Investment and operating synergy pertains to the economies of scale applicable to costs of investment and operation. It is clear that, in case of a diversification, we have to analyze the extent to which the joint use of facilities, personnel, common raw materials inventories, research and development capabilities, etc., can result in economies of scale. Sales synergy may result from the common use of distribution channels, sales administration, warehousing, and promotion and advertising procedures.

Positive management synergy may result from a new venture in a closely related diversification since management is likely to find itself in a position to provide forceful and effective guidance. It is also possible in market-related, production-related, or technology-related diversifications. On the other hand, management synergy is likely to be low or negative if the problems in the new area are unfamiliar, as may be the case in an unrelated diversification. This is not to be construed as suggesting that unrelated diversifications should be avoided. The following essential conditions should, however, be present for a successful entry in an unrelated field: recognition of the differing requirements for success in different industries; competent managers who are motivated to perform well, and who can quickly adjust to being responsible for doing business in a new industry; and a venturesome, risk-taking management point of view.

The additional data mentioned above can be collected from Dun and Bradstreet reports, Moody's, Standard and Poor's, trade literature, business periodicals, association publications, U.S. Department of Commerce statistics and industry reports, the *Wall Street Journal*, the specific company's marketing and purchasing organizations, and special reports issued by investment firms. A source which is frequently overlooked by members of industry study groups is the company's own employees. However, obtaining a flow of information upward through succeeding echelons of management requires active work by those at the top. Some of the candidate industries on the preliminary list may be disqualified after the evaluation of these data.

A further screening is required in view of internal and external constraints. Internal constraints result from self-imposed policy limitations such as the avoidance of industries with unions hostile to the unions of our firm, industries with salary and wage scales out of line with those of our firm, and industries with price-earning ratios out of line with those of our firm. An example of an external constraint is compliance with the Sherman and Clayton Antitrust Acts. Legal advice is necessary to determine the risk of violation of the provisions of these acts, since they are vaguely worded.

After the consideration of internal and external constraints, we have a list of acceptable industries. Normally, this list should contain only a few candidates.

Projecting Consequences

In addition to the identification of promising diversification fields, diversification planning should consider the "hereafter" effects of any future action. To some degree, this has already been done in the previous screening (the consideration of economic and technical factors). It is advisable, however, to examine the "hereafter" effects in more detail. For instance, the effects of the following activities require scrutiny.

a. Reallocations of senior management's time to provide for managing the new venture.
b. Possible realignment of the organization structure, management, and controls of a new venture in order to fit into the firm's existing operations.
c. Integration of requirements and costs which may be involved when the new activities are related in certain ways to existing operations.
d. Expansion onto adjoining land and/or securing of additional management and labor in the future, if necessary.
e. Negotiations with existing and, possibly, new unions.
f. Possible competition of new products with the firm's products.

The above items are examples of hereafter effects. It is clear that each diversification includes a unique bundle of consequences, since it must be remembered that the diversification of a company is a unique experience.

The list of acceptable industries may be further reduced after the projection of consequences in combination with current operations and other planned developments. Thus, we now have a list of final industries which will be used for the selection of the appropriate action or actions.

Selecting the Appropriate Action or Actions

The main problem of the selection of the appropriate action or actions (realization of full potentials of development of the existing product-market position, diversification, or both) is that each of the criteria used and each of the final industries are likely to contribute to a different aspect of the firm's performance. In addition, each criterion (economic, costs of entry and exit, and synergy) is measured by a different yardstick. An obvious way in which these can be combined to give a single figure of merit for each scope does not exist. Therefore, a rank ordering of criteria followed by a rank ordering of the final industries is suggested.

The rank ordering of criteria should be done in terms of contribution to a firm's objectives. Thus, the criterion which contributes most to the firm's objectives is assigned the highest number. The industries are then rank ordered under each of the criteria. That is, the potential industry which satisfies the criterion better than any other one is assigned the highest number under that criterion.

The rank ordering of criteria and the rank ordering of the industries under each criterion facilitate the final selection of an industry since the result will show which industry satisfies the important criteria more than any other one. This is the industry to be selected. It is noted that the rank ordering may be facilitated by a consolidation of criteria, if we are faced with many different ones. For instance, a multitude of economic criteria can be consolidated into one or two standards.

After the definite selection of an industry, we must return to our analysis of the possibility of realizing the full potentials of development of the existing product-market position. A choice must be made to pursue this realization, diversification, or both. If no diversification opportunity is sufficiently superior to the expansion of the existing product-market position in order to justify the added risks, we must maintain the previous commitment of resources to this expansion. Consequently, diversification is limited to the use of the residual resources. It is possible that upon completion of the diversification analysis, we find the opportunities so attractive that it is justified to sacrifice the planned expansion of the existing product-market position or even to relinquish some parts of the present business. In this case, we adjust the diversification gap and resources for diversification upward and decrease the resources for the planned expansion (and, possibly, present operations) correspondingly. Naturally, it is also possible that one or more of the reasons for diversification force the choice into the direction of diversification. Management may also decide that the information obtained during the planning of diversification is inadequate to commit the firm either way, and that additional information should be obtained.

Heretofore, we have analyzed diversification without making a distinction between internal and external expansions. This distinction has not yet been made since we first have to decide whether a diversification strategy should be pursued. It must be recognized, however, that the observations of this section apply equally to internal and external expansions.

4. NONFINANCIAL EVALUATION OF COMPANY ACQUISITIONS

The sources of information mentioned in Section 3 (Dun and Bradstreet reports, Moody's, Standard and Poor's, etc.) are also useful in locating candidate companies to be required. These sources may be supplemented by suggestions from our firm's board of directors, investment bankers, commercial banks, consultants, and business brokers.

Investment bankers have proved particularly helpful in locating prospective companies for acquisition since their staffs typically include experienced partners with wide business acquaintances. Commercial banks frequently know of companies where capital for growth is constrained by a company's borrowing capacity, where the management is getting old and seeking retirement or anxious to devote full time to research and development or other activities. Reliance on consultants rather than the establishment of an acquisition staff group is frequently less expensive for smaller organizations where the need to acquire another company is rather sporadic. A disadvantage of this approach is that the accumulated knowledge and information do not inure to the benefit of the company.

It is evident that a prospectus is useful if a company has had a public offering. In addition, the 10-K report, which is filed with the stock exchange and the Securities and Exchange Commission if a company is listed, is public information in the United States.

In general, the assessment of the information used in the preparation of a list of acceptable industries should, as a minimum, be supplemented by the collection and evaluation of the following data in order to prepare a list of acceptable companies:

a. Balance sheets, income statements, earnings per share, and price-earnings ratios (Chapter 1).

b. Ownership of a company's stock.

c. Identity, ages, and compensation of officers and directors.

d. Product line.

e. Number and location of plants and offices.

f. Research and development areas.

g. Company markets.

h. Existence of good will—the reputation a business enjoys with its customers.

i. Contractual relationships (with customers, suppliers, and staff).

j. History of recent labor relations.

k. Legal considerations such as pending lawsuits, licensing arrangements, exclusive selling franchise rights, and patent rights.

The reader may wonder why item 1 (balance sheets, income statements, and so on) is included here, since these data are considered in more detail in the assessment of a company's worth later on. This is done because a crude examination of these data may result in the exclusion of potential companies from the acceptable list. The assessment of a company's worth is generally limited to a rather small number of potential companies on the final list, since it is a time-consuming analysis.

The list of acceptable companies is further screened in view of the "hereafter" effects. Potential company acquisitions may have specific hereafter effects in addition to those common to diversification moves. For instance, a change of ownership in a business often has far-reaching tax implications. The potential company may have substantial capital allowances or other tax carry forwards. On the other hand, it may have tax losses on its books which can be used to offset tax on the profits of the acquiring firm.

The required further screening before arriving at a list of final companies also involves the disqualification of companies on the acceptable list in view of certain undesirable qualities of the management, personnel, and/or organization of the company to be acquired. It is clear that these ingredients will be dominated by other standards if the objective of the acquisition is to increase borrowing capacity or if the management of the acquiring firm wishes to acquire companies for the purpose of liquidating the physical assets at a profit, thereby increasing the acquirer's earnings per share. Most acquisitions are, however, made with the intent that the acquired organizations continue operating as going concerns. Consideration of the above intangible qualities is perhaps more important than the assessment of reasonably measurable quantitative factors (see the next section) since competent top-level management is a scarce commodity.

Conversations with former employers and employees of the key people of a potential company can reveal much about their management qualities. This knowledge is supplemented by information gained during interviews, which generally are conducted with the management of one or more companies of the list of final candidates (those companies left after the above successive screening). The interviews take place either after or concurrently with the assessment of a company's worth. They should not be limited to the top one or two executives. It is important that the management of both the acquiring company and the one to be acquired give ample time to get to know each other. Clear understanding must be reached on vital issues such as what both parties can contribute to each other, the place of the company to be acquired in the organization of the acquired company, and the division of responsibilities. It is recommended that both parties give adequate thought to anticipatory questions in order to avoid a premature termination of negotiations.

The initial approach to the management and/or owners of a potential company should be made by one or more key executives of the acquiring company. If possible, the experience and personal idiosyncrasies of these people should match those of the company to be approached. Sometimes it is desirable to

Table 4.1
P/E and EPS Methods

	Acquiring Company	Company to be Acquired	Combined Company (after acquisition)
Forecast net earnings[1]	$1,300,000	$1,000,000	$2,300,000
Shares in issue	11,000,000	10,000,000	17,666,666
Earnings per share	$0.12	$0.10	$0.13
Price per share	$2.10	$1.40	$2.28
Price earnings ratio	17.5	14.0	17.5

[1] Forecast for the year immediately following the acquisition.

include a distinguished member of the board of directors of the acquiring company in the first visit.

Secrecy of approach is frequently of vital importance, since an organization's morale may suffer when employees learn that consideration is being given to a possible sale. In addition, rumors about a possible acquisition can lead to a premature termination of negotiations.

An item often overlooked in the assessment of a potential acquisition is the pension plan in the firm to be purchased. Where pension arrangements are less adequate than those for the acquiring firm's staff, they will need to be improved, and vice versa—where more adequate, they may result in the acquiring firm needing to increase its benefits.

The discussion of the nonfinancial evaluation of company acquisitions has primarily been presented from the acquiring company's viewpoint. Clearly, the wise owners and/or management of a company who have concluded to sell should proceed with a similar screening procedure.

5. ASSESSMENT OF A COMPANY'S WORTH

The price-earnings ratio (P/E) and the earnings per share (EPS) methods often are used in acquisition appraisals. These methods can best be explained with the example of Table 4.1. This table shows that the net earnings predicted for the year immediately following the acquisition are $1.3 million and $1.0 million for the acquiring company and the one to be acquired, respectively.

The acquiring company offers two of its shares for every three shares of the company to be acquired. Thus, the offer would involve the issue of 6,666,666 shares at $2.10 per share by the acquiring company. It would obtain $1 million for its $14 million of shares, which represents an acquisition's "exit" P/E of 14. The P/E method compares the 14 to the P/E of the acquiring company, 17.5, and possibly other companies which might be acquired. In other words, the comparison of P/E's is used to determine the relative attractiveness of one or more potential acquisitions.

The EPS for the acquiring company, the one to be acquired, and the combined company (after the acquisition) are $0.12, $0.10, and $0.13, respectively. Consequently, the bid will have brought about an improvement in earnings per share of $0.01. Table 4.1 also shows that the share price would rise to $2.28 provided the price-earnings ratio remains at its pre-bid level of 17.5. Thus, the EPS method focuses on the degree of improvement in EPS of the existing shareholders of the acquiring company. The P/E, on the other hand, focuses on the multiple of earnings for which the acquiring company is paying.

Both the P/E and EPS statistics are insufficient indicators for the attractiveness of an acquisition, although they can be used as supplemental tools of evaluation. Particularly, the computation of the EPS statistic is desirable since the realization of an improvement in the earnings per share of the acquiring company is normally a prior condition of a bid. The main shortcoming of the P/E and EPS methods is the disregard of the growth of earnings after the first year. Another problem inherent in the P/E statistic is the possibility of under- or overvaluation of the shares of the company after acquisition (Chapter 2). With the EPS method, we do not consider the share price directly. The latter method has, however, the disadvantage that a modest increase in EPS does not necessarily reflect adversely upon an acquisition's attractiveness. Such an increase can be the result of the relatively small size of the company to be acquired.

A sound acquisition appraisal includes collecting such information as: (a) estimates of profit—future, net of tax, and annual; (b) necessary adjustments to these profits; (c) estimates of the value of surplus assets; and (d) estimates of replacement costs of nonsurplus assets.

Estimates of Annual Profits

This estimation normally begins with an analysis of the performance of the company to be acquired during the past 5–10 years, since the acquiring company usually plans to continue the operation of the acquired company in its existing line of activity. The analysis should consider net of tax profits, since maximization of such profits is our goal.

Accounting and financial reports and statements form the basis for the evaluation of a company's past performance (Chapter 1). A problem arising with

Table 4.2

Illustrative Difference in Profit Reporting Caused by Ill-Defined Accounting Standards[1]

Income Statement of Company XYZ - Year 1997

	A		B	
Net Sales	$11,000,000		$11,000,000	
Cost of Sales and Operating Expenses				
Cost of goods sold	$6,500,000		$6,500,000	
Selling and administrative expenses	1,500,000		1,500,000	
Inventory reserve	600,000		-	
Depreciation	500,000		400,000	
R&D costs	100,000		20,000	
Pension costs	300,000	9,500,000	70,000	8,490,000
Operating Profit		$1,500,000		$2,510,000
Other Income				
Dividends and interest		50,000		50,000
Total Income		$1,550,000		$2,560,000
Less: Interest on bonds		70,000		70,000
Profit before Provision for Federal Income Tax		$1,480,000		$2,490,000
Provision for Federal Income Tax		710,000		1,200,000
Net Profit for the Year		$ 770,000		$1,290,000

[1] Income Statements A and B apply to the same company and are both prepared in conformity with generally accepted accounting principles.

the examination of these reports and statements stems from the fact that generally accepted accounting principles have never been well defined in most countries, although industry has placed great emphasis on such principles. For instance, a typical auditor's certificate reads "In our opinion, the balance sheet and statement of income present fairly the position of Company XYZ at December 31, 1997, and the results of its operations for the year then ended in conformity with generally accepted accounting principles applied on a basis consistent with that of the preceding year." What do phrases like "fair presentation" and "general acceptance" mean? Are there any standards for these value judgements? What are the accounting principles referred to in the auditor's opinion? Consistent answers to these questions do not exist since both the accounting profession and industry have never accepted consistent, underlying accounting postulates and standards. Consequently, the amount of net profit reported depends on the concepts used by the persons who performed the audit.

Table 4.2 represents two income statements of the same company. Both statements are prepared in conformity with "generally accepted" accounting principles; however, Statement A shows a net profit of $770,000, and Statement B shows $1,290,000. The difference in profit reported may be the result of the use of different standards in one or more of the following reporting areas.

a. Work in process and inventory evaluations. For instance, Statement A of Table 4.2 is based on the Lifo (last in, first out) principle, while Statement B uses the Fifo (first in, first out) principle.

b. Rates of depreciation applied to the various categories of assets. For instance, Statement A uses accelerated depreciation, while Statement B uses straight-line depreciation.

c. Capitalization of interest or commissioning costs. For instance, Statement A charges R&D costs to current expenses and funds the current pension costs, while Statement B capitalizes and amortizes the R&D costs over a five-year period and funds only the present value of pensions vested.

d. Provisions for deferred taxes, bad debts, renegotiation settlements, and devaluation and exchange losses.

e. Commitments for royalty payments, consulting fees, and other fixed contractual liabilities.

Balance sheets and income statements sometimes disclose the standards used in the above reporting areas. A cursory examination of explanatory notes in auditors' certificates also reveals inconsistencies.

The discussion of problems related to what constitutes general acceptance should not be construed to suggest that audited statements have little value. It is clear that a statement certified by a well-known organization is more likely to reflect fairly the status of a company than an unaudited statement. The purpose of mentioning the problems is to stress the importance of examining the accounting systems of the acquiring company and the one to be acquired for compatibility.

We should also recognize that the complete information required for accounting realignment can seldom be obtained until after the acquisition is completed. Complete evaluations of work in process and inventory are particularly difficult to accomplish prior to the completion of an acquisition. In addition, an audit prior to acquisition, although desirable, is frequently difficult to achieve since full audits require considerable time, may indicate distrust on the part of the purchaser, and are disruptive in attempts to maintain the secrecy of negotiations. In practice, an audit is often provided for as one of the warranties of the contract and serves as the basis for acquisition changes in the purchase price. It is desirable, however, to undertake a complete audit as soon as the acquisition is legally completed.

Accounting realignment may have to be supplemented by other corrections in order to arrive at a useful evaluation of a company's past performance. Reasons for such allowances include the following.

a. Reductions in advertising and sales promotion expenditures during recent years and other attempts of "dressing up a company for sale."

b. The enhancement of a company's reported profits by the possession of free-hold property or low rental leases.

c. The impossibility of realizing profits on sales and order backlogs at the same rate as that disclosed by historical experience.

d. Stock appreciation or depreciation in view of changes in material prices which are not in line with variations in the general price level.

After making the necessary corrections of trading profits for the firm under consideration, it is useful to compare the profits to those of other companies in the same industry as a measure of the performance of the present management. The next step is to predict the future trading profits. This involves an estimation of (1) the rate of growth of the total market relative to the capacity of the industry, (2) the effect of any relevant government action, and (3) the firm's market share in the future. The results of the evaluation of a company's past performance are used in the determination of this market share. The estimation should be made for the firm's end-products as well as its basic raw materials. It is advisable to get a second opinion from a capable market research firm, since the estimation of these factors is very important.

Forecast earnings based on the above estimation have to be adjusted in view of synergy effects and, possibly, other factors, such as savings through the termination of personnel, legal, auditing, and appraisal costs, "country-club dues," and employee benefit plans. Consideration of synergy effects stresses the importance of evaluating the joint incremental net profit. We should also include any loss averted by the acquisition. Thus, an unsuccessful termination of acquisition negotiations between companies X and Y may result in the purchase of company Y by company Z, and subsequent failure on the part of company X to expand as rapidly. Finally, we should recognize that the cost in executive time devoted to integrating the acquired organization is frequently greater than anticipated. Measurement of the cost of executive time is difficult, although the related expenses are real.

It is evident that future earnings and costs have to be discounted. Naturally, we should use the acquirer's net-of-tax equity cost of capital in discounting computations.

Necessary Adjustments

Discounted forecasts of trading profits may have to be adjusted in view of financial and legal considerations as well as tax aspects. When a business is acquired, the acquirer becomes responsible for its short-, medium-, and long-term debts. A company's balance sheet shows these debts under the heading of "Current Liabilities" (Chapter 1). Except for allowances for seasonal fluctuations, the assessment of the short-term debts poses no new problems. Provisions of additional short-term finance in view of significant seasonal fluctuations increase the purchase price of a business.

Medium- and long-term debts differ from short-term ones in that they fall due after one year. They include various forms of medium- and long-term loans and preference shares. The basic approach to loans is to discount interest payments and the terminal repayment to their present values. As mentioned earlier, the acquirer's net-of-tax equity cost of capital is to be used for the discounting computations. It is clear that we may wish to consider a renewal of the loan as an alternative to the terminal repayment.

The assessment of the medium- and long-term liabilities stemming from preference shares is more difficult than that of loans, although the method also involves the discounting of all future net-of-tax outgoings. It is more difficult since preference shares may carry the right to further participation in profits when equity shareholders have received a given amount of dividends. Such right calls for the estimation of related outgoings. Preference shares may also be redeemable at the company's option, in which case we should examine the available alternatives in order to determine the minimal price of the company to be acquired. Allowance must be made for paying outstanding past dividends related to cumulative preference shares.

We must reduce the forecasts of trading profits by the costs of legal services necessary for the acquisition. These services may be required for an investigation of the position of preference shareholders, minority shareholders, and owners of debentures; an examination of licensing arrangements, patent rights, and terms of leases; and investigation of pending lawsuits, a scrutiny of exclusive franchise rights and contracts to customers, and, possibly, many other issues.

Estimates of the Value of Surplus Assets

Assets which may be surplus to the requirements of the acquirer have to be identified, since they constitute a different value than assets required for the continuation of operations. The identification calls for the consideration of synergy effects.

Surplus assets may include surplus equipment, surplus buildings, unused land, investments, and cash reserves. They are those assets which are not required in the realization of the forecast profits. Except for cash reserves and investments, we should use current market values in the assessment of surplus assets. Cash reserves and investments must be subjected to the evaluation method which the acquiring company applies to such assets.

Estimates of Future Replacement Costs of Nonsurplus Assets

A business is usually worth continuing until its operating costs—costs of maintenance, power, tooling, and labor—become so high that they can no longer be justified. At this point, we can either reconstruct it, sell it, or close it down. In all these cases, we should estimate the terminal value.

It is evident that the various assets which are to be continued in their present use will not wear out at the same time. The estimation of the costs to replace the assets obviously cannot be done for every single item. Instead, broad categories such as buildings, main equipment, and vehicle fleet have to be made. The appraisal of fixed assets calls for technical expertise such as engineers and surveyors.

The determination of the timing and costs of replacements and the terminal value of assets to be replaced is discussed in detail in Chapter 8. During this determination, it is important to remember that the concept of replacement implies that we wish to maintain the function of an existing asset. For instance, milling machines are not replaced by milling machines, but rather milling capacity is replaced by milling capacity.

The evaluation of net current assets such as cash, marketable securities, accounts receivable less accounts payable, and taxes due is easier than evaluation of fixed assets. Net current assets and contingent liabilities are usually best assessed by accountants (Chapter 1).

The establishment of terminal values and future replacement costs is necessary for the determination of the net cash flow resulting from an acquisition (see next section). It is noted that a present value of replacement expenditures which exceeds that of net income does not necessarily mean that an acquisition is not worthwhile to pursue. It does mean that it would not be worthwhile to undertake the replacement or to continue the business beyond the point in time when the replacement should be made. The acquisition can, however, still be profitable as an investment with a limited life.

The estimates of adjusted, future, annual profits, value of surplus assets, and replacement costs of nonsurplus assets provide us with the data necessary to compute the net present value (NPV) of an acquisition. More precisely, the net present value of the adjusted annual profits and replacement costs of nonsurplus assets measures the value of the company to be acquired from the viewpoint of continuing the operation. The value to the acquirer of any surplus assets should be added to this present value in order to arrive at the NPV of the potential acquisition. This NPV sets the maximum value to the acquirer from continued operation.

It is obvious that the collection and evaluation of the data required to compute the NPV of a potential acquisition is a time-consuming task. For most cases, it is, therefore, recommended to start with the nonfinancial evaluation of a company acquisition. This nonfinancial evaluation results in a final list of a few candidate companies, which can be ranked in order of descending priority. The assessment of a company's worth may be limited to the company with the highest priority on the final list. Alternatively, this assessment may be extended to two or more companies of the final list if the investment in question is a major one and/or if the estimates of projected earnings are subject to a high element of risk.

6. PRICE OF A COMPANY

The price of a company can usually not be taken as fixed but is open to negotiation. Disagreement over the purchase price offered is most frequently given as the reason for premature termination of acquisition discussions. It is, therefore, important to establish a number of bench marks for bargaining.

The first and most important benchmark from the acquirer's viewpoint is the NPV of the potential acquisition. This NPV sets the upper limit to the cash price it is worth paying to acquire a business, provided the acquisition also satisfies the criteria discussed in Section 4. In addition, we assume that a decision has already been made in favor of external expansion rather than internal expansion. The computation of the NPV poses no new problems. In case of potential acquisitions, this index of project appraisal is based on net cash flows resulting from the adjusted, future, annual net profits, and estimates of the value of surplus assets and replacement costs of nonsurplus assets.

It is recommended that the NPV computation be based on equity net cash flows in order to ensure that the benefits accruing to the equity shareholders in the acquiring company are sufficient for the resources involved. Concentration on equity net cash flows is particularly desirable since the acquiring company will be trusted with the responsibility of looking after the interests of lenders, minority shareholders, and so on. These interest groups represent obligations on the total net cash flow before the residual amounts available for equity compensation.

Another benchmark is obtained by going through the valuation procedure and the related NPV computation from the vendor's point of view. The resulting NPV is indicative of the value of the potential acquisition to the vendor. In addition, the minimum acceptable price to be paid for a company with listed or actively traded over-the-counter securities is often established by the market value. The problems of determining a minimum acceptable price for an unlisted company are complicated by the absence of a stock market appraisal. Owners of unlisted companies sometimes attempt to place a value on their firms by negotiating with prospective acquirers for the sole purpose of getting a bid. The minimum acceptable price for an unlisted company can also be established on the basis of the market value of a comparable company, which involves the comparison of price-earning ratios.

It is obvious that minimum acceptable prices based on current market values of shares may not be acceptable to prospective acquirers. Shares are frequently overvalued (Chapter 2). Another benchmark is obtained by determining the break-up value of the company to be acquired. The break-up value is the sum of the resale values of all the assets (surplus as well as nonsurplus) assuming they will be sold in sufficiently small lots such that the business is discontinued. It represents the absolute minimum value to the existing owner of his business.

7. POOLING OF INTERESTS

The method of accounting for an acquisition affects net worth (book value), capital surplus, retained earnings, and earnings per share (EPS). Financial analysts, stockholders, management, and the stock market frequently pay much attention to these factors, although they should concentrate on the NPV of an acquisition since this is the best indicator of profit-making ability. However, the NPV computation requires more time than the determination of the above factors.

The accounting method may also affect the amount of taxes payable and, therefore, the NPV of the combined company (after the acquisition). Thus, the choice of the accounting method to be used is important from several viewpoints. The principal methods of accounting for an acquisition are the pooling of interests and the purchase methods.

In *Accounting Research Bulletin No. 48*, the American Institute of Certified Public Accountants describes the pooling of interests as follows.

When a combination is deemed to be a pooling of interests, a new basis of accountability does not arise. The carrying amounts of the assets of the constituent corporations, if stated in conformity with generally accepted accounting principles and appropriately adjusted when deemed necessary to place them on a uniform accounting basis, should be carried forward; and the combined earned surpluses and deficits, if any, of the constituent corporations should be carried forward, except to the extent otherwise required by law or appropriate corporate action. Adjustments of assets or of surplus which would be in conformity with generally accepted accounting principles in the absence of a combination are ordinarily equally appropriate if effected in connection with a pooling of interests; however, the pooling-of-interests concept implies a combining of surpluses and deficits of the constituent corporations, and it would be inappropriate and misleading in connection with a pooling of interests to eliminate the deficit of one constituent against its capital surplus and to carry forward the earnings surplus of another constituent.

The procedure applicable to accounting for purchase of assets is, according to the aforementioned Institute: "When a combination is deemed to be a purchase, the assets acquired should be recorded on the books of the acquiring corporation at cost, measured in money, or in the event other consideration is given, at the fair value of such other consideration, or at the fair value of the property acquired, whichever is more clearly evident."

The quotations indicate that accounting principles are not very well defined. Who determines what the "fair value" is in case of a purchase? The description of the pooling of interests refers to "generally accepted accounting principles," which, as we have discussed, are vaguely defined. The requirements for an acquisition to qualify as a pooling of interests are also vague. In case of a transaction involving listed securities, the Securities and Exchange Commission makes the final decision. For unlisted companies, this decision hinges on the interpretation of the Securities and Exchange rulings by accounting experts.

Two methods of accounting can best be described in terms of the hypothetical example of Table 4.3. Part A of this table gives the relevant information about the acquiring company and the one to be acquired, while parts B and C present the effects on the balance sheet and EPS of the purchase and pooling of interest methods, respectively. Notice that according to the purchase method, the retained earnings are equal to the earned surplus of the acquiring company ($3,500,000), and the capital surplus equals $40,000 \times (\$60 - \$2) = \$2,320,000$. The difference between the purchase price ($2,400,000) and the book value for the seller ($1,000,000) is recorded on the buyer's balance sheet as "good will."

According to the pooling of interests method, the retained earnings are equal to the earned surpluses of the acquiring company and the one to be acquired ($3,500,000 + \$880,000 = \$4,380,000$). The capital surplus amounts to only $40,000, while no good will item is created if the combination is accounted for as a pooling of interests.

The pooling of interests method takes into account the results of operations of the two companies during the preceding part of the fiscal period in which the acquisition takes place, as well as the results of the operation of the combined company during its existence over the remaining part of the fiscal period. For instance, if the acquisition takes place on the first day of the tenth month of the fiscal year for the purchasing company, the buyer can report its own earnings for the 10 months prior to the closing, the seller's 10-month earnings, and the combined company's earnings on its income statement for the first two months of the combination. Clearly, this can affect the amount of taxes payable.

In Table 4.3, the acquisition is assumed to take place in December, the last month of the fiscal year for the purchasing company. Consequently, the seller's earnings for the year are, according to the pooling of interests method, included in the buyer's combined earnings for the year. This results in an EPS of $2.67 as compared to an EPS of $2.40 in accordance with the purchase method.

Let us assume that in the year after the acquisition, the earnings of the combined company amount to $1,600,000 before amortization of good will. Good will is amortized over a 10-year period. The EPS of the combined company the year after the acquisition would be $(\$1,600,000 - \$140,000)/540,000 = \$2.70$ according to purchase accounting, and $\$1,600,000/540,000 = \$2.96$ with pooling of interests accounting.

Table 4.3

Illustrative Differences in Net Worth, Capital Surplus, Retained Earnings, and EPS Caused by Accounting Methods

A. Information about the acquiring company and the one to be acquired prior to the acquisition in December 1997:

Item	Acquiring Company	Company to Be Acquired
Net Assets	$4,500,000	$1,000,000
Common Stock	$1,000,000	$ 120,000
Number of Shares	500,000	120,000
Par Value	$ 2.00	$ 1.00
Earned Surplus	$3,500,000	$ 880,000
Book Value	$4,500,000	$1,000,000
1997 Income Statement:		
Net Income	$1,200,000	$ 240,000
EPS	$ 2.40	$ 2.00
Market Price per Share at		$ 20.00
Closing Date	$ 60.00	(Price paid[1])

B. Relevant items of the December 31, 1997, balance sheet and EPS of combined company according to accounting for acquisition as a purchase:

Net Assets	$5,500,000	Common Stock (540,000	
Good Will	1,400,000	@ $2.00)	$1,080,000
		Capital Surplus	2,320,000
		Retained Earnings	3,500,000
Total Net Assets	$6,900,000	Net Worth	$6,900,000

EPS = $2.40

C. Relevant items of the December 31, 1997, balance sheet and EPS of combined company according to accounting for acquisition as a pooling of interests:

Net Assets	$5,500,000	Common Stock (540,000	
		@ $2.00)	$1,080,000
		Capital Surplus	40,000
		Retained Earnings	4,380,000
Total Net Assets	$5,500,000	Net Worth	$5,500,000

EPS = ($1,200,000 + $240,000)/540,000 = $2.67

[1] The company to be acquired is privately owned; the acquiring company issues 40,000 new shares of $2.00 per common stock to pay the owners $2,400,000 worth of its stock.

SUGGESTIONS FOR FURTHER READING

American Institute of Certified Public Accountants. *Accounting Research Bulletin No. 48* (January 1957).

Cody, T. G. *Strategy of a Megamerger: An Insider's Account of the Baxter Travenol-American Hospital Supply Combination.* Westport, CT: Quorum Books, 1990.

Halperin, M., and S. J. Bell. *Research Guide to Corporate Acquisitions, Mergers, and Other Restructuring.* Westport, CT: Quorum Books, 1992.

Mace, M. L., and G. G. Montgomery. *Management Problems of Corporate Acquisitions.* Boston: Graduate School of Business Administration, Harvard University, 1962.

Nahavandi, A., and A. R. Maleikzadeh. *Organizational Culture in the Management of Mergers.* Westport, CT: Quorum Books, 1993.

CHAPTER 5

Cost of Capital

No blister draws sharper than interest on money. It works day and night; in fair weather and foul. It gnaws at a man's substance with invisible teeth. It binds industry with its film, as a fly is bound with a spider's web. Debt rolls a man over and over, binding him hand and foot, and letting him hang on the fatal mesh, till the long-legged interest devours him. One had better make his bed of Canada thistles, than attempt to lie at ease upon interest.

—Henri W. Beecher

As we will see in the next chapter, decisions regarding whether or not to invest in fixed assets, that is, capital budgeting decisions, involve discounted cash flow analysis. We estimate a project's cash flows, find their present value (PV), and if the PV of the inflows exceeds the cost of the project, we undertake the investment. This chapter deals with determining the proper discount rate for use in calculating the PV of the cash inflows, or the cost of capital for private firms and government organizations.

A private firm's cost of capital (COC) is determined by the organization's cost of debt, cost of preferred stock, and cost of common equity (retained earnings plus common stock). Governments sometimes borrow money from other governments, private banks, or international organizations such as the World Bank. The objectives used in arriving at appropriate rates for the COC differ in the private and public sectors. The term interest rate rather than the COC may be more appropriate for use in public investment analysis, since its value may be based on a government's choice between increase in savings or consumption. In addition, public authorities can manipulate interest rates to affect stabilization goals; that is, the rates are increased to arrest excess economic activity and thereby control inflation, while they are reduced to induce borrowing and investment to combat depression. Interest rates are also influenced by imbalances in foreign trade. The larger a country's trade deficit, the more it must borrow. As borrowing increases, interest rates are driven up. Also, foreigners are willing to hold U.S. debt if the interest rate on this debt is competitive with interest rates of other countries. Thus, if the Federal Reserve attempts to lower interest rates in the United States, foreigners are likely to sell U.S. bonds thereby depressing bond prices, and the result will be higher U.S. rates. In other words, the existence of a deficit trade limits the Fed's measures to combat a recession by driving interest rates down.

Sections 2 and 3 deal with the determination of the COC in the private and public sectors, respectively. First, however, we must make a number of observations that apply to the use of COC in both sectors. The last sections of this chapter discuss uncertainty and risk aspects of private and public investments, and introduce methods of dealing with them.

1. GENERAL OBSERVATIONS ABOUT THE COST OF CAPITAL

The first observation concerns whether to use one value for the COC or the interest rate i for all future time periods or different values for different points in time in the future.

Normally, we associate a higher COC with investments subject to more risk. It is logical that investments with more chance of failure can demand a higher rate of return than investments with less chance of failure. Consequently, the use of one value for i for all future time periods may seem unrealistic if the uncertainty or riskiness of future returns is expected to vary over time.

It can be shown, however, that the use of one value for i is valid if the risk is expected to change over time at a constant rate. In this situation, we can find a constant COC or interest rate that is an unambiguous measure of return under risk. For instance, if the interest rate applicable to the first year return of an investment is 10%, and thereafter is expected to increase as the result of risk increasing at an annual constant rate, we can find one constant rate applicable to the returns of all years of the investment's expected life and which is equivalent to the increasing annual interest rates.

Significant changes in risk from one year to another are not characteristic of the typical pattern of cash flows experienced in most investment analyses. In addition, situations where we are able to specify the exact change in risk from one year to another with a high degree of accuracy are exceptional. Therefore, in this book we will use a COC or rate of interest that is constant over all future time periods. The use of a constant interest rate simplifies the analysis of capital investments significantly. In fact, the application of different interest rates is ordinarily too cumbersome for anything other than expository purposes.

The second observation concerns the manner in which the rate of interest has been introduced in Appendix 1. Specifically, it discusses the rate of interest as a way of expressing the price ratio between current and future claims. This is sometimes referred to as the agio or premium concept of interest. The term "premium" suggests that current dollars trade for future dollars at better than one for one. In line with the pragmatic approach followed in this book, we will not consider the interest rate against a detailed background of productive transformations between the present and future time. Such a treatment concerns the principles of intertemporal choice or the allocation of resources for consumptive and productive purposes over time.

The third observation concerns the real risk-free rate of interest, r^*, which is defined as the interest rate that would exist on a riskless security if no inflation were expected. It may be thought of as the interest rate which would exist on short-term U.S. Treasury securities in an inflation-free world. It is difficult to measure the real risk-free rate precisely; most experts in the United States think that it has fluctuated in the range of 1% to 4% in recent years.

The nominal, or quoted, risk-free rate of interest, r_{RF}, is the real risk-free rate plus a premium for expected inflation: $r_{RF} = r^* + IP$. (To facilitate notation, Chapter 3 uses the symbol r for r_{RF}.) Strictly speaking, the nominal risk-free rate means the interest rate on a totally risk-free security or one that has no risk of default, no maturity risk, no liquidity risk, and no risk of loss if inflation increases. Naturally, such a security does not exist. A U.S. Treasury (T)-bill or a short-term security issued by the U.S. government is, however, a security that is free of most risks. Treasury (T)-bonds or longer-term securities issued by the U.S. government are free of default and liquidity risks, but are exposed to some risk due to changes in the general level of interest rates. If the term "risk-free rate" is used without the modifier "real" or "nominal," people generally mean the nominal risk-free rate, which includes an inflation premium equal to the expected inflation rate over the life of the security. T-bill and T-bond rates are generally used to approximate the short-term and the long-term risk free rates, respectively.

2. COST OF CAPITAL IN THE PRIVATE SECTOR

A firm can finance new projects by borrowing, issuing preferred stocks, using its retained earnings, and/or issuing common stocks. Financing new projects only by borrowing is normally not recommended since, at some point, the firm will find it necessary to use one of the other forms of financing to prevent the debt ratio from becoming too large. Alternatively, financing new projects by issuing too many preferred stocks is not desirable since it is riskier to guarantee a given dividend to many persons. A firm should, therefore, be considered as an ongoing concern, and the COC used in capital budgeting should be established as a weighted average of the various types of funds it generally uses, regardless of the specific financing used to fund a particular project.

We introduce the following notation:

$$k_d = \text{interest rate on a firm's new debt; it is the before-tax cost of debt}$$

$k_d(1-T) = $ after-tax cost of debt, where T is the firm's marginal tax rate

$k_p = $ cost of preferred stock

$k_s = $ cost of retained earnings (or internal equity); it is identical to the required rate of return on common stock as defined in Chapter 2 (Section 2)

$k_e = $ cost of external equity obtained by issuing new common stock as opposed to retained earnings

$WACOC = $ the weighted average cost of capital.

Cost of Debt

We use the after-tax cost of debt, $k_d(1 - T)$, to calculate the WACOC. It is the interest rate on debt, k_d, less the tax savings that result because interest is deductible, which is the same as k_d multiplied by $(1 - T)$, where T is the firm's marginal tax rate. In other words, the government pays part of the cost of debt because interest is deductible. In the United States, the federal rate for most corporations is 34%, while most of them are also subject to state income taxes, so that the marginal tax rate on most corporate incomes is about 40%. For instance, if a company can borrow at an interest rate of about 10% and has a marginal federal-plus-state tax rate of 40%, then its after-tax cost of debt is:

$$k_d(1 - T) = 10\% \ (1.0 - 0.4) = 10\% \ (0.6) = 6\%$$

The following observations are made regarding the cost of debt.

a. For a firm with losses, the tax rate is zero so that the after-tax cost of debt equals k_d.

b. The cost of debt is the interest rate on new debt, not that on already outstanding debt since our primary concern is the use of the COC in capital budgeting decisions rather than a rate at which a firm has borrowed in the past, which is a sunk cost.

c. The above discussion of cost of debt ignores flotation costs (the costs incurred for new issuances on debt) since the vast majority of debt is privately placed and, consequently, has no flotation cost; however, if bonds are publicly placed and do involve flotation costs, the after-tax cost of debt is determined by

$$M(1 - F) = \sum_{t=1}^{n} [INT(1 - T) / (1 + k_D)^t] + M/(1 + k_D)^n$$

where

$M = $ the maturity value of the bond

$F = $ the percentage amount of the bond flotation cost

$n = $ the number of periods to maturity

$INT = $ the dollars of interest per period

$T =$ the corporate tax rate

$k_D =$ the after-tax cost of debt adjusted to reflect flotation costs.

Cost of Preferred Stock

The cost of preferred stock, k_p, used to compute the COC, is defined as the preferred dividend, D_p, divided by the net issuing price, P_n, or the price the firm receives after deducting flotation costs: $k_p = D_p/P_n$. Thus, if a firm has preferred stock that pays a $10.00 dividend per share and sells for $100.00 per share in the market, and if it incurs a flotation (or underwriting) cost of 2.5% or $2.50 per share, then it will net $97.50 per share. Consequently, the firm's cost of preferred stock is $k_p = \$10.00/\$97.50 = 10.3\%$. No tax adjustments are made when computing k_p because preferred dividends, unlike interest expense, are not deductible.

Cost of Retained Earnings

The cost of retained earnings, k_s, is the rate of return stockholders require on equity capital the firm obtains by retained earnings, or that part of current earnings not paid out in dividends and, hence, available for reinvestment. Thus, it refers to the income statement item "addition to retained earnings" (Chapter 1). It does not refer to the balance sheet item "retained earnings" since this item consists of all the earnings retained in the business throughout its history. The earnings remaining after interest payments to bondholders and dividends to preferred stockholders belong to the common stockholders, and these earnings serve to compensate them for the use of their capital. A firm may pay out the earnings in the form of dividends or retain them and reinvest the earnings in the business. If the management of a firm decides to retain earnings, there is an opportunity cost involved since shareholders could have received them as dividends and invest the money in real estate, bonds, or other stocks. Consequently, the firm is expected to earn on its retained earnings at least as much as the shareholders could earn on alternative investments of comparable risk.

Whereas debt and preferred stock are contractual obligations with easily determined costs, it is not easy to measure k_s. In practice, three methods are commonly used to determine k_s: the bond-yield-plus-risk-premium approach, the discounted cash flow approach, and the Capital Asset Pricing Model (CAPM) approach.

The bond-yield-plus-risk-premium approach is an ad hoc, subjective procedure consisting of a firm's long-term debt plus a risk premium of three to five percentage points. For instance, according to this approach, a well-established computer firm with bonds yielding 9% has a cost of retained earnings determined as follows:

$$k_s = \text{bond yield} + \text{risk premium} = 9\% + 4\% = 13\%$$

A riskier firm may have bonds yielding 12% and, therefore, its estimate cost of equity is:

$$k_s = 12\% + 4\% = 16\%$$

It makes sense that a firm with risky, low-rated, and (hence) high interest-rate long-term debt also has risky, high cost of equity.

It is clear that the 4% risk premium and the estimated value of k_s based on this premium are judgmental estimates. The aforementioned range of three to five percentage points for the risk premium is based on recent empirical work in the United States.

According to the discounted cash flow approach, the k_s is determined by equation (1) of Chapter 2:

$$V_S = \sum_{t=1}^{t=\infty} D_t / (1 + k_s)^t$$

where

V_S = present value of stock
t = term indicating year
D_t = dividend in year t (expected to be paid at the end of year t)
∞ = symbol indicating that the value of "t" is infinitely large.

Note that in the notation of equation (1) of Chapter 2, the "i" has the same definition as the k_s in the above expression of V_s.

If dividends are expected to grow at a constant rate "g," then, as we saw in Chapter 2, the expression for V_s reduces to the following formula:

$$V_S = D(1+g)/(k_s - g) = D_1/(k_S - g) \tag{1}$$

where

D = the stock's last dividend (which has already been paid)
D_1 = the estimated dividend one year hence.

Expression (1) may be written as:

$$k_s = (D_1/V_S) + \text{expected } g.$$

Thus, the cost of retained earnings equals an expected dividend yield, D_1/V_S, plus a capital gain, g.

It is relatively easy to determine the expected dividend yield; however, the establishment of the proper growth rate is difficult if growth rates in earnings and dividends have not been relatively stable. In other words, the projection of the growth rate cannot be based on a firm's historic growth rate if the firm's growth has been abnormally low or high due to general economic fluctuations or its own unique situation. Merrill Lynch, Salomon Brothers, and other organizations make forecasts of earnings and dividend growth based on projected sales, profit margins, and competitive factors. In addition, publications such as *Value Line* provide growth rate factors for a range of companies. One could, therefore, obtain several available forecasts of a company's dividend growth rate, average them, and use the average as a proxy for the growth expectations of investors in general.

To illustrate the discounted cash flow approach, consider a firm's stock which sells for $25.00. Its next expected dividend is $1.25, and its expected dividend growth rate is 7%. The firm's expected and required rate of return and, hence, its cost of retained earnings is:

$$k_s = (\$1.25/\$25.00) + 7\% = 5\% + 7\% = 12.00\%$$

This 12.00% is the minimum rate of return that management is expected to earn to justify retaining earnings and plowing them back into the business rather than paying them out to stockholders as dividends.

The CAPM approach determines k_s with the help of the following equation:

$$k_s = k_{RF} + (k_M - k_{RF})\beta_i \qquad (2)$$

where

k_{RF} = the risk-free rate, generally taken to be either the U.S. Treasury bond rate or the short-term Treasury bill rate

k_M = the expected rate of return on the market (or on an "average" stock)

β_i = the stock's beta coefficient (the "i" signifies the ith company's beta).

Thus, the CAPM estimate of k_s consists of the risk-free rate, k_{RF}, and a risk premium, $k_M - k_{RF}$, scaled up or down to reflect the particular stock's risk as measured by its beta coefficient.

The meaning of β_i will become clearer when we discuss the Capital Asset Pricing Model later in this chapter. Let it suffice to say now that the parameter β indicates the relationship between the return on a portfolio of stocks and the average return on the market, while β_i indicates the relationship between the return of the ith stock of the portfolio and the average return on the market. Although the CAPM approach appears to yield precise estimates of k_s, in practice, there are several problems: (a) it is difficult to estimate the beta that investors expect the firm to have in the future, (b) there is controversy about whether to use long-term or short-term Treasury yields for k_{RF}, (c) it is especially hard to estimate the market risk premium, and (d) a firm's true investment risk is not measured by its beta if a firm's stockholders are not well diversified and, consequently, are more concerned with total risk rather than market risk.

To illustrate the CAPM approach, suppose that $k_{RF} = 7\%$, $k_M = 12\%$, and $\beta_i = 0.7$ for a given stock. Hence, the stock's k_s is calculated as follows:

$$k_s = 7\% + (12\% - 7\%)\,0.7 = 7\% + 3.5\% = 10.5\%$$

Had β_i been 1.7—indicating that the stock was riskier than average—its k_s would have been

$$k_s = 7\% + (5\%)\,(1.7) = 7\% + 8.5\% = 15.5\%$$

For an average stock,

$$k_s = k_M = 7\% + (5\%)\,(1.0) = 12\%$$

Cost of Newly Issued Common Stock

The cost of new common equity or external equity capital, k_e, is higher than the cost of retained earnings, k_s, because of flotation costs involved in selling new common stock. A firm's existing stockholders expect it to pay a stream of dividends, D_t, which will be derived from existing assets with a per-share value of V_S. Likewise, new investors expect to receive the same stream of dividends, but the funds available in assets will be less than V_S because of flotation costs. Funds obtained from the sale of new stock must be invested at a return high enough so as not to impair the D_t stream of existing stockholders. In other words, funds obtained from the sale of new stock must provide a dividend stream whose present value equals the price the firm will receive:

$$V_S\,(1 - F) = \sum_{t=1}^{\infty} D_t\,/(1 + k_e)^t = V_N \qquad (3)$$

where

V_S = the present value of an existing stock
V_N = the present value of a newly issued stock
F = the percentage flotation cost incurred in selling the new stock issue
D_t = dividend to be paid to existing and new stockholders at the end of year t
k_e = cost of new outside equity.

When growth is constant, expression (3) reduces to:

$$V_S(1 - F) = D_1/(k_e - g)$$

or

$$k_e = [D_1/V_S(1 - F)] + g. \tag{4}$$

Note that $V_S(1 - F)$ is the net price per share received by the firm when it issues new common stock. We also note that expression (4) may be written as

$$k_e = [(D_1/V_S)/(1 - F)] + g = [\text{dividend yield}/(1 - F)] + g.$$

Let us consider again the example described under the discounted cash flow approach toward computing k_s; that is, a firm's stock sells for $25.00 and its next expected dividend and dividend growth rate are $1.25 and 7%, respectively. The flotation cost is 10%. The cost of retained earnings and the cost of new outside equity are, respectively:

$$k_s = (\$1.25/\$25.00) + 7\% = 12.00\%$$
$$k_e = [\$1.25/\$25.00 \ (1 - 0.10)] + 7\% = 12.56\%$$

Investors require a return of $k_s = 12.00\%$ on the stock; however, the firm must earn more than 12.00% due to flotation costs. Specifically, the firm's expected dividend can be maintained, and the price per share will not decline if the firm earns 12.56% on funds obtained from new stock. If the firm earns less than 12.56%, then earnings, dividends, and growth will fall below expectations, causing the stock's price to decline. If it earns more than 12.56%, the stock's price will rise.

Another way of looking at the flotation adjustment is as follows. Consider a company with $1,000,000.00 of assets and no debt. It earns a 14% return (or $140,000.00) on its assets, and it pays all earnings out as dividends, so its growth rate is zero. The company has 10,000 shares of stock outstanding so its earnings per share (EPS) and dividends per share (DPS) are: EPS = DPS = $14.00, and $V_S = \$100.00$. Thus, $k_s = (\$14.00/\$100.00) + 0 = 14\%$. Now suppose the company can get a return of 14% on new assets. Should it sell new stock to acquire new assets? If it sold 10,000 new shares of new stock for $100.00 per share, and if it incurred a 10% flotation cost on the issue, the company would net $100.00 − 0.10 ($100.00) = $90.00 per share, or $900,000.00 in total. Next, the company would invest the $900,000.00 and earn 14%, or $126,000.00. Its new total earnings would be $140,000.00 from the old assets plus $126,000.00 from the new, or $266,000.00 in total, and the company would now have 20,000 shares of stock outstanding. Thus, its EPS and DPS would fall from $14.00 to $13.30, because the new EPS and DPS are: EPS = DPS = $266,000.00/20,000 = $13.30. Since the company's EPS and DPS would decline, the stock's price would also decline from $V_S = \$100.00$ to $13.30/0.14 = $95.00 because investors have put up $100.00 per share but the company has received and invested only $90.00 per share. The $90.00 must, therefore, earn more than 14%

to provide investors with 14% return on the $100.00 they put up. Had the company earned a return of k_e based on equation (4), we would have:

$$k_e = [\$14.00/\$100.00\ (0.90)] + 0 = 15.56\%$$

New total earnings $= \$140,000.00 + \$900,000.00\ (0.1556)$
$$= \$280,000.00$$
New EPS and DPS $= \$280,000.00/20,000 = \$14.00$
New price $= \$14.00/0.14 = \$100.00 =$ original price.

Thus, if the return on the new assets is based on the k_e of equation (4), then EPS, DPS, and the stock price will remain constant.

Weighted Average Cost of Capital

The WACOC is a weighted average of the component costs of debt, preferred stock, and common equity. Consider, for instance, a firm with a capital structure consisting of 45% debt, 1% preferred stock, and 54% common equity (retained earnings plus common stock). Suppose its before-tax cost of debt, k_d, is 10%; its marginal tax rate is 40%; its cost of preferred stock, k_p, is 11%; its cost of common equity from retained earnings, k_s, is 13%; and all of its new equity will come from retained earnings. We now determine the firm's WACOC as follows:

$$\text{WACOC} = w_d k_d\ (1 - T) + w_p k_p + w_s k_s$$
$$= 0.45\ (10\%)\ (0.6) + 0.01\ (11\%) + 0.54\ (13\%)$$
$$= 10\%$$

The w_d, w_p, and w_s are the weights used for debt, preferred, and common equity, respectively. They are based on the accounting values shown on the firm's balance sheet (book values). It is noted that, theoretically, the weights should be based on the market values of the different securities; however, book value weights can be used as a proxy for market value weights if a firm's book value weights are reasonably close to its market value weights.

Each firm has an optimal capital structure, defined as the capital structure with the lowest WACOC. Such a capital structure is a combination of debt, preferred stock, and common equity which causes its stock price to be maximized. The concept of optimal capital structure is based on a capital structure policy which involves a tradeoff between risk and return; that is, using more debt raises the riskiness of a firm's earnings. However, a higher debt ratio generally leads to a higher expected rate of return. In other words, higher risk associated with greater debt tends to decrease the stock's price, but the higher expected rate of return increases it. The optimal capital structure is the one that strikes the optimal balance between risk and return, and by doing so maximizes the stock's price.

Financial leverage, which is the extent to which fixed-income securities (debt and preferred stock) are used in a firm's capital structure, affects the firm's expected earnings per share (EPS), their riskiness, and, consequently, its stock price. As a result of using financial leverage, an additional risk is placed on common stockholders. This additional risk, called the financial risk, is the portion of the stockholders' risk, over and above the basic business risk.

The following example illustrates how financial leverage affects a company's EPS and stock price. Suppose a company's annual sales are $400,000.00; its fixed costs $80,000.00; its variable costs 60% of sales, or $240,000.00; and its marginal tax rate, T, is 40%. The company's total assets are worth $400,000.00. We consider two cases:

—debt assets ratio (D/A ratio) = 0, or zero debt and 20,000 shares outstanding, and

—D/A ratio = 50%; an interest rate, k_d, equal to 12%; and 10,000 shares outstanding.

Thus, in the first case, the company is capitalized with 0% debt and 100% equity; while in the second case, the company is capitalized with 50% debt and 50% equity.

We determine the EPS for the above-mentioned two cases with equation (5):

$$EPS = (Sales - Fixed\ costs - Variable\ costs - Interest)$$
$$(1 - T)/shares\ outstanding. \tag{5}$$

for D/A = 0, expression (5) becomes:

$$EPS = (\$400,000 - \$80,000 - \$240,000 - 0)\ (0.6)/20,000$$
$$= \$2.40$$

for D/A = 50%, we have:

$$EPS = (\$400,000 - \$80,000 - \$240,000 - \$24,000)\ (0.6)/10,000$$
$$= \$3.36$$

Let us assume that the company pays all of its earnings out as dividends, so EPS = DPS, and no retained earnings will be plowed back into the business. Consequently, growth in EPS and DPS will be zero. Suppose the risk-free rate of return, k_{RF}, is 6%; the required return on an average stock, k_M, is 10%; the beta pertaining to the D/A = 0 case is 1.50; and the beta pertaining to the D/A = 50% case is 2.35. Application of expressions (2) and (1) gives:

for D/A

$$k_s = 6\% + (10\% - 6\%)\ 1.50 = 12.0\%$$
$$V_S = DPS/k_s = \$2.40/0.120 = \$20.00$$

for D/A = 50%,

$$k_s = 6\% + (10\% - 6\%)\ 2.35 = 15.4\%$$
$$V_S = DPS/k_s = \$3.36/0.154 = \$21.82$$

Next, we determine the price earnings (P/E) ratio and WACOC for each of the cases considered:
for D/A = 0,

$$
\begin{aligned}
\text{P/E ratio} &= V_S/EPS = \$20.00/\$2.40 = 8.33 \\
\text{WACOC} &= w_d k_d\ (1 - T) + w_s k_s \\
&= (D/A)\ (k_d)\ (1 - T) + (1 - D/A)k_s \\
&= 0 + k_s = 12.0\%
\end{aligned}
$$

for D/A = 50%,

$$
\begin{aligned}
\text{P/E ratio} &= V_S/EPS = \$21.82/\$3.36 = 6.49 \\
\text{WACOC} &= (D/A)\ (k_d)\ (1 - T) + (1 - D/A)k_s \\
&= 0.5\ (12\%)\ (0.6) + 0.5\ (15.4\%) \\
&= 3.6\% + 7.7\% = 11.3\%
\end{aligned}
$$

The above example illustrates that changing a company's capitalization from 0% debt and 100% equity to 50% debt and 50% equity decreases the WACOC from 12.0% to 11.3%, increases the EPS from $2.40 to $3.36, and increases the company's estimated stock price from $20.00 to $21.82. In other words, using financial leverage is to the advantage of the company, since it increases the company's stock price. How far should the company go with substituting debt for equity? The answer is that the company should choose the capital structure that will maximize the price of its stock. To elucidate this concept, we consider the same example as the one discussed above, and increase the number of cases pertaining to different D/A ratios as given in Table 5.1.

The values of columns (2) and (4) of Table 5.1 are given, while the values of the other columns are calculated in the same manner as we computed them for D/A = 0 and D/A = 50%. For instance, for D/A = 20%, we have:

$$
\begin{aligned}
EPS &= (\$400,000 - \$80,000 - \$240,000 - \\
&\quad \$6,800)\ (0.6)/16,000 \\
&= \$2.75 \\
k_s &= 6\% + (10\% - 6\%)\ 1.65 = 12.6\% \\
V_S &= \$2.75/0.126 = \$21.83 \\
\text{P/E ratio} &= \$21.83/\$2.75 = 7.94 \\
\text{WACOC} &= 0.2(8.5\%)\ (0.6) + 0.8\ (12.6\%) = 11.10\%
\end{aligned}
$$

Table 5.1 shows that at a 40% debt ratio, the expected stock price is maximized and the WACOC is minimized. Thus, the optimal capital structure calls for 40% debt and 60% equity. The company should set its target capital structure at these ratios; it should move toward this target when new securities offerings are made if the existing ratios are off target.

Table 5.1
Stock Price and Cost of Capital Estimates for a Company with Different D/A Ratios

D/A (%)	k_d (%)	Exp. EPS and DPS[1]	Est. β	k_s^2 (%)	V_S^3	P/E[4]	WA-COC[5] (%)
(1)	(2)	(3)	(4)	(5)	(6)	(7)	(8)
0	-	$2.40	1.50	12.0	$20.00	8.33	12.00
10	8.0	2.56	1.55	12.2	20.98	8.20	11.46
20	8.5	2.75	1.65	12.6	21.83	7.94	11.10
30	9.0	2.97	1.80	13.2	22.50	7.58	10.86
40	10.0	3.20	2.00	14.0	22.86	7.14	10.80
50	12.0	3.36	2.35	15.4	21.82	6.49	11.30
60	15.0	3.30	2.75	17.8	18.54	5.62	12.52

[1] The company pays all of its earnings out as dividends, so EPS = DPS.
[2] $k_s = [k_{RF} + (k_M - k_{RF})\beta]$ with $k_{RF} = 6\%$ and $k_M = 10\%$.
[3] Estimated price.
[4] Resulting P/E ratio.
[5] Weighted average cost of capital.

The following observations are made about the figures of Table 5.1.

a. Column (2) shows that the company's cost of debt varies if different percentages of debt are used in its capital structure. The higher the percentage of debt, the riskier the debt and, consequently, the higher the interest rate lenders will charge.

b. Column (3) demonstrates that the expected EPS is maximized at a D/A ratio of 50%. However, this does not mean that the company's optimal capital structure calls for a 50% debt, since the optimal capital structure is the one that maximizes the price of the company's stock, and this always calls for a D/A ratio which is smaller than the one which maximizes expected EPS.

c. The beta coefficients of Column (4) measure the relative volatility of the company's stock compared to that of an average stock (Section 5 of this chapter discusses the manner in which beta coefficients are established). It has been demonstrated both empirically and theoretically that a company's beta increases with its degree of financial leverage.

d. Column (5) shows that the values of k_s increase when the estimated beta coefficients increase (by definition of k_s).

e. As mentioned above, the values of Column (6) are computed to establish the optional capital structure or the one which results in the highest estimated stockprice.

f. The P/E ratios of Column (7) demonstrate that, other things held constant, these ratios should, of course, decline as the riskiness of a company increases. The P/E ratios are computed as a check on the reasonableness of the other data of Table 5.1, and they can be compared for consistency to those of zero growth competitive companies with varying amounts of financial leverage.

g. Column (8) shows that as the D/A ratio increases, the costs of both debt and equity rise, and the increasing costs of the two components begin to offset the fact that larger amounts of the lower-cost components are being used. At 40% debt, WACOC hits a minimum, and it rises after that as the D/A ratio is increased.

3. INTEREST RATE IN THE PUBLIC SECTOR

Depending on a government's objectives, the following interest rates may be distinguished: opportunity cost of capital, social rate of discount, and accounting rate of discount. These different names reflect different aims a government has formulated for an investment program. The three "types" of interest rates are used in the same manner in investment appraisals—either for computation of present values of future money outlays and receipts, or for comparison to internal rates of return of individual projects.

Opportunity Cost of Capital

The opportunity cost of capital is defined as the return on capital which might be obtained by its employment when the central objective of planning policy is to use capital so its return to employment in any one investment is at least as high as its return from employment in any alternative investment. Similar to the cost of capital to equity shareholders, we have to allow for any risk differential.

In other words, the opportunity cost of capital is the marginal productivity of additional investment in the best alternative uses. It is, therefore, not surprising that the marginal productivity of capital in the private sector is frequently suggested as an appropriate value for the opportunity cost of capital to be used in public investment projects. It seems reasonable to say that if the marginal investment can earn x percent in the private sector, no public investment project should be allowed to earn less, and vice versa. However, the suggestion does not lead to a solution, since measurement of marginal productivity of capital is a formidable (if not impossible) task due to the fact that capital is not a homogeneous good. That is, marginal products from different capital goods may differ. A more practical way to determine the value of the opportunity cost of capital is to use some market rate of interest.

The use of a market rate of interest corresponds to the neoclassical approach of perfect competition, which assumes the existence of a capital market that generates efficient prices. That is, the price system equates marginal costs and benefits and results into efficient allocation of resources. Thus, efficient prices are the prices at which there would be a competitive equilibrium between supply and demand. In other words, they are equilibrium prices for the various factors in an optimum situation when all alternative uses have been taken into account. Naturally, an efficient price system rarely exists due to various market imper-

fections—tariffs, taxes, quotas, increasing returns to scale, monopoly and mo-
nopsony power by various buyers and sellers, or a lack of necessary market
institutions. Nevertheless, the use of a market rate of interest for the opportunity
cost of capital is often a good approximation.

In practice, the use of a market interest rate follows the following procedure:
(1) selection of relevant interests rates; (2) estimation of the prime interest rate
or the rate charged borrowers having the highest credit training; and (3) adjustment of the prime interest rate by including a corresponding risk premium, if
necessary. From a broad viewpoint, the selection of relevant interest rates calls
for a reflection of what determines the rate of interest in an economy. In brief,
it is the result of the interplay between the supply of and demand for capital.
Basically, the supply depends on the level of savings in a country and the flows
of capital from abroad. The demand stems from investment plans by private
business and government. Thus, we could consider the following array: interest
rates related to the short-term funds, medium- and long-term loans, preferred
shares and equity capital, interest rates on time deposits, rates for consumer
credits, rates of return on real assets (fixed assets and inventories), and interest
rates charged by private money lenders operating in unorganized markets.

The selection of relevant interest rates relates to the choice of the interest rate
that is a prime rate (as free of risk as possible) and not subject to random short-
term fluctuations. Consequently, we eliminate from the above array interest rates
related to equity capital, preferred shares, and short-term funds.

The rates of return on real assets are not recommended for consideration
either, since the establishment of these rates calls for the evaluation of such
assets, which is a Herculean task if one considers the variety of existing real
assets. Moreover, prices of similar fixed assets vary from location to location.

Interest rates charged by private money lenders in unorganized markets primarily take place in developing countries where private money lending sometimes accounts for a large portion of the total volume of credit extended.
However, such rates are also not recommended for consideration since they often
reflect the default of borrowers, and frequently exist in quasi-monopolistic en-
vironments (the loans are frequently made by small businessmen and farmers
in rural areas with a lack of good communications and money markets).

The above eliminations leave us with interest rates of medium- and long-term
loans, interest on time deposits, and rates for consumer credits to estimate the
prime interest rate. In the United States, Canada, and most western European
nations, the capital markets are essentially free, and governments, in their bor-
rowings, pay a competitive price. In addition, government bonds in these countries are regarded as the prototype of investments with a prime interest rate.
Therefore, it is reasonable to use the yields on long-term government bonds for
the opportunity cost of capital in the United States, Canada, and most western
European nations.

In developing countries, however, capital markets are usually imperfect, and
governments do not always enjoy the highest credit rating. Depending on local

conditions, it is frequently better to use first-rate corporate bond yields, long-term private borrowing rates on high-grade loans of commercial and specialized credit institutions, first trusts granted by mortgage banks, or a weighted average of these.

The adjustment of the prime interest rate by including a corresponding risk premium is necessary when there are risky investment plans. The correct adjustment relies largely on judgment, since there is no practicable way to analyze systematically and to transform price risks and risk of failure of the investment into one risk premium. The difference between short-term and long-term lending rates for prime risk capital may give an indication of the market's assessment of the adjustment necessary for price risks. In addition, the yields on purchasing-power bonds (those bonds whose nominal value is tied to a value standard such as a general price index) may, if they exist, be compared to ordinary financial bonds of similar terms. An indication of the adjustment necessary for risk of failure of the investment may also be obtained on the basis of past trends and forecasts of probable failures of ventures.

The use of competitive growth models is sometimes suggested for the determination of the opportunity cost of capital. The models are based on highly abstract production functions of the Cobb-Douglas type with variables and parameters that are difficult or impossible to measure empirically. In addition, the underlying assumptions appear to be unrealistic in real-world situations. The application of growth models to the establishment of the opportunity cost of capital may become more promising once the approach has been further developed through the relaxation of unrealistic assumptions and the inclusion of variables which are easier to measure. So far, little progress along these lines has been made.

Social Rate of Discount

The method of establishing the opportunity cost of capital is based on the objective of an efficient allocation of resources, although this may not be realized due to market imperfections. The method implies, moreover, that aggregate private savings are determined by the division of value added between workers and owners of capital, with workers consuming almost their entire income, and capitalists saving most of their profits.

The social rate of discount realizes that society may wish to attach relative weights to objectives other than the efficient allocation of resources as well. For instance, society may decide that growth is important and justifies the sacrifice of present consumption.

Let us introduce the following three simple equations to obtain a better understanding of the concept of social rates of discount:

$$P_{j,t} = \sum_i p_{i,j,t} X_{i,t} \qquad (6)$$

$$P_t = \sum_j w_{j,t} P_{j,t} \tag{7}$$

$$P = \sum_t v_t P_t \tag{8}$$

where

$p_{i,j,t}$ = the marginal value to objective j of one unit of good (or factor) i during year t

$X_{i,t}$ = the input (if negative) or output (if positive) of good i in year t

$P_{j,t}$ = net profit to objective j in year t

$w_{j,t}$ = weight given to objective j in year t (these weights indicate the marginal substitution rates between different objectives)

P_t = annual net profit

v_t = weight given to the net profit in year t

P = net profit

$\sum_i, \sum_j, \sum_t$ = summation over all goods i, all objectives j, and all years t of the expected life of the project, respectively.

Equations (6)–(8) relate to a specific project or investment plan being considered. Inputs consist of factors of production such as capital, labor, intermediate goods, raw materials, and land; while outputs consist of goods and services produced. In our discussion of the social rate of discount method, we will assume that the implementation of this project or plan itself has a negligible effect on the relative marginal values for different physical units ($p_{i,j,t}$), the weights for aggregating net benefits to different objectives ($w_{j,t}$), and the weights for time aggregation (v_t). General equilibrium methods, which are beyond the scope of this book, are necessary to relax this assumption. Examples of situations where this assumption may be invalid are the societies of oil-rich countries like Saudi Arabia.

Notice the similarity between the weights v_t of expression (8) and the single payment present worth factor (sppwf) of Appendix 1. Both the sppwf and the v_t intend to aggregate net benefits which accrue in different time periods. However, there is a difference in the interpretation of these two factors. The sppwf is an "exchange rate" between present and future pecuniary values. The v_t represents a time preference—such as present consumption is more preferable than future consumption—and may reflect a diminishing marginal utility for the realization of objectives a government has formulated. For instance, society may derive less utility from additional increments of a good or service in the future once it expects to be richer. These time preferences and diminishing marginal utilities are directly related to demand and social preferences.

The use of the social discount rate may be particularly desirable in developing countries with a disequilibrium between supply and demand in the choice between consumption and investment. The impact of time preferences and diminishing marginal utilities in developing countries is usually reflected in a v_t value that declines over time.

The computational difficulties involved in the use of different values of the interest rate over time have been pointed out. Use of different v_t values over time is also too cumbersome. We will, therefore, make the working assumption that the weights v_t decline at a constant rate. Thus,

$$[v_t - v_{t+1}]/v_{t+1} = \text{constant}. \tag{9}$$

The ratio of expression (9) is called the social rate of discount. Using i to represent this rate, we can rewrite expression (8) as follows:

$$P = \sum_t P_t / (1 + i)^t. \tag{10}$$

Expression (9) defines the social rate of discount only partly, since we have to indicate the common yardstick or numeraire used in establishing the weights. Generally, the use of this rate is based on the assumption that P_t of expression (7) is measured in aggregate consumption units. Thus, it includes the aggregation of other objectives through the weights $w_{j,t}$. The choice of the numeraire essentially establishes the absolute value of the weights to be applied to benefits accruing to different groups of society since the weight attached to the numeraire (aggregate consumption) is, by definition, set equal to unity.

Expressions (6) and (7) clearly indicate that proponents of the social discount rate wish to consider net contributions to all relevant objectives. In other words, the criterion for public project selection is social profit rather than monetary profit. Note that either the weights $w_{j,t}$ or the weights v_t may include a risk premium.

The difference between the determination of the opportunity cost of capital and the social rate of discount is that the former uses market prices of goods and services for the weights $p_{i,j,t}$ of expression (6) and market interest rates representative of the opportunity cost of capital for the weights v_t of expression (8), while the latter uses shadow prices of goods and services and the social rate of discount. In addition, the procedure for establishing the opportunity cost of capital does not use expression (7) since it is only associated with the achievement of one objective (efficient allocation of resources). In brief, the philosophy of the social rate of discount is that market prices are not necessarily representative of the marginal social benefits and costs of a scarce commodity.

Shadow prices are defined as the values of inputs and outputs associated with the optimal development program, given the weights attached to the basic social/economic objectives, and given all the various constraints which limit the extent to which these objectives can be achieved. Thus, shadow prices are introduced to correct distortions which, due to administrative costs or political pressure, cannot be removed. For instance, the possibilities of taxing certain commodities may be limited by the costs of collection and administration, or the political power of the rich may be too strong to prevent income distribution to the poor by a government. In other words, shadow prices are prices which, despite the distortion, attempt to ensure the realization of the objectives of a government's development program. They imply that a government is using project selection to achieve its goals rather than, for instance, fiscal policy.

The rate of savings in a country depends on the distribution of income between various classes of wage and profit earners and the government. Generally, workers have a higher marginal propensity to consume than profit earners. Therefore, two investments producing the same product and with comparable costs per unit of output will affect future savings differently, if in one project the value added goes primarily to workers as wages, while in the other one the value added is paid largely to profit earners as return for their invested capital. Acceptance of the former project would imply less future savings. Thus, if a government's objective relates to emphasis on current consumption rather than the accumulation of future savings, then it should include an extra value to the society of workers' consumption as part of the computations for the objectives other than aggregate consumption.

It is clear that the establishment of a value for the social discount rate is no simple task. First, expressions (6) and (7) indicate that the computations involved may be cumbersome. Second, the choice of the weights $w_{j,t}$, which relate the various objectives, is subjective and, in the last analysis, must be decided by the political process. Third, the determination of the marginal values for $p_{i,j,t}$ is not easy either. Fourth, the previous paragraph shows that the implementation of a specific project may affect the distribution of income between consumption and savings.

In view of the problems related to the determination of the social discount rate, we may conclude that it cannot be estimated and it must be set exogenously by political authority. Naturally, such a conclusion is of no help to governments which rely on expert planning organizations to make recommendations for the value of the social discount rate. In such a situation, it is recommended that investment appraisal be done with a number of alternative discount rates lying between lower and upper bounds which are based on some knowledge of a nation's national economic plan. For instance, the evaluation of projects could be done with discount rates falling between the economic growth rate and the opportunity cost of capital.

Alternatively, we may compute the cross-over discount rate to examine alternative values of the social discount rate. The concept of a cross-over discount rate applies to the examination of two alternative investment appraisals. It is defined as the discount rate which equalizes the present values of the cash flows of two alternative investments. In practice, the cross-over discount rate is found by subtracting the undiscounted cash flow of the investment with the lower net present value (NPV) year by year from that with the higher NPV, and then finding the discount rate which will make the present value of the stream of differences equal to zero. Thus, the concept of a cross-over discount rate is that the preference ranking of alternatives may change between lower and higher discount rates. It is the rate at which the preference changes.

Readers interested in case studies that use the social rate of discount are referred to the UNIDO Guidelines mentioned at the end of this chapter. Chapters 19, 20, 21, and 22 of these guidelines present examples pertaining to a pulp and paper mill, a chemical plant, a water project, and a fiberboard plant, respectively.

Accounting Rate of Discount

Like the social rate of discount, the concept of the accounting rate of discount is that society may wish to attach relative weights to objectives other than the efficient allocation of resources. The difference between the social and accounting rates of discount lies in the numeraire used; the former uses aggregate consumption, while the latter uses uncommitted public income as numeraire. The accounting rate of discount may be used by a government if in its view additional savings and future consumption are as valuable as additional present consumption. The government wishes, however, to concentrate on income, irrespective of its use for consumption or savings, since both are presumed to be of the same value.

Expressions (6) through (8) may also be used to obtain a better understanding of the concept of accounting rates of discount since the only difference between social and accounting rates of discount is the choice of numeraire. Consequently, the shadow prices (and the associated weights) used in the determination of the social rate of discount are different from those used in the determination of the accounting rate of discount.

Alternatively, we may use equation (11) to elucidate the concept of using shadow prices in establishing either the social rate of discount or the accounting rate of discount.

$$\text{Shadow Price} = \text{Efficiency Price} \pm \text{Impact.} \qquad (11)$$

Efficiency price has been defined in the discussion of the opportunity cost of capital.

Suppose that labor, an input factor of a project, enjoys an increase in consumption. The increased demand on the part of labor comprises various commodities or services that directly or indirectly reduce the quantity of uncommitted income available to a government. As such, the increased demand represents an additional cost incurred by the project, which should be considered when determining the shadow price of labor.

Suppose also that increased consumption is a goal of the government considered in our example. In this case, the increased demand also represents a benefit. Through the use of weighted factors, we now have to value the aforementioned additional cost and the benefit related to increased consumption in terms of our numeraire (units of public income), while the efficiency price will also have to be expressed in this numeraire. Let us call the above additional cost and the benefit related to increased consumption and expressed in the chosen numeraire, C and B, respectively. Equation (11) becomes:

$$\text{Shadow price} = \text{Efficiency Price} + (C - B).$$

Thus, $(C - B)$ represents the "impact" of the increased consumption as a reduction in the government's uncommitted income (C) and an increase in consumption (B).

The discussion related to the above example explains the concept of the accounting rate of discount in a rather simplistic manner. The determination of this rate is, however, as complex as the establishment of a value for the social rate of discount. No matter how sophisticated an approach is followed, the procedure of expressing all relevant variables in the same numeraire is time consuming (unless unrealistic assumptions are introduced) and subject to judgment. Again, an easy solution would be to have public authority establish the accounting rate of discount.

In principle, the accounting rate of discount should be selected such that the demand for public investment resources just exhausts the available supply, since too high a rate would result in an excess supply of public investment funds, and too low a rate would give a demand for public investment resources which exceeds the supply. This is so because too high a rate would result in too few projects passing the test of a positive net present value (NPV), which is required for acceptability of a project. On the other hand, too many projects would have a positive NPV if the rate were too low. Similar to our discussion of the determination of the social discount rate, we recommend the examination of alternative accounting discount rates between lower and upper bounds and the computation of cross-over discount rates.

4. RISK, UNCERTAINTY, AND CERTAINTY

How to deal with risk through risk loading on the interest rate has already been discussed. Now we will analyze what risk actually is before examining additional ways to treat risk.

Investment decisions deal with future outcomes. We may view the future as taking the following four basic forms.

1. *Ignorant.* The future is seen as a blank about which we are unwilling or unable to make any useful statement. Decisions made under such conditions may be called "heroic" rather than "rational" decisions.
2. *Uncertain.* A variety of future outcomes are possible but we are unable to make any statement about the probability of occurrence of each of these outcomes.

3. *Probabilistic.* The inability to predict exactly what is going to happen in the future is recognized. However, we are able to say that several possible outcomes may occur with stated probability.

4. *Certain.* The outcome of an investment is known. For example, the decision to purchase a U.S. government bond is one in which it is reasonable to assume complete information about the future outcome.

It is impossible to analyze the ignorant form of the future or the heroic decisions. We will, therefore, limit our discussion to the last three forms of the future. Accordingly, we may classify investment decisions as decisions under uncertainty, under risk, and under assumed certainty.

A decision for which the analyst elects to consider several possible futures, the probabilities of which cannot be stated, is called a decision under uncertainty. An investment decision for which the analyst elects to consider several possible futures, the probabilities of which can be stated, is called a decision under risk. For some investment decisions, it is practical to assume that there is no uncertainty connected with the analysis of the decision. These decisions are referred to as decisions under assumed certainty or deterministic decisions.

Sources of risk and/or uncertainty include the following.

1. *Insufficient numbers of similar investments.* Generally, the number of investments of a particular type considered by an organization is relatively small. This means that there will be insufficient opportunity for the effect of unfavorable outcomes to be cancelled by favorable outcomes.

2. *Bias in the data and its assessment.* For example, it is not uncommon to find that those involved in cost-benefit analysis are frequently eager to raise estimates of benefits but not of costs.

3. *Changing external economic environment.* Estimates of future conditions are often based on past results, and changing economic conditions invalidate past experience.

4. *Misinterpretation of data.* A high danger of this misinterpretation exists if the relationship among parameters influencing the investment decision is not clear.

5. *Errors of analysis.* These errors can occur in the analysis of the investment decision as well as in the analysis of the technical operating characteristics of a project.

6. *Managerial talent availability and emphasis.* Generally, management talent is a limited resource within an organization. Thus, there is a risk that insufficient management talent is applied to the implementation of investment projects.

7. *Salvageability of investment.* In judging risk, it is important to consider the relative recoverability of investment commitments if a project, for performance considerations or otherwise, is to be liquidated. The salvage value expressed as a percentage of the original price of special-purpose equipment is likely to be less than that of general-purpose equipment.

8. *Obsolescence.* The problem of predicting obsolescence is complex since technological change and progress may occur more rapidly than anticipated.

It should be noted that the aforementioned definitions of investment decisions under risk or uncertainty are not universally accepted in the literature of managerial economics. Uncertainty sometimes refers to investments whose outcomes are uncertain, while risk is used for the consequential effect of possible uncertain outcomes. Consequently, risk exists if the future outcome of an investment is uncertain. We will not use these definitions of uncertainty and risk.

We have referred to a risk premium or risk loading on the interest rate. Strictly speaking, we should, according to our definitions of uncertainty and risk, talk about an uncertainty or risk premium (or loading), depending on whether probabilities related to various possible future outcomes are used in order to arrive at a value of a risk premium. In practice, this value is usually based on previous experience, intuition, or random guess. Thus, the terms "uncertainty premium" and "uncertainty loading" may be more appropriate.

Risk or uncertainty loading on the interest rate results in a decrease in the net present value (NPV) of a project with no negative terms in its cash flow. Extreme caution is called for if some negative terms exist in the cash flow, since the loading on these terms counter-affects the loading on positive terms of the cash flow. The following simple example illustrates that in this case the NPV can increase rather than decrease.

Consider a cash flow consisting of +$50.00 at the end of the first year, +$100.00 at the end of the second year, −$160.00 at the end of the third year, and +$30.00 at the end of the fourth year. NPVs of this cash flow with interest rates of 10% and 15% are as follows:

$$10\%: 0.9091(\$50) + 0.8264(\$100) - 0.7513(\$160)$$
$$+ 0.6830(\$30) = \$28.39$$
$$15\%: 0.8696(\$50) + 0.7561(\$100) - 0.6575(\$160)$$
$$+ 0.5718(\$30) = \$31.05$$

A lower NPV reduces the chances of acceptance for a project when competing with other projects. It is clear that this is what we want for projects with uncertainty and/or risk involved. It is noted that the method of loading on the interest rate fails to be effective if a project has so short a life that discounting cannot take effect.

Relatively simple methods other than uncertainty loading on the interest rate to deal with uncertainty are sensitivity analysis and the allowance of contingencies. The principle of sensitivity analysis consists of the examination of the impact of variations in the values of the input variables of a decision process on the final decision. For instance, we may make various contingency assumptions with respect to the main variables or the ones that most profoundly affect the analysis. Naturally, if the proceeds of an investment project are not affected much by the variations in the value assumed by a given variable, there is no need to incur the cost of developing an accurate estimate of that variable. A range of assumptions—at least an optimistic and a conservative extreme—may be assumed for each variable that has a major effect on the costs and benefits of the investment project. In some situations, the investment decision will be the same under both optimistic and pessimistic assumptions. In other cases, one investment will be preferred under one realistic set of assumptions, and another on the basis of a different set of realistic assumptions. In these circumstances, experienced judgment, with an awareness of the importance of the various assumptions, must be exercised.

A traditional engineering method of handling uncertainties has been to allow for "contingencies"—adverse events or conditions that are expected to occur with sufficient probability to require explicit provision for their costs. If escalation clauses are included in contracts for equipment or construction, the contingency allowances include payments which can be anticipated in addition to bid prices due to the effect of such clauses. Contingencies may be classified as physical and price contingencies.

It is clear that physical contingencies vary with the nature and size of a project. The investment analyst is well advised to seek engineering assistance to determine the nature of the physical contingency allowances. The nature may relate to difficult access to the project site, the degree to which field work has been completed, geophysically difficult areas, design work quality, contract supervision, degree of precision with which quantity estimates have been prepared, unusually adverse weather conditions, or unforeseen technical difficulties.

We should consider the justification of incurring additional costs for the refinement of designs, improvement of supervision, or further site investigations if the physical contingencies are relatively large. Physical contingencies should be expressed as a percentage of the base costs rather than as a percentage of the costs including the price contingencies.

Price contingencies are allowances for cost increases arising from expected increases in prices after the date specified for the prices used in the same estimation of the base costs of a project. Price contingencies may be due to domestic or foreign inflation, the extent to which a large project may increase the cost of local resources, and possible delays in time of implementation of a project.

Note that the adjustment for price risk related to inflation should only be made in appraisals if inflation is expected to result in changes in relative prices. Thus, price contingency allowances should not be made if general inflation is expected to affect prices proportionally. General inflation is really a change in the value of the monetary unit in which costs are measured; it does not result in changes in commodity values in relation to each other. Higher prices due to general inflation should not be considered when determining price contingency allowances (or interest rates), since potential investments are always analyzed in terms of costs expressed in constant prices. This is explained in detail in Chapter 6.

Other methods of dealing with uncertainties are the application of one of the following rules: maximin, minimax, maximax, Laplace, Hurwicz, and minimax regret rules. These rules provide a logical framework for the study of the strat-

Table 5.2
Example Problem Involving Uncertainty

		States of the World			
		S_1	S_2	S_3	S_4
Alternatives	a_1	5	5	0	3
	a_2	3	3	3	3
	a_3	0	9	0	0
	a_4	3	6	0	0
	a_5	0	2	2	0

egies open to an investment analyst in the face of total uncertainty. The framework enables the investment analyst to choose an alternative action (or project) from a group of mutually exclusive actions (or projects).

The aforementioned rules typically recognize the existence of a number of alternative, possible actions (a_1, a_2, etc.) and a number of possible states of the world (S_1, S_2, etc.) whose effect on each outcome, as measured by a net present value (NPV), can be calculated. The alternatives may relate to sizes of proposed factory buildings needed to supply a certain size market. The states of the world could represent the possible points in the market cycle when the factory comes into production. The decision to be made concerns the optimum factory size.

The above rules may also be used to analyze the effects of uncertainties involved in determining capital costs. The alternative actions would relate to alternative approaches to this determination, while the state of the world would represent alternative, prevailing future conditions.

The maximin rule suggests that we examine the minimum NPV associated with each alternative. Next, we select the alternative which maximizes the minimum NPV. This is clearly a conservative or pessimistic rule that directs attention to the worst outcome and makes it as desirable as possible. As an example of the maximin rule, consider the decision matrix of Table 5.2. Five different alternatives are considered, while each of these can result in four different future outcomes. The numbers in the matrix are the NPV values in thousands of dollars. According to the maximin rule, we select alternative a_2 from the decision matrix of Table 5.2. It is clear that this rule does not make sense if all the minimal net present values associated with each alternative are negative.

The maximin principle would be reinterpreted if we were dealing with a decision in which costs instead of net present values were given. In this case, we examine the maximum cost associated with each alternative, and then select the alternative that minimized the maximum cost. In this form it is called the minimax rule. Too frequent application of the maximin or minimax rules may lessen the available opportunities for profit that normally only result from a willingness to take some risks.

The obvious antithesis of the maximin principle is the maximax principle, which suggests examination of the maximum NPV associated with each alternative. Next, we select the alternative which maximizes the maximum NPV. In the example of Table 5.2, the maximax rule selects alternative a_3. The maximax rule is as optimistic and adventurous as the maximin rule is pessimistic and conservative.

The Laplace rule, sometimes called the principle of insufficient reason, assumes that all possible outcomes are equally likely and that we can choose on the basis of expected outcomes based on equal probabilities for all outcomes. This assumption is usually of highly questionable merit. In the example problem of Table 5.2, we assume that the probabilities related to the four outcomes are $p_1 = p_2 = p_3 = p_4 = 1/4$ and the expected NPVs are $E(a_1) = 3.25$, $E(a_2) = 3.00$, $E(a_3) = 2.25$, $E(a_4) = 2.25$, $E(a_5) = 1.00$. The Laplace rule would lead then to the selection of a_1.

The purpose of the Hurwicz rule is to reflect any degree of moderation between extreme optimism and extreme pessimism which the investment analyst may wish to select. The rule says explicitly: select an index of optimism, α, such that $0 \leq \alpha \leq 1$. For each alternative, compute the weighted outcome: α(NPV or cost if most favorable outcome occurs) $+ (1 - \alpha)$ (NPV or cost if least favorable outcome occurs). Select the alternative that optimizes the weighted outcome. The weighted outcomes associated with the five alternatives of Table 5.2 and $\alpha = 0.75$ are 3.75, 4.50, 6.75, 3.10, and 1.50. Thus, alternative a_3 with a weighted outcome of 6.75 is selected if $\alpha = 0.75$. A practical difficulty of the Hurwicz rule involves the determination of a proper value for α, the weighing factor. In case of extreme optimism ($\alpha = 1$), the Hurwicz rule becomes the maximax rule; the case of extreme pessimism ($\alpha = 0$) gives the minimax rule.

The minimax regret rule, sometimes called the Savage principle, calls for the examination of the maximum possible regret associated with each alternative. Next, the alternative which minimizes the regret is selected. The regret represents the possible loss due to not having selected the best alternative for each possible outcome. Consider the matrix of Table 5.3, which is the regret matrix for the problem of Table 5.2. For instance, the regret for a_1 and S_2 is found by subtracting the NPV = 5 from the maximum NPV that could be obtained given S_2, which is 9. The difference of 4 is the regret for the cell (a_1, S_2) of Table 5.3. The other regrets of this table are found in a similar manner. Table 5.3 shows that the alternative which minimizes the maximum regret is a_4. It is clear that the minimax regret rule intends to counter some of the ultraconservative results given by the maximin and minimax rules.

Note that in the example problem of Table 5.2, only two rules lead to the same selection:

Table 5.3
Example Regret Matrix[1]

		Possible Outcomes				Maximum Regret
		S_1	S_2	S_3	S_4	
Alternatives	a_1	0	4	3	0	4
	a_2	2	6	0	0	6
	a_3	5	0	3	3	5
	a_4	2	3	3	3	3
	a_5	5	7	1	3	7

[1] Related to the example problem of Table 5.2.

Maximin rule	a_2
Maximax and Hurwicz ($\alpha = 0.75$) rules	a_3
Laplace rule	a_1
Minimax regret rule	a_4

Generally, there is a difference between the rules, although in some cases they may yield the same results.

We also note that none of the rules selects alternative a_5. This is evident since alternative a_2 is always preferred to alternative a_5. If of two alternatives one would always be preferred no matter what future occurs, this preferred alternative is said to dominate. The other alternative may then be discarded, since there is no further reason to consider it. To reduce the range of alternatives to be considered, and, consequently, to facilitate the analysis, we should check for dominance before using the maximin, minimax, maximax, Laplace, Hurwicz, and minimax regret rules.

The six rules for dealing with uncertainty reflect various degrees of optimism or pessimism with which the management of an organization views the future. Naturally, the actual assessment of uncertainty is done by management. In addition, management's preference for activity (or project) A versus activity (or project) B depends upon its preferences with respect to uncertainty. These preferences will vary according to the size of the investment project relative to the size of the organization. For instance, the management of a company with a net worth of $1.5 million is likely to be more adverse to uncertainty with respect to an investment project costing $2 million than a company with a net worth of $50 million.

The practical value accruing from any of the above rules lies in the array of information on a project in matrix form and its subsequent manipulation. In other words, the more alternative courses of action we examine, the more likely our final decision will be optimal. It is clear that the above rules can only be used if each alternative action does not affect the outcome of another action. It would not be wise to eliminate one action if it would affect the outcome of another one.

5. PORTFOLIO RISK AND THE CAPITAL ASSET PRICING MODEL

Let us consider the following two examples to illustrate the riskiness of financial assets. First, suppose an investor buys $100,000.00 of short-term government bonds with an expected return of 10%. The rate of return of this investment can be estimated rather precisely; the investment is defined as being risk-free and the investment decision is referred to as a decision under certainty. Next, suppose the investor buys a $100,000.00 stock of a recently organized firm with the sole purpose of prospecting oil in the North Sea. In this case, the investor's return cannot be estimated precisely. After having analyzed the investment, one might conclude that in a statistical sense the expected rate of return is 30% but the actual rate of return could range from, for instance, +500% to −100%. The stock is called a relatively risky one because there is a danger of actually earning less than the expected return. Thus, investment risk relates to the probability of actually earning less than the expected return. The greater the chance of low or negative returns, the riskier the investment. This brings us to the concept of probability.

Probability is defined as the chance that an event will occur. To illustrate the probability of an event, we consider the example of Table 5.4. Columns (1) and (2) of the table recognize three states of the economy, that is, boom, normal, and recession with related probabilities of 0.3, 0.4, and 0.3, respectively. Since these states are the only ones considered, their probabilities must add up to 1.0. Columns (3) and (4) show the possible rates of return (dividend yield plus capital gain or loss) that one might earn next year on $100,000.00 in the stock of either Company A or Company B. Company A produces computer equipment for a rapidly growing data transmission industry with profits rising and falling with the business cycle, and an extremely competitive market. Company B is an utility company with city franchises which protect it from competition. Its sales and profits are, therefore, relatively stable and predictable. The table shows that there is a 30% chance of a boom, in which case both companies will have high earnings and pay high dividends and/or capital gains. There is a 40% chance of a normal economy and moderate returns, and a 30% probability of a recession, in which case both companies will have low earnings and dividends as well as capital losses. The riskier a stock or the higher the probability that a firm will fail to pay expected dividends, the higher the expected return must be to induce one to invest in it.

Table 5.4
Probability Distributions of Two Companies A and B

State of Economy	Prob. of State	ROR[1]		Product	
		A	B	A $(2) \times (3)$	B $(2) \times (4)$
(1)	(2)	(3)	(4)	(5)	(6)
Boom	0.3	90%	20%	27%	6%
Normal	0.4	15	15	6	6
Recession	0.3	(60)	10	(18)	3
	___ +			___ +	___ +
	1.0			$\hat{k} = 15\%$	$\hat{k} = 15\%$

[1] ROR = rate of return if state of column (1) occurs.

Columns (5) and (6) of Table 5.4 present the result of multiplying each possible outcome by its probability of occurrence. The sum of these products represents the weighted average of outcome, where the weights are the probabilities and the weighted average is the expected rate of return, $\hat{k}$, called "k-hat." It is noted that the first three percentages of columns (5) and (6) represent the k_s defined in Section 2 of this chapter; it is not necessary to use the subscript s, since we discuss only returns on stocks here.

Equation (12) represents the definition of the expected rate of return, or $\hat{k}$:

$$\hat{k} = P_1 k_1 + P_2 k_2 + \cdots + P_n k_n = \sum_{i=1}^{n} P_i k_i \qquad (12)$$

where

P_i = the probability of the ith outcome
k_i = ith possible outcome.

Using the data of Table 5.4, we calculate $\hat{k}$ as follows:

Company A: $\hat{k} = P_1 (k_1) + P_2 (k_2) + P_3 (k_3)$
$= 0.3 (90\%) + 0.4 (15\%) + 0.3 (-60\%) = 15\%$
Company B: $\hat{k} = 0.3 (20\%) + 0.4 (15\%) + 0.3 (10\%) = 15\%$

So far, we have assumed that only three states of the economy can occur (boom, normal, or recession). Naturally, we could assume that the state of the

Figure 5.1
Continuous Probability Distributions of Rates of Return of Companies *A* and *B*

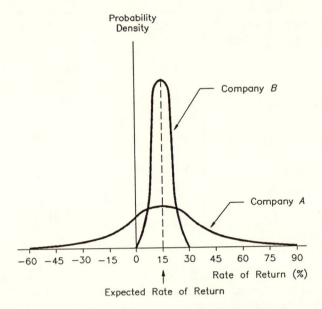

economy ranges from a fantastic boom to a deep depression with various possibilities in between (for example, moderate boom, small boom, slight recession, recession, depression). If we would consider an unlimited number of possibilities between a fantastic boom and a deep recession, the discrete probability distribution of Column (2) of Table 5.4 would become a continuous probability distribution with the sum of the probabilities still equaling 1.0. In that case, the probability of obtaining exactly a rate of return of 15% for the normal state of economy with companies *A* and *B* would be much smaller than 40% since there are many possible outcomes instead of just three. In fact, as covered in detail in statistics courses, it is more appropriate to ask what the probability is of obtaining at least some specified rate of return than to ask what the probability is of obtaining exactly that rate when dealing with continuous probability distributions. Consequently, we introduce the probability density indicating the probability of obtaining at least some specified rate of return.

Figure 5.1 shows the continuous probability distributions of the rates of return of companies *A* and *B*. In this figure, we have changed the assumptions so that there is essentially a zero probability that the return of Company *A* will be more than 90% or less than −60%, or that the return of Company *B* will be more than 20% or less than 10%; however, virtually any return within these limits is possible.

Figure 5.1 shows that the tighter the probability distribution, the more likely it is that the actual outcome will be close to the expected value and, therefore,

Table 5.5
Calculating Company A's Standard Deviation

$k_i - \hat{k}$	$(k_i - \hat{k})^2$	$(k_i - \hat{k})^2 P_i$
90 - 15 = 75	5,625	1,687.5
15 - 15 = 0	0	0.0
-60 - 15 = -75	5,625	1,687.5
		$\sigma^2 = 3,375.0$
		$\sigma = \sqrt{\sigma^2} = 58.09\%$

the less likely it is that the actual return will be far below the expected return. In other words, the tighter (or more peaked) the probability distribution, the lower the risk assigned to a stock. Because Company B has a relatively tight probability distribution, its actual return is likely to be closer to its 15% expected return than is that of Company A.

To measure risk, we need a measure of the tightness of the probability distribution. One such measure is the standard deviation, the symbol for which is σ (pronounced "sigma"). The smaller the σ, the tighter the probability distribution and, consequently, the smaller the risk of a given investment. To calculate the σ, we first compute the variance, σ^2, which is defined as:

$$\text{Variance} = \sigma_2 = \sum_{i=1}^{n} (k_i - \hat{k})P_i \qquad (13)$$

where the symbols are as defined previously. Taking the square root of the variance gives the standard deviation. Table 5.5 shows the computations to arrive at the σ of Company A of Table 5.4.

Using the same procedure, we find the σ of Company B to be 3.87%. Since Company A has a larger σ, it is the riskier stock, according to this measure of risk.

One type of continuous probability distribution, which emerges commonly enough, is a symmetrical distribution which is bell-shaped and shows some tendency for there to be a few cases at some distance from the mean in each direction, that is, the frequencies do not stop abruptly. We call this the normal type. Other types are unsymmetrical, and rarely a J-shaped or U-shaped distribution occurs. Figure 5.2 shows the probability ranges for a normal distribution. We make the following observations about this figure.

Figure 5.2
Probability Ranges for a Normal Distribution

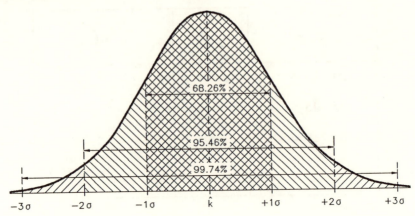

a. The area under a normal curve equals 100%.

b. Half of the area under a normal curve is to the left of the mean, $\hat{k}$, indicating that there is a 50% probability that the actual outcome will be less than the mean; and half is to the right of $\hat{k}$, indicating a 50% probability that it will be greater than the mean.

c. Of the area under the curve, 68.26% is within $\pm 1\sigma$ of the mean, indicating that the probability is 68.26% that the actual outcome will be within the range $\hat{k} - 1\sigma$ or $\hat{k} + 1\sigma$. Figure 5.2 illustrates this point and shows the situations for $\pm 2\sigma$ and $\pm 3\sigma$.

d. For a normal distribution, the larger the value of σ, the greater the probability that the actual outcome will vary widely from the expected outcome.

We saw that for Company A, $\hat{k} = 15\%$ and $\sigma = 58.09\%$. Thus, there is a 68.26% probability that the actual return for Company A will be in the range of $15 \pm 58.09\%$, or from -43.09 to 73.09%. For Company B, the 68.26% range is $15 \pm 3.87\%$, or from 11.13 to 18.87%. In other words, there is only a small probability that the return of Company B will be significantly less than expected and, hence, the stock is not very risky. For the average company listed on the New York Stock Exchange, the standard deviation has been about 30% in recent years.

The coefficient of variation, CV, defined as $\sigma/\hat{k}$, is a better measure of risk in situations where investments with substantially different expected returns are being compared. The CV indicates the risk per unit of return. Since companies A and B of Table 5.4 have the same expected return, the CV is not necessary. Figure 5.3, which shows two projects, X and Y, with different expected rates of return, illustrates a situation where the CV is necessary. The expected rates of return, standard deviations, and CVs for projects X and Y are as follows:

Figure 5.3

Comparison of Probability Distributions and Rates of Return for Projects *X* and *Y*

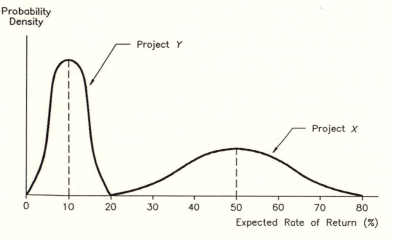

Project X: $\hat{k} = 10$, $\sigma = 5\%$, and CV $= 5/10 = 0.5$
Project Y: $\hat{k} = 50$, $\sigma = 15\%$, and CV $= 15/50 = 0.3$

Is Project *Y* riskier than Project *X* because its σ is larger than that of Project *X*? No, because the CV of Project *X* is larger than the CV of Project *Y*. In other words, Project *X* has more risk per unit of return than Project *Y*, in spite of the fact that *Y*'s standard deviation is larger. In still other words, by the CV measure, Project *X* is riskier. Figure 5.3 clearly shows that the chances of a really low return are higher for *X* than for *Y*, because *Y*'s expected return is so high.

A person who chooses a less risky investment is risk-averse. The average investor is risk-averse, at least with regard to his/her own money. What are the implications of risk aversion for stock prices and rates of return? To answer this question, we analyze the situation of the stocks of companies *A* and *B* of Table 5.4. Suppose each stock sold for $100.00 per share and each had an expected rate of return of 15%. There would be a preference for Company *B* since investors are risk-averse. People with money to invest would buy stock of Company *B* rather than that of Company *A*, and stockholders of Company *A* would start selling their stock and using the proceeds to buy stock of Company *B*. Buying pressure would drive up the price of the stock of Company *B*, and selling pressure would simultaneously cause the stock price of Company *A* to decline. These price changes, in turn, would cause changes in the expected rates of return on the two stocks. Suppose, for example, that the price of Company *B* was bid up from $100.00 to $140.00, and the price of the stock of Company *A* declined from $100.00 to $80.00. This would cause the expected return of Company *B* to fall to 10%, while the expected return of Company *A* would rise to 20%. The difference in return—10%—is a risk premium representing the compensation investors require for assuming the additional risk of Company *A*. This example illustrates an important principle, that is, in a market dominated by risk-averse investors, riskier stocks should have higher expected returns, as estimated by the average investor, than less risky stocks; if this situation would not hold, stock prices will change in the market to force it to occur.

Heretofore, we discussed the riskiness of stocks held in isolation. Let us now move on and analyze the riskiness of stocks held in portfolios or a collection of investment securities. To do so, we introduce the Capital Asset Pricing Model (CAPM) which is a model based on the proposition that any stock's required rate of return equals the risk-free rate of return plus a risk premium, where risk reflects diversification. We will see that a stock held as part of a portfolio is less risky than the same stock held in isolation.

The concept of CAPM is that risk and return of an individual security should be analyzed in terms of how that security affects risk and return of the portfolio in which it is held. Consider, for instance, a not-well-known collection agency with earnings which have fluctuated a lot in the past, a record of not paying dividends, and stock which is not very liquid. In other words, we would expect that the agency is risky and, therefore, its required rate of return should be relatively high. In reality, however, its rate of return has been low in relation to those of most other companies, indicating that investors regard it as a low-risk company despite its uncertain profits and nonexistent dividend stream. The reason is that a stock of the collection agency provides diversification. Its stock price will rise during recessions while other stocks tend to decline when the economy slumps. Consequently, including the agency's stock in a portfolio of "normal" stocks tends to stabilize returns on the entire portfolio.

As shown in equation (14), the expected return on a portfolio, $\hat{k}_p$, is the weighted average of the expected returns on the individual stocks in the portfolio, where the weights represent the fraction of the total portfolio invested in each stock:

$$\hat{k}_P = w_1\hat{k}_1 + w_2\hat{k}_2 + \cdots + w_n\hat{k}_n = \sum_{i=1}^{n} w_i\hat{k}_i \qquad (14)$$

where

$\hat{k}_i$ = expected return on stock i
w_i = the weight allocated to stock i
n = number of stocks in the portfolio.

It is noted that a weight given to Stock i is the proportion of the portfolio's dollar value invested in Stock i, and that the weights must add up to 1.0. For instance, a \$100,000.00 portfolio consisting of \$50,000.00 in Stock *A* with an expected return of 15%, \$25,000.00 in Stock *B* with an expected return of 20%, and \$25,000.00 in Stock C with an expected return of 30% has an expected return of 0.50 (15%) + 0.25 (20%) + 0.25 (30%) = 20%.

Contrary to a portfolio's expected return, the standard deviation of a portfolio is not the weighted average of the individual stocks' standard deviations; it is smaller than this weighted average. To elucidate this point, we consider a simple, hypothetical portfolio consisting of two stocks X and Y in which we invested an equal amount of money. If the stocks' returns move countercyclically to each other, that is, when X's returns fall, those of Y rise, and vice versa, then the portfolio would be riskless. In statistical terms, we say that the returns on stocks X and Y are perfectly negatively correlated, with a correlation coefficient, r, equal to − 1.0. The correlation coefficient can range from + 1.0, denoting that the two variables move up and down in perfect synchronization, to − 1.0, denoting that the variables move in exactly opposite directions. A correlation coefficient of zero suggests that changes in one variable are independent of changes in the other. Returns on two perfectly positively correlated stocks would move up and down together, and a portfolio consisting of two such stocks would be exactly as risky as the individual stocks. In reality, most stocks are positively correlated, but not perfectly so. On average, the r for most pairs of stocks would lie in the range of + 0.5 to + 0.7. Thus, combining stocks into portfolios reduces risk but does not eliminate it completely.

For the companies A and B of Table 5.4, we calculated the standard deviations for each of them and found that A has a σ = 58.09% and B a σ = 3.87%. The expected return on a portfolio consisting of 50% of stocks of Company A and 50% of stocks of Company B is [(90 + 20)/2 + (15 + 15)/2 + (−60 + 10)/2]/3 = 15%. With the help of expression (13), we determine that the variance is equal to 1,700.00 and, therefore, the σ = 22.58%, which is indeed smaller than the weighted average of 58.09 and 3.87 or 30.98.

It is virtually impossible to find stocks whose expected returns are not positively correlated since most stocks tend to do well when the national economy is strong, and badly when it is weak. The collection agency discussed earlier is one of the rare exceptions.

Figure 5.4 shows how portfolio risk is affected by portfolio size. It has been lrawn by forming larger and larger portfolios of randomly selected NYSE tocks. Thus, standard deviations are plotted for an average one-stock portfolio, two-stock portfolio, etc., up to a portfolio consisting of 1,500-plus common .ocks which were listed on the NYSE at the time the figure was prepared.

Figure 5.4 shows the following.

a. The σ of an average one-stock portfolio is approximately 28%.

b. The σ of a portfolio consisting of all stocks (called a market portfolio) is about 15%.

c. The riskiness of a portfolio consisting of average NYSE stocks generally tends to decrease and to asymptotically approach a limit as the size of the portfolio increases.

d. Almost half (28%–15%) of the riskiness of an average individual stock can be elim-

Figure 5.4
Effects of Portfolio Size on Portfolio Risk for Average Stocks

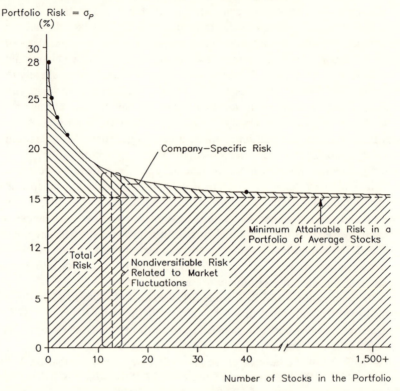

inated if the stock is held in a reasonably well-diversified portfolio, for example, one consisting of about 45 stocks.

e. It is virtually impossible to diversify away the effects of broad stock market movements.

That part of the risk of a stock which cannot be eliminated is called nondiversifiable, systematic, or market, risk; the part which can be eliminated is called diversifiable, unsystematic, or company-specific, risk. Market risk is caused by factors which affect most companies (high interest rates, recessions, inflation, and so on), while company-specific risk stems from events that are unique to a particular firm (lawsuits, strikes, the losing of major contracts, and so on). Total risk is the sum of market and company-specific risks. We have seen that the higher the riskiness of an individual security, the higher the expected return required to induce the investor to buy it. How should the riskiness of an individual stock be assessed if the investor is concerned about the riskiness of his or her portfolio? According to the CAPM, the relevant riskiness of an individual stock is its contribution to the riskiness of a well-diversified portfolio. The riskiness of an individual stock might be high if held by itself, but if most of its risk can be eliminated by diversification, then its relevant risk may be small. Different stocks will affect the portfolio differently, so different stocks have different degrees of relevant risk. To measure this relevant risk, we define an average stock as one that tends to move up and down in step with the general market as measured by some index such as the S&P 500, Dow Jones Industrials, or the NYSE index.

A stock has, by definition, a beta (β) equal to 1.0 if the stock moves up or down by a specific percentage if the market moves up or down by this percentage. A portfolio of such $\beta = 1.0$ stocks will move up or down with the broad market averages, and its riskiness is the same as that of the averages. A $\beta = 0.5$ means that a stock moves up or down by half as much as the market moves up or down, or the stock is half as volatile as the market. A portfolio of $\beta = 0.5$ stocks is half as risky as a portfolio of $\beta = 1.0$ stocks. On the other hand, if $\beta = 2.0$, the stock is twice as volatile as an average stock, and a portfolio of such stocks will be twice as risky as an average portfolio. The β coefficients of thousands of companies are calculated and published by organizations like Value Line and Merrill Lynch. Most stocks have betas in the range of 0.50 to 1.50, and the average of all stocks is by definition 1.0. In general, a β coefficient is calculated by using data from some past period and assuming that the stock's relative violability will be the same in the future as it was in the past. Next, a statistical technique called regression analysis is used to calculate the coefficient. The beta of a set of securities is the weighted average of the individual securities' betas. For instance, a $100,000.00 portfolio consisting of $50,000.00 in Stock A with a $\beta = 0.60$, $25,000.00 in Stock B with a $\beta = 0.70$, and $25,000.00 in Stock C with a $\beta = 1.50$, has a portfolio β equal to 0.50 (0.60) + 0.25 (0.70) + 0.25 (1.50) = 0.85. Suppose Stock B is sold and replaced by Stock D with a $\beta = 1.10$. This action will increase the portfolio's β from 0.85 to 0.50 (0.60) + 0.25 (1.10) + 0.25 (1.50) = 0.95. Adding a stock with a $\beta = 0.20$ instead of Stock D would have reduced the riskiness of the portfolio.

The above discussion of a portfolio's expected return, standard deviation, diversifiable and nondiversifiable risks, and β coefficients is the principal part of the CAPM. A more detailed analysis would require a level of mathematical analysis which is beyond the scope of this book, and would add little practicability. Finally, a word of caution about the CAPM and the β coefficients is in order. As mentioned earlier, the betas are calculated on the basis of a stock's past violability, while the stock's future violability, which is the real concern to investors, might be different from its past violability. However, the concepts underlying the CAPM are logical.

6. POLICY TOWARD RISK

The prerequisite to allowing for risks in investment decisions is for an organization, whether it is private or public, to establish its own policy toward risk. The amount of risk an organization is prepared to take to secure an actual or apparent monetary return is a general question of values, and there is no logical criterion by which the choice can be made. The lines of policy a company may have in this respect will largely be determined by the preferences of its stockholders, the amount of risk the company is already exposed to, and its reputation. Thus, a company may opt for a policy of taking greater risks, or for one of conservatism demanding a high return for risk. The choice is one of value judgments, in which the financial manager may have no special competence once the issues are clearly stated and understood. It is essential, however, that the issues are clearly understood by those making the judgments. Often a policy of conservatism is inconsistent within its own assumptions, in that, by rejecting some forms of risk investment, a company merely exposes itself to risks of a different type. This occurs frequently where a company refuses to undertake risky investments in research, new methods and/or products, while failing to recognize that this policy exposes it to even greater risks of loss through the successful investments of this type that its rivals may undertake. In a competitive industry, the maximum safety generally lies in the intelligent balancing of risks.

Once an organization has decided on its general policy of risk, it needs to make it clearly understood at all levels where investments are under consideration. Thus, it is generally advisable to establish specific rates of return requirements for different types of investments. For instance, a company may establish that it is prepared to invest in relatively risk-free projects if these offer a return on total capital in excess of, say, 8% after tax. Projects in this category include those involving revenues or saving expenditures which are largely determined by contractual obligations such as lease decisions, and cost-saving investments which are relatively immune from the risks involved in the sale of the final product. These acceptable return figures are not merely helpful with regard to relatively risk-free investments, but are also useful benchmarks for more risky investments. The aim of this strategy is to try to ensure that all projects are afforded equal consideration once due allowance for the differential risks involved has been made. It avoids a situation where one type of project is favored over another one without considering the general policy of risk. It is not suggested that this is an easy or exact task; but, hopefully, the treatise on uncertainty and risk given above demonstrates that it is worth attempting.

SUGGESTIONS FOR FURTHER READING

Dasgupta, P., and A. Sen. *Guidelines for Project Evaluation.* Vienna: UNIDO, 1972.
Hirshleifer, J. *Investment, Interest, and Capital.* Englewood Cliffs, NJ: Prentice-Hall, 1970.
Mackinnon, N., and P. Neal. *Economics: A Guide for the Financial Markets.* London: IFR Publishing, 1992.

CHAPTER 6

Project Appraisal

There are some minds like either convex or concave mirrors, which represent
objects such as they receive them, but they never receive them as they are.
                                                              —Joseph Joubert

In the widest sense, project appraisal is defined as a partial equilibrium technique
for estimating the net contribution of a project to some set of objectives. We
may distinguish the following three phases of project appraisal.

1. Consideration of alternatives—the single most important feature, since we should
   never incur a capital expenditure for a specific project before making certain that there
   is not a better way to achieve the same objectives.
2. Examination of whether a proposed, independent project should be accepted.
3. Selection of a project from a set of mutually exclusive projects.

Each calls for an estimation of costs and benefits. This chapter discusses
various types of costs and the effects of inflation in project appraisals. The term
"project appraisal" is also known as "cost–benefit analysis." The latter term
will be used here to refer to the analysis of costs and benefits.

The literature of managerial economics and engineering economy proposes a
variety of different and not generally consistent indices for project selection.
We will evaluate and compare these indices together with rules for project acceptance, that is, rules for the acceptance of an independent project and for the
selection of a project from a set of mutually exclusive projects. Next, we will
examine the manner in which risk is to be treated, and when we use these rules.

The basic methodology presented in this chapter applies to the appraisal of

Table 6.1
Classification of Costs

Managerial Concept	Economic Concept	Socioeconomic Concept	Value Engineering Concept
Costs of direct materials	Fixed Costs	Opportunity costs	Costs to produce
Costs of direct labor	Increment costs[2]	Social costs	
Overhead costs[1]	Marginal costs	External costs	
	Sunk costs	Associated costs	
		Sunk costs	

[1] Sometimes called indirect costs or burden.
[2] Sometimes called differential costs or variable costs.

both private and public investments. Consistent with this approach, we emphasize the similarity in technique between public and private decision making. The dissimilarities involve the use of different criteria and different prices but not the application of different methodology. We have seen the use of different criteria in the discussion of the cost of capital for private and public sectors in Chapter 5. However, once the cost of capital is established, it is used in the same manner in project appraisals by private and public organizations.

The terms project appraisal and cost-effectiveness analysis are sometimes used interchangeably. However, the latter term primarily refers to an analysis where the output or level of effectiveness is taken as given, while several methods of achieving it with minimal costs are examined. Typically, cost-effectiveness analysis is applied to analyses dealing with national security, such as the protection against enemy missiles at minimum costs. The analyses of the investments of Sections 1 and 2 of Chapter 8 are examples of the application of cost-effectiveness analysis to projects other than those dealing with national security.

1. COST ANALYSIS

Table 6.1 presents various ways in which costs may be classified. Understanding the different cost components and their functions is vital to the performance of a sound cost analysis since a given classification identifies which costs are obvious and readily calculable as out-of-pocket dollar costs, and which ones are not. Knowledge of these cost components is helpful in the performance of a sensitivity analysis (Section 4 of Chapter 5) and minimizes the occurrence of cost overruns.

The classification of costs as costs of direct materials, direct labor, and overhead is the managerial viewpoint in manufacturing enterprises. Direct materials costs are those directly related to the making of a product; they are, in general, readily measurable, of the same quantity in identical products, and used in economically significant amounts. Direct labor costs normally include the wages, salaries, and fringe benefits costs of those people processing the material. Thus, the fringe benefits are those which are approximately proportional to direct labor costs, such as Social Security, pensions, and health and accident insurance.

Those materials and labor force that do not meet the above criteria are overhead costs. Thus, overhead costs may include costs of indirect materials; salaries and fringe benefits of foremen, supervisors, managers, and employees of accounting and personnel departments; costs of buildings, equipment, electricity, and property taxes. The literature suggests a number of methods of allocating overhead costs among products manufactured or services rendered. These methods, based on the determination of an overhead rate, differ in that they allocate overhead costs in proportion to either costs of direct labor, costs of direct materials, or the sum of direct labor and materials costs. The last method is recommended if costs of direct labor and direct materials are both significant.

For instance, the overhead rate based on the assumption that overhead is incurred in direct proportion to the costs of direct materials is:

overhead rate = (total overhead in dollars for period under consideration)/
(total direct materials in dollars for period under consideration).

The overhead cost per unit is, in this case, the product of the overhead rate and the costs of materials per unit. Suppose, for example, that for the coming month the totals of overhead costs and direct materials costs are estimated at $100,000.00 and $400,000.00, respectively. From this, the overhead rate is $100,000/$400,000 or $0.25 per dollar of costs of direct materials. Thus, the overhead cost for a unit of production with a cost of direct materials of $100.00 per unit is $25.00.

It is clear that it may not always be easy to establish the distinction between direct materials, direct labor, and overhead. In these situations, we must draw a reasonable line beyond which no further attempt is made to measure directly the materials and labor which are used for each unit of production.

The classification of fixed costs versus increment costs is applied to investment analyses where we consider the economic results of changes from pre-established and/or existing conditions. Fixed costs are those that will continue, unchanged, whether or not a given change in operations or policy is adopted. Increment costs are those that arise as the result of a change in operations or policy. Marginal costs are a special case of increment costs. That is, a marginal cost is the increment cost of one added unit of output. It is also frequently used in the more restrictive sense to mean the increment cost of that unit for which the resulting revenue is equal to the increment cost.

Increment cost studies may be performed according to one of the following two approaches: (1) examination of increment costs and increment revenues or savings related to the alternatives being considered, and (2) comparison of the total of all costs and revenues of each of these alternatives. The first approach usually involves fewer data but has the disadvantage of having to separate all increment costs from the fixed costs.

Increment costs are also known as differential costs or variable costs. However, it is better to avoid the synonymous use of these terms in view of possible confusion about the interpretation of the words "differential" and "variable." The mathematical connotation of "differential" is an extremely small change, while the term "variable costs" is frequently employed for ordinary accounting purposes.

Unit or standard costs are sometimes used in investment analyses involving changes from a specified level of activity. The use of increment costs is, however, preferred, since unit or standard costs are frequently based on accounting records and, consequently, may be established on somewhat arbitrary cost allocations and levels of activity.

Sunk costs are those costs incurred on a project prior to its appraisal and which can no longer be retrieved. They are costs already paid or committed which are irrelevant to a future investment decision that is being made. Thus, they should be excluded from the cost of a project for the purpose of reaching a decision as to whether to proceed further with it. For instance, the economic merit of a project designed to complete a project started earlier and left unfinished does not depend on the costs already incurred but only on the costs of completion. In addition to situations of projects left unfinished, sunk costs may arise as the result of error in estimating a project's economic life or salvage value and/or below-normal activity. Section 2 discusses benefits associated with the completion of a project started earlier and left unfinished, or those arising over and above the benefits that may already accrue from the old, uncompleted works.

Opportunity costs, social costs, external costs, and associated costs are frequently considered in the analysis of public investments. Decision makers of private investments are generally not concerned about these costs. Opportunity costs are the value of a foregone opportunity of which we have not taken advantage. For instance, public spending may preempt private investment.

Social costs are subsidies to each person who would suffer from a public project if he or she did not receive a subsidy. Ideally, these subsidies are sufficient to persons indifferent between (1) no project and no subsidies, and (2) the project with the subsidies. For instance, the construction of a highway or railway may involve social costs. In this case, these costs relate to costs of dislocation effects including the direct property losses of the affected parties along the right-of-way, the moving costs of relocatees, utility losses caused by the loss of preferred locations of relocated households, and increased transaction costs of relocates. In the United States, the Uniform Relocation Assistance and Real Property Acquisition Policies Act provides relocation expenses to persons (with houses or businesses) who are displaced by a federally funded project. The act provides for (1) actual reasonable expenses in moving a person, his family, his business, or other personal property; (2) actual direct losses of tangible personal property as a result of moving or discontinuing a business, but not to exceed an amount equal to the reasonable expenses that would have been required to relocate such property; (3) actual reasonable expenses in searching for a replacement business; and (4) replacement housing if housing is not available on the open market. It is clear that social costs are not always so easily measured in commensurable terms as in the example of dislocation effects. They may involve intangible values ranging from ideological values to clean air. We are also faced with the problem of market prices being inadequate measures of the real social costs of the resources in a fully employed economy since market prices neglect consumers' surplus that would accrue in their alternative use.

Consumer surplus is defined as a measure of the difference between what a consumer is prepared to pay for a product and what is actually paid. Thus, it is a private measure of the cost, and does not necessarily correspond to market prices. It is of interest to note that the literature on cost-benefit analysis frequently refers to consumer surplus in connection with benefits but rarely with regard to costs. This may be indicative of the motivations of those involved in cost-benefit analysis, that is, they often appear to be eager to raise the estimates of benefits but not of costs.

External costs are costs imposed on parties other than the one sponsoring the project. Sometimes the word "externality" is used to refer to the effects of a project which do not impose a cost or confer a benefit within the confines of the project itself. Various forms of pollution and congestion, use of water affecting yields of wells elsewhere, or side effects from irrigation schemes on health or fisheries are some of the standard examples of external costs. It is recommended to discuss external (as well as social) costs in qualitative terms in public investment analyses, if they cannot be quantified.

Price effects caused by a project are often included in the definition of externalities. That is, a project may lead to higher prices (external costs) for the inputs which it requires and lower prices (external benefits) for the outputs which it produces. In addition, the project may result in higher demand and prices for complementary products or services, or lower demand and prices for competing ones. From our discussion of opportunity, social, and external costs, we conclude that social costs may include opportunity costs and external costs.

Associated costs are sometimes determined in a public investment analysis to obtain an index of willingness to pay for project outputs. We define associated costs as any costs involved in utilizing project services in the process of converting them into a form suitable for use or sale at the stage of the evaluation of benefits. An example of associated costs relates to the beneficiary of educa-

Figure 6.1
Pattern of Typical Costs-to-Produce Estimates

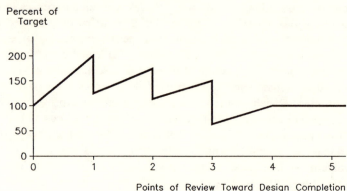

tional opportunities who foregoes income he could have been earning had he not been occupied in classes. Thus, income foregone constitutes a cost.

During the last three decades, costs-to-produce have been the subject of discussion in the literature about concepts of value engineering. The principle of costs-to-produce is that their estimates are made early during the development of a project and subsequently refined and/or corrected as the development and design proceeds. Thus, rational estimates of costs-to-produce are necessary when the development commences. In addition, feedback of increasing precision is needed as the design evolves to initiate corrective action. The feedback should go to management as well as the designer, since future costs are frequently more a function of basic design than any other factor.

We should emphasize that for costs-to-produce to be a useful concept, their estimates must be available early. It is recommended to apply Pareto's principle when early cost estimates have to be prepared. In simple words, Pareto's principle states that emphasis should be placed on the significant few rather than the insignificant many. It is widely used in economics, value engineering, inventory control, and quality control. With the application of Pareto's principle, the sequence of development can be arranged so that the basic production costs can be verified during the expenditure of, say, the first quarter of the development budget. Figure 6.1 illustrates the fluctuations of typical costs-to-produce estimates of a commercial concern whose costs-to-produce requirements exceed the target and are subject to corrective action several times during development.

The concept of costs-to-produce is used in both private and public investment analyses. Companies apply it since it is vitally important to know whether the costs of a major appliance being developed will be competitive. Its use in public projects is by contractors who design new systems (such as defense or transportation systems for the government). During recent years, the U.S. government has placed emphasis on improving cost estimates. Another way of improving cost estimates is through the application of the principles of regression analysis.

Multiple regression analysis can be used to determine variations in costs to changes in the configuration of the product desired or in the quantities of output. It may also be extremely useful in providing independent verification of detailed estimates of costs-to-produce when developing a new product or system. However, the treatment of multiple regression analysis is the proper subject for standard statistics texts, and so is not presented here. Let us just caution that multiple regression analysis can only be used if a sufficient amount of statistical data is available, and if the assumptions underlying its principles are not violated. Too often, multiple regression analysis is used while these assumptions are violated. This may result in incorrect conclusions.

Emphasis on the improvement of cost estimates is desirable in view of historical evidence that they have often been wrong—estimates generally are too low rather than too high. Prime reasons for these errors include: (1) uncertainties present in analyzing future costs, (2) changes in configuration of the product desired by the procuring service during the implementation phase, (3) changes in quantities of output originally projected, (4) deliberate underbidding by contractors, and (5) inflation. Inflation is, in practice, frequently overemphasized in relation to the other reasons, although it is often the least serious one. This is so since inflation affects costs as well as benefits and, consequently, may have little effect on the internal rate of return or net present value of a project (see Section 3).

To end our discussion of cost analysis, let us consider the determination of one of the most difficult cost estimates—those related to family planning (birth control) programs. These costs include the costs of providing family services and the opportunity costs related to the productive contribution to the economy that an additional person would have made through a lifetime.

The estimation of the costs of providing family services is difficult, although not as complex as the establishment of the aforementioned opportunity costs. The determination of the former costs is difficult since the treatment of services (contraceptive supplies, medical and training equipment, and time on radio and television) is frequently free of charges. That is, the services are either provided by the government or by foreign sources (in which case they will not involve the use of national resources). In addition, many family planning programs are integrated with other health services, and budgeted expenditures do not reflect the additional use of health resources. The only way to arrive at the costs of a family planning program in such a situation is to use rough rules of thumb to determine the costs which correspond to the proportion of the time that health facilities are used and paramedical and medical personnel are working for family planning purposes.

The determination of the opportunity costs related to the reduced output (resulting from the slower rate of growth of the labor force under conditions of declining fertility) can only be done in a rather approximate manner. An estimate of the marginal product of labor, starting at the time the averted birth would have entered the labor force and extending over the whole of his/her productive life, is necessary to measure the effect of the above decline per averted birth. Ideally, a detailed projection of a country's economy for, say, 60 years should be made. As an approximation, we may take the prevailing marginal product as an approximation of future productivity.

Several difficulties remain, however. For instance, we have to estimate when children start working; mostly this age differs for rural and urban areas. Another problem relates to the establishment of the possible increase in productivity as the children become older. In addition, we have to estimate whether the lost productive contribution to the economy is that which an additional farmer, mechanic, nurse, or engineer (for example) would have made through his or her lifetime. From the point of view of a country in which unemployment in prevalent, the opportunity cost would be zero if the unborn child would have been unemployed.

Finally, a family planning program may result in a reduction of external costs related to less concentration of persons. This is, however, the subject of our next section in which we shall come back to family planning projects when discussing various benefits.

2. BENEFIT ANALYSIS

Benefits are defined in terms of their effect on fundamental objectives. In the private sector, the fundamental objective is mostly maximization of profits or profit rate. Sometimes this objective is minimization of costs to achieve a certain goal. Naturally, we cannot maximize profits and minimize costs simultaneously. We can minimize costs by spending nothing and doing nothing, but in that case no benefits result. Benefits of a particular project can be maximized by spending until marginal benefits are zero, but that action may require more capital than is available.

Other fundamental objectives may be stated by private investors in addition to those related to profit maximization or cost minimization. Examples are maximization of a firm's growth rate; maximization of sales; maximization of a firm's prestige; improvement of quality of service; excellent economic, physical, and psychological security of employees; excellent safety records; service of community needs; creation of a certain type of public image; and minimization of a firm's cyclic fluctuations. Some of these objectives may not be entirely compatible. From a corporation's viewpoint, the benefit analysis can, therefore, not be done in isolation of the corporate development plan. In practice, corporations are sometimes tempted to evaluate investments on their own merits, independent of ancillary benefits or adverse effects on the rest of the business, since this simplifies the evaluation process. This approach can, however, result in a somewhat inaccurate picture of the true impact of investments on the attainment of objectives. The best practice is to call for consideration of the desirability of the combined benefits of alternative development patterns and operations.

The remaining part of this section is primarily of interest to public investment analysts since it deals with the measurement of the effects related to socioeconomic objectives. Socioeconomic "profit" measures the effect of a project on the fundamental objectives of the whole economy.

A government may, in a broad sense, state that its prime objective is the realization of an efficient economy. An efficient economy may be defined as one in which it is possible to (1) reallocate inputs among firms in such a way that the output of some products is increased and the outputs of others are not reduced, (2) reallocate products among consumers in such a way that some become better off and none become worse off, (3) increase the output of some products and reduce the output of others in such a way that some consumers become better off and none become worse off, or (4) alter the amount of leisure time or income that people consume and find that what they gain is worth more to them than what they lose. Naturally, it is difficult or impossible to fully realize the goals identified by this definition. Nevertheless, such an economy would probably have the largest possible national income.

National income measures the flow of goods and services in pecuniary units (such as dollars) to aggregate diverse outputs. In view of their desire to achieve an efficient economy, economists sometimes suggest national income as the quantitative indicator of benefits from public investments. The use of this indicator is, however, not recommended since it has many pitfalls, among which the most serious ones are the following three. First, national income values government output at factor cost and, therefore, defines away the problem of evaluating government output. Second, increased leisure, which increases welfare if chosen freely, is not included in national income. Third, pecuniary effects such as increased national income due to inflation are reflected in national income. Although we may correct the national income for such effects, available methods do not guarantee their complete elimination.

Our discussion of the measurement of socioeconomic benefits from public investments will be in terms of pecuniary values. This should not be construed as suggesting that the wider moral, religious, and political considerations are in any sense less important than the more narrowly economic ones. Pecuniary aspects, however, constitute the most important ingredients in any rational discussion of public investments. In addition, the measurement of benefits from public investments in terms of pecuniary units can be adjusted through the use of shadow prices (Section 3 of Chapter 5), which then enables us to measure socioeconomic profits of a project.

Alternatively, we may divide all relevant objectives into two categories—absolute and relative ones. The absolute objectives are those which must be met by any alternative project to be acceptable, and relate to social and aesthetic dimensions. The relative objectives are those which are expressed in pecuniary units for purposes of economic evaluation.

Before reviewing the measurement of benefits from public investments, we should discuss "externalities," "induced benefits," and "secondary benefits." Externalities were defined as the wide class of benefits and costs that accrue to parties other than the one sponsoring a project. On the benefit side, demonstration and training effects are often cited as externalities. Another example of external benefits pertains to the development of a water resource which, in addition to increased agricultural production, gives an improved situation of public health.

Effects such as higher rent payments to landlords, greater profitability of industries along an improved road, and employment of more labor resulting from the improvement of a road, are generally not considered as external benefits. This is because side effects should not be considered if the sole effect is via prices of products or services. In other words, external effects should only be taken into account insofar as they alter the physical production possibilities of other producers or the satisfactions that consumers can get from given resources. A net rise in rents in the above example of a road improvement is simply a reflection of the benefits of more journeys being undertaken than before. Treatment of such a net rise in rents as an external benefit would result in double counting.

Externalities of various kinds are often difficult to identify. It should be emphasized, however, that the purely transfer or distributional items from a benefit evaluation are not to be considered as external benefits. The distinction between transfer and nontransfer items is valuable as a general guiding principle, although it is recognized that the making of such a distinction is often not a simple task in practice.

Another problem related to externalities such as demonstration or training effects is that these are difficult to quantify. These problems should, however, not be cited as an excuse not to identify and, if possible, quantify external benefits. The problem of quantification may, in some cases, be made easier by internalizing externalities, which means that a "package" of closely related activities is considered as one project. For instance, the concept of "internalization of market externalities" is frequently used in urban renewal projects. Internalizing market externalities is, in this case, defined as the improvement of efficiency in resource allocation which can be achieved when a neighborhood is regarded as a unit where previously each of the separate owners in it paid no regard to the adverse effects upon other owners' property due to the inadequate maintenance of his. The social benefit of urban renewal projects may be represented by the increase in the total site value of the redevelopment area, which is measured by the present values of the rental or sales values to be had from the new buildings less the present values of the costs of erecting and maintaining those buildings.

Induced benefits are those related to additional activities generated as the result of an investment. They are accountable without double counting only if (1) no similar economic activity is displaced elsewhere, (2) nonpecuniary resources utilized would have otherwise been unemployed, and (3) possible costs incurred to generate the aforementioned additional activities would not have been incurred in the absence of the investment under consideration. Naturally, these additional costs have to be deducted from the generated benefits. Induced benefits are also known as "stemming," "generated," or "distributional" benefits.

An example of induced benefits would be the income generated in processing the outputs of grain due to irrigation water. The increased grain output is likely to involve increased activity by grain merchants, transport concerns, millers, bakers, and so on. The induced benefits may also consist of income generated in activities that sell to farmers (for example, tractors).

Another example of induced benefits are the benefits related to generated traffic due to road improvements. In transport investments, we frequently divide future traffic into three components—normal, diverted, and generated traffic. Normal traffic is the expected traffic growth that would have taken place on existing transport facility in any case, even without the new investment. Diverted traffic is traffic diverted from an existing facility to the new or improved facility. Generated traffic is traffic arising from economic and social activity which would not develop without the lowering of transport costs and the improvement in transport services caused by the new investment.

We define secondary benefits as benefits for which one imputes a value to the output. For instance, it is necessary to impute a value to the output of an irrigation project in a country where "water" is an output which is either not sold (or is free) or is sold at a price fixed solely with reference to cost-sharing considerations. The benefits of such a project may be measured as the value of the increase in grain output less the associated increase in farmers' costs.

It is clear from our definitions of external, induced, and secondary benefits that certain benefits may be classified as being of an external, an induced, as well as a secondary nature. The main reason for introducing these definitions is to make the reader aware of the various types of benefits that may accrue from public investments.

The measurement of benefits from public investments may involve the quantification of benefits related to: prevention of loss of life, reduction of accidents or illnesses, improved education, time savings, reduction of pollution, increase of comfort, slum clearance, additional recreational facilities, or prevention of births.

Economic benefits stemming from the prevention of loss of life concern the avoidance of a loss of production. The first step in estimating them is to ascertain what the average person whose life is made safer will earn over the rest of his/her life. Naturally, this depends on age at death, the probability of survival to each higher age, the proportion of people at each age who will both be in the labor force and employed, and their contribution to production at each age. It is clear that consideration of these factors can only be done for large population groups (for example, groups according to professions and ranges of age). Age at death of those whose lives are expected to be saved as the result of a project can be assumed to equal the average age of all those who die from whatever it is. "Life tables," like those used by insurance companies, may be consulted to determine the probability of survival at each age for the group at risk. This probability should be amended to account for any projected changes in age-specific death rates.

In principle, the estimation of the economic benefits from a reduction in accidents or illnesses can be done in a manner similar to the evaluation of benefits related to the prevention of loss of life. Additional problems arise, however, since estimates of productivity and the effects of disability (loss of working time) and debility (loss of capacity while at work) must be considered.

The benefits of an educational program are often measured by the higher incomes possibly resulting from such a program. This approach, which requires census information to classify individuals by education and region, assumes that differences between cross-sectional income streams of people with varying levels of education are only attributed to differences in education levels. Such an assumption may be unrealistic, since education does not necessarily confer the ability to make more money. On the other hand, education may confer other benefits such as a greater possibility to choose a pleasant occupation, and benefits to society not captured by persons who receive an education.

Estimation of the pecuniary value of time savings, which is mostly an issue in the evaluation of alternative transport investments, varies considerably from one study to another. In addition, the estimation of dollar values of time savings is not always done on a formal basis. Some studies deal with information on consumers' choices between alternative modes or routes with different time and money outlay characteristics. Thus, estimates are made of the amount trip makers are willing to pay in the form of higher gasoline costs, tolls, and so on, in order to obtain a faster route. Other studies have combined the method of consumers' choices between alternative modes with the income or productivity approach which values travel time according to the time value in work.

The determination of the economic benefits related to reduction of air or noise pollution may be done by considering the relation between pollution effects and their capitalization into real estate values. This approach, which uses actual or constructive market prices, is based on the assumption that the market mechanism will operate through land and property values to capitalize the external disadvantages of pollution. It is clear that the estimation of benefits from pollution reduction projects through the aforementioned capitalization into real estate values has many pitfalls. For instance, the increase in market values of real estate resulting from reduction of pollution is uncertain since it is difficult to estimate these market values with and without pollution. In addition, increases in land values may be caused by other projects such as the rezoning of a city. Another approach to the estimation of the economic benefits of a reduction of air pollution is to compare the direct costs (such as costs of house painting, curtain cleaning, and car wash) of living among areas with different air pollution levels.

The estimation of the economic benefits from an increase in comfort, which is sometimes attempted in hospital and transportation projects, is a formidable task, if we recognize that comfort is determined by such factors as humidity, noise level, temperature, lighting, and vibration. Little is known about the degree to which different levels of comfort effect occupancy rates of hospitals and usage of transport vehicles. Mostly adequate levels are assumed. Attempts to quantify benefits of comfort include the estimation of the increased probability of getting a seat in the Victoria Underground Line in London.

The application of the concept of internalization of market externalities to the evaluation of benefits of slum clearance has already been mentioned in our discussion of externalities. Other benefits to be had from slum clearance stem from reduction in disease, crime, and fire risks. Records kept by hospitals and police and fire departments may be consulted to estimate this reduction. The valuation of reductions in disease and crime involves the assessment of human lives as discussed in the reduction in accidents and illnesses and the prevention of loss of human lives.

One of the earliest approaches toward the evaluation of economic benefits related to recreation projects is based on Dupuit's concept of consumers' surplus. According to this method, we postulate that if visitors to a recreational area come from a series of concentric zones, any visitor coming from the nearest zone enjoys a consumer's surplus which can be measured by the difference between his travel costs and those incurred by a person coming from the farthest zone. This postulation implies that the inner-zone resident would derive as much satisfaction from a recreational area as the outer-zone one. Another approach to the valuation of benefits to be had from recreation projects is the previously mentioned capitalization into real estate values.

The economic benefits related to averting a birth, which is of interest to governments facing overpopulation, may be measured by the value of the consumption stream necessary to support a person through life. This stream consists of the personal consumption of the unborn child throughout his or her life plus such social services as medical care or education that the government would have provided to this unborn child. The consumption stream represents a reduction in the claim on national income. In addition, there are external benefits since this reduction is likely to result in a better-fed and healthier labor force, and, possibly, larger private and public savings. There are many difficulties inherent in measuring these external benefits. For instance, how do we measure increases in productivity resulting from a healthier labor force? How much healthier will the labor force be as a result of a family planning program?

It should also be noted that measurement of the aforementioned external benefits hardly seems to be necessary since almost all family planning programs have a rather high net present value (NPV) or internal rate of return. This is because the initial capital outlay required for providing family services is small while the opportunity costs related to the productive contribution to the economy that an additional person would have made throughout a lifetime are not incurred for at least 12 to 15 years after the averted birth. The benefits represented by the consumption stream are, however, to be had immediately after this birth.

In the above discussion, we have learned ways to measure benefits of public investments which involve prevention of loss of life, reduction of accidents or illnesses, improved education, time savings, reduction of pollution, increase in comfort, slum clearance, additional recreational facilities, and prevention of births. Any single public investment may involve one or more of these issues. In such a situation, we can simply add the benefits of these issues, provided they are independent. However, we cannot add benefits if, for instance, an increase in time savings has an adverse effect on the number of accidents. In this case, we have to establish this adverse effect.

Obviously we cannot discuss all possible projects that a public investment analyst may be faced with. The intent of the above discussion is to provide guidelines for the evaluation of benefits in a consistent manner. After general agreement on the principles to be followed, we should be able to extend the guidelines to other projects. In our description about the evaluation of benefits from public investments, we estimate these benefits in principle according to: (1) potential cost savings (for example, reductions in vehicle operating and maintenance costs related to a transport investment); (2) capitalization into real estate values (for example, pollution reduction); (3) willingness of beneficiaries to pay (for example, the amount trip makers are willing to pay in the form of higher costs, such as tolls, to take a faster route); or (4) estimation of future income of a person (for example, education and health projects).

In some cases, we should include complementary investments in the benefit analysis. For instance, an area into which the construction of a highway is proposed may not fully develop unless other investments are made. The best practice for such interdependent development projects is to consider all benefits and costs of the total investment plan rather than to evaluate the individual projects of this plan.

A word of caution should be given to public investment planners in developing nations—that is, these planners should not overambitiously attempt to homogeneously quantify the benefits of project investments, because the existing reality of many of these countries indicates that this is a time-consuming exercise aimed at singular directional perfection. In countries with a limited professional and administrative capability, it is frequently preferable to direct efforts to effectively organize, coordinate, and manage the execution and operation of a project.

3. INFLATION

General inflation exists if all current prices increase at approximately the same rate both at home and abroad, or if domestic current prices increase at one rate and foreign current prices at another rate, but these differential rates of inflation are completely offset by exchange rate adjustments. Thus, if domestic and foreign inflation of all project prices is estimated at a rate of, say, 8% per year, or if domestic and foreign inflation is expected at respective yearly rates of 8% and 11% and domestic currency is estimated to appreciate at 3% per year, then all real project prices remain the same. These observations are made based on the fact that we have to look beyond our own borders in view of foreign trade and competition, which is a reality.

Current prices are prices prevailing in successive periods. They are unadjusted prices which reflect any inflation or deflation occurring over time. Constant prices relate the value of one good or service to other goods and services in terms of a constant unit of measurement. Constant prices may be obtained by denominating all prices in terms of a numeraire value, such as a unit of either domestic or foreign currency of a certain date. For instance, all prices may be denominated in terms of the 1996 purchasing power of the U.S. dollar.

Cost benefit analysis should be performed in terms of constant rather than current prices. Further adjustment of constant prices is not necessary if we are faced only with general inflation, with changes in the general price level resulting from inflation, or with price changes that do not affect the relation of the value of one good or service to other goods and services. This is because the constant prices would remain the same even if we would make corrections for the general increase in current prices by converting the latter prices into constant prices.

Constant prices are constant for given intervals of time. Further adjustment of constant prices is necessary if they change during subsequent time intervals. This situation arises when inflation or price changes during subsequent time intervals affect the relation of the value of one good or service to other goods and services. Thus, general inflation no longer exists. Some economists prefer the term "real price" to "constant price" because constant prices do not necessarily remain constant over time. Current prices are sometimes called nominal prices.

In other words, constant prices do not remain constant during subsequent time intervals if price changes of specific project items are expected to differ significantly from changes in the general price level. In this case, we have to reflect the changes in relative prices of the costs and benefits in project appraisals. Naturally, all prices are still expressed in terms of constant or real prices. Suppose, for instance, that the overall price index is estimated to increase by 8% per year, but that the prices of items A and B are expected to rise at 5% and 11% per annum, respectively. In this case, we must decrease the constant price of item A by 3% and increase the one of item B by 3%. All other constant prices in the costs and benefits streams remain the same. Clearly, this assumes that the prices of the costs and benefits related to all but items A and B will follow the general price trends. It is evident that constant prices may also change if differentials between domestic and foreign price changes are not offset by exchange rate adjustments over significant periods of time.

In brief, adjustments to constant prices are only to be made in project appraisals if prices of one or more project items do not follow the general price trends. General inflation does not affect project appraisals in terms of constant prices. The preparation of price forecasts in specific cases is no mean task. Sometimes the changes in costs over time are recorded in price indices, which assists the preparation of price forecasts. In the absence of clear indications to the contrary, we may, however, assume that most relative prices remain constant, and that where differentials exist between domestic and foreign rates of inflation, exchange rate adjustments will be made to correct the imbalance.

4. COST BENEFIT INDICES AND RULES FOR PROJECT ACCEPTANCE

Cost benefit indices are used in the comparison of costs and benefits of a proposed project or investment. An examination of the literature of managerial economics and engineering economy reveals that a variety of different, and not generally consistent, indices have been proposed for deciding whether a given investment project should be executed. Perhaps one of the oldest indices is the payoff period (sometimes called the payback period), which is still used in industry. This index corresponds to the length of time up to payoff—the date when the summed benefits have recovered the summed costs. Usually, the benefits and costs are summed without discounting future cash flows. The payoff index has been applied to the examination of whether a single, independent project should be accepted as well as to the choice between mutually exclusive projects. In the former case, the payoff period is compared to a pre-established number (for example, "no project with a payoff period greater than 15 years should be accepted"); in the latter case, the project with the shorter payoff period is selected.

Even if discounting is used in summing up benefits and costs, we generally should avoid the use of a payoff period since it ignores the expected life of a project, savings after the payoff period, and the salvage value. In addition, there is a danger that the payoff period lends itself to serious misinterpretation. It is, for instance, not unusual to encounter a businessperson who concludes that the rate of return on an investment that will pay for itself in, say, five years, is 20%. Even worse, some may conclude that this rate of return can be increased to 40% by simply decreasing the payoff period requirement to two and a half years! This reasoning fails to realize that rates of return are determined by the excess of revenues over costs, and there is nothing in the payoff period calculation to indicate what this is. The survival of the payoff period in business practice may be due to its ease of application or the fact that it provides a very crude way of allowing for risk of the future in that it presents a calculation of how soon the investor will get his/her money back.

Table 6.2
Cost-Benefit Indices

Name	I_j^1	G^1
Benefit-Cost Ratio (B/C)	B_j/C_j	1
Net Benefit-Cost Ratio (NB/C)	$[B_j - C_j]/C_j$	0
Eckstein's Benefit-Cost Ratio (EB/C)	$b_j/[C_j + c_j]$	1
Internal Rate of Return (IRR)	R_j	i
Modified Internal Rate of Return (MIRR)	MR_j	i
Net Present Value (NPV)[2]	$B_j - C_j$	0
Equivalent "Annual" Value (EAV)[3]	$[B_j - C_j](\text{crf } i, n_j)^4$	0

[1] I_j = index of the worth of a project j; G = constant against which I_j is compared.
[2] Also called present worth.
[3] "Annual" is put in quotation marks since the corresponding compounding interval can be any length of time, not necessarily a year.
[4] crf = capital recovery factor (see Appendix 1).

The sinking fund return index, which is defined as the net profit after sinking fund depreciation expressed as a percentage of the initial capital cost of a project, is seldom used as an index. Its use is not recommended, since it is a clumsy way of assessing an investment. In addition, the sinking fund depreciation method frequently employs some conventional interest rate which has little or no relation to the cost of capital.

Table 6.2 presents various indices currently proposed in the literature. The benefit-cost ratio (B/C), net benefit-cost ratio (NB/C), and Eckstein's benefit-cost ratio (EB/C) are frequently proposed for public investment planning, while the internal rate of return, net present value (NPV), and equivalent annual value (EAV) are widely suggested for managerial economics. It is no surprise that there appears to be considerable confusion as to which index to use. We will, therefore, examine the equivalences and differences between the indices of Table 6.2. Upon completion of this comparison, we shall be able to make recommendations for the use of specific indices.

The second column of Table 6.2, which defines the indices of worth of a project according to the various cost-benefit indices, uses a number of symbols. These symbols have been introduced to easily identify the parameters of the

Figure 6.2
Net Cash Flow Pattern for Project *j*

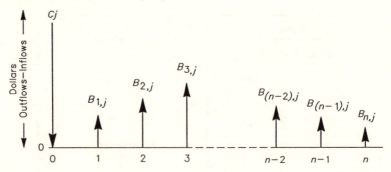

various indices and to facilitate our comparison. The following notation is introduced to define the symbols:

j = index denoting a specific project j (j = 1 means project 1, j = 2 means project 2, and so on)

i = interest rate in the public sector, or weighted average cost of capital in the private sector

$b_{t,j}$ = gross receipt, in dollars, procurable from project j at time t (note that $b_{t,j} \geqslant 0$)

$c_{t,j}$ = gross cost, in dollars, to be incurred by project j at time t (note that $c_{t,j} \geqslant 0$)

$B_{t,j} = b_{t,j} - c_{t,j}$ = net receipt, in dollars, procurable from project j at time t (note that $B_{t,j}$ is unconstrained in sign)

n_j = expected life of project j

$b_j = \sum\limits_{t=1}^{n_j} b_{t,j}/(1 + i)^t$ = discounted gross receipts, in dollars, procurable from project j

$c_j = \sum\limits_{t=1}^{n_j} c_{t,j}/(1 + i)^t$ = discounted gross costs, in dollars, to be incurred by project j.

With the above symbols, we now define

$$B_j = b_j - c_j = \sum\limits_{t=1}^{n_j} B_{t,j}/(1 + i)^t.$$

In addition, we define

C_j = initial capital outlay, in dollars, required for project j at time 0 (note that $C_j > 0$).

Figure 6.2 depicts graphically the above-described net cash flow pattern of project j. Note that Table 6.2 and the above notation define B/C, NB/C, EB/C, NPV, and EAV. For instance, Eckstein's benefit-cost ratio (EB/C) is defined as $b_j/[C_j + c_j]$, or the discounted value of gross receipts procurable from project j, divided by the sum of the initial capital outlay and the discounted value of the gross costs to be incurred by it. We still have to define the internal rate of return and the modified internal rate of return.

The internal rate of return is defined as the rate of interest which equates the present values of capital outlays and their resultant cash flows. With the aforementioned notation, the internal rate of return for project j is an interest rate R_j such that

$$[\sum_{t=1}^{nj} B_{t,j} / (1 + R_j)^t] - C_j = 0.$$

The internal rate of return method assumes no knowledge of an external rate of interest. As a result, it is a rough indicator of relative profitability since it ignores a company's cost of capital which depends on the prevailing borrowing rate of corporations and the rate of return equity shareholders expect (see Section 2 of Chapter 5 for details). In other words, the internal rate of return assumes that net receipts or cash flows from a project are reinvested at the project's rate of return, which is not realistic since future investments will most likely have a different rate of return. In still other words, it would be preferred to assume that all net receipts from a project are reinvested at a company's cost of capital.

To overcome the above-mentioned shortcoming of the internal rate of return, we introduce the modified internal rate of return (MIRR). With the aforementioned notation, the MIRR for project j is an interest rate MR_j such that

$$C_j = [\sum_{t=1}^{nj} B_{t,j} (1 + i)^{n_j - t}] / (1 + MR_j)^{n_j}.$$

We can illustrate the computation of MIRR with the following example:

```
                |--------|--------|--------|--------|
Cash Flows:  -2,000    1,000     800      600      200
                         |        |        |    i = 10%
                         |        |        L- - - - - - ->660
                         |        |    i = 10%
                         |        L- - - - - - - - - - - ->968
                         |    i = 10%
                         L- - - - - - - - - - - - - - - - ->1,331

                    Value at end of 4 years (F):    3,159
                            MIRR = 12.1%
PV of F:    2,000<- - - - - - - - - - - - - - - - - - - - -
```

Note that in the above example, we first compute the values of $1,000.00, $800.00, $600.00 at the end of the fourth year with spcaf (given P, find F) and $n = 3$, $n = 2$, and $n = 1$, respectively. Next, we add the four values at the end of the fourth year ($200.00, $660.00, $968.00, and $1,331.00). Finally, we compute the interest rate which transforms the present value of $2,000.00 into a value of $3,159.00 at the end of the fourth year; this gives a MIRR of 12.1%.

The above-mentioned value of 12.1% for the MIRR can be obtained with a financial calculator. Using the symbols introduced in the section entitled "Financial Calculators" of Appendix 1, the operations are as follows: start with f CLEAR REG, next enter 2,000, CHS, g, CFo; 1,000, g, CFj; 800, g, CFj; 600, g, CFj; 200, g, CFj, and press f IRR to obtain the value of 12.1%.

The third column of Table 6.2 represents a constant (G) against which the index I_j is compared in rules for project acceptance. The rules of interest to us are as follows.

Rule 1. A given independent project, j', should be accepted if and only if $I_j' \geq G$.

Rule 2. For a set, J, of mutually exclusive projects, a given project j' belonging to set J should be accepted if and only if $I_j' \geq G$ and $I_j' \geq I_j$ for all other projects j belonging to set J.

The interpretation of these rules when, for instance, we employ the NPV index is as follows.

Rule 1. A given independent project, j', should be accepted if and only if $NPV_j' \geq 0$.

Rule 2. For a set, J, of mutually exclusive projects, a given project j' belonging to set J should be accepted if and only if $NPV_j' \geq 0$ and $NPV_j' \geq NPV_j$ for all other projects j belonging to set J.

Alternatively, if we use the internal rate of return, the rules are interpreted as follows.

Rule 1. A given independent project, j', should be accepted if and only if $R_j' \geq i$.

Rule 2. For a set, J, of mutually exclusive projects, a given project j' belonging to set J should be accepted if and only if $R_j' \geq i$ and $R_j' \geq R_j$ for all other projects belonging to set J.

Rule 1 applies to the examination of whether a proposed independent project should be accepted. The independent project is given a name, viz. project j'.

Rule 2 applies to the selection of a project (called project j') from a set or group of mutually exclusive projects. A set or group of projects is mutually exclusive if the implementation of one project of this set makes the implementation of the other projects of this set impossible. This may be the case if the mutually exclusive projects have the same objective (a highway or railway track to connect two locations) or if resource constraints (money or manpower) limit the implementation to one project. Thus, in the case of Rule 2, we are faced with the problem of selecting one project from a group of alternative projects.

It can be shown mathematically that: (1) use of the NPV and EAV indices and their associated constants (see column G of Table 6.2) give identical results in the application of Rules 1 and 2; (2) use of the B/C, NB/C, and MIRR and their associated constants gives identical results in the application of Rules 1 and 2; and (3) use of the NPV, EAV, B/C, NB/C, EB/C, and MIRR and their associated constants gives identical results in the application of Rule 1. The above three points only partly resolve the confusion as to which index to use. We only know that, for instance, it does not make any difference whether we

Table 6.3
Illustrative Differences in Project Selection Caused by Indices[1]

(1) j^2	(2) C_j	(3) c_j	(4) b_j	(5) $B_{1,j}$	(6) $B_{2,j}$	(7) B_j	(8) B_j-C_j	(9) B_j/C_j	(10) R_j	(11) $\dfrac{b}{[C_j+c_j]}$
1	2.00	1.00	5.89	2.00	8.00	4.89	2.89	2.44	1.56	1.96
2	1.00	0.00	2.22	2.00	2.00	2.22	1.22	2.22	1.73	2.22
3	1.50	0.64	4.54	0.60	7.88	3.90	2.40	2.60	1.50	2.12
4	2.01	0.00	4.89	2.00	8.00	4.89	2.88	2.43	1.54	2.43

[1] The four projects are assumed to be subject to the same degree of risk.
[2] Project number.

use the NPV or EAV index in Rules 1 and 2, and it does not make any difference whether we use the B/C, NB/C, or MIRR in Rules 1 and 2. However, recommendations or selections can be different if we use the NPV index rather than, say, the B/C. Thus, we now have to decide which indices we should use in project appraisals. The above three points inform us that we have to be particularly careful when employing Rule 2.

In view of the identified identicalness of indices, it is (for Rule 2) sufficient to examine only the results of the use of NPV, B/C, internal rate of return, and Eckstein's benefit-cost ratio. The simple example of Table 6.3 shows that these four indices can select a different project when inserted in Rule 2. The example pertains to the selection of one project from four mutually exclusive projects. Columns (2) through (7) of this table present the initial capital outlay, gross costs, gross receipts, net receipts in the first and second year, and $B_j = b_j - c_j$, respectively. Suppose that the interest rate $i = 0.50$. Columns (8) through (11) show the NPV, B/C, internal rate of return, and EB/C, respectively. Table 6.3 shows that the NPV index selects project 1; the B/C selects project 3; the internal rate of return selects project 2; and the EB/C selects project 4.

It can also be shown mathematically that only the use of the NPV and EAV indices in Rule 2 guarantees a correct decision. Intuitively this makes sense, since the goal of investment analysis is maximization of overall net present value adjusted for risk, if necessary, rather than some ratio.

The conclusion of the above discussion is that both private and public investment analysts should avoid the use of the B/C, NB/C, and EB/C. Notice that we make an exception for the internal rate of return and its modified version. Does this mean that these rates of return will, like the NPV and EAV indices, always result in a correct decision when used in Rules 1 and 2? Except that MIRR guarantees a correct decision when used in Rule 1, the answer is no. An exception is made for the internal rate of return and the modified internal rate of return, since they offer the following important advantages when compared to the NPV and EAV indices. (1) They are widely understood concepts and have merit as a *compact summary measure of the economic evaluation of a project* (NPV and EAV are, on the other hand, *absolute quantities*); (2) they often *obviate the difficult task of establishing the cost of capital* (see Chapter 5) *with great exactitude* (we can avoid needless dispute about the precise magnitude of the cost of capital as long as the IRR and/or MIRR are reasonably larger than the cost of capital); and (3) they provide a *margin of error* (for instance, if the IRR or MIRR is 50% and the cost of capital is 15%, then the realized return could fall substantially and the project would still be profitable). In addition, as we will see in Chapter 7, the internal rate of return is a useful index in the capital budgeting process.

If we wish to employ the internal rate of return in view of the advantages, we should be aware of the possibility of incorrect (nonoptimal) decisions when it is applied to Rule 1. An example of such an incorrect decision is the following.

Suppose that the capital outlay of a project j is 1 unit, its expected life is two years, while its net receipts amount to 6 and -6 units in the first and second years, respectively. The units are in thousands of dollars, and the cost of capital is $i = 0.10$. Consequently, the NPV is -0.51 and the internal rate is either 3.73 or 0.27. This simple example shows two problems inherent in the use of the internal rate of return in Rule 1. First, our NPV criterion shows that the project should not be recommended, which is a correct decision. However, both of the internal rates of return indicate that the project should be recommended. Second, the answer obtained with the internal rate of return is ambiguous, since more than one rate equalizes costs and discounted benefits.

It can be shown that multiple solutions with the use of the internal rate of return may appear when there are periodic negative net benefits during the expected life of a project. Particularly, the presence of large negative net receipts in the later life of a project (for example, major restoration of property or land when a project terminates) can give rise to more than one internal rate of return (multiple solutions of R_j). Multiple solutions are avoided with the use of the modified internal rate of return. It is noted that a situation where the IRR index does not give a correct solution when applied to Rule 1 seldom happens.

The example of Table 6.3 illustrated that the use of the internal rate of return may lead to nonoptimal decisions when applied to Rule 2. The risk of getting a nonoptimal decision is particularly high when there is a large difference in initial capital outlays of the mutually exclusive projects, and/or when some of these projects have net receipts in the early years and others have net receipts in later years of their expected lives. It can be shown that the use of the internal rate of return in Rule 2 will only guarantee an optimal decision in the special case of constant benefits ($B_{1,j} = B_{2,j} = \cdots = B_{n_j,j}$ for each project j) and all projects requiring the same initial capital outlay. In addition, the internal rate of return can provide the correct decision if applied to the difference in net benefits between two mutually exclusive projects. The disadvantage of this solution to the problem of incorrect decisions is that it increases the possibility of multiple solutions to the internal rate of return calculation. The use of the modified internal rate of return may lead to nonoptimal decisions when applied to Rule 2 when the initial capital outlays of the mutually exclusive projects are not the same; otherwise it will provide a correct decision.

For private and public investments, we conclude the following.

a. The use of the NPV and EAV indices always results in correct decisions.

b. In view of their advantages, the internal rate of return or its modified version should be used; however, since their use does not guarantee a correct decision with Rule 2 and IRR does not guarantee a correct decision with Rule 1, the simultaneous use of one of these rates and the NPV (or EAV) is recommended. Such practice will identify incorrect decisions obtained with the use of the internal rates of return while maintaining their advantages when selections made with them and the NPV (or EAV) are identical. Obviously, the simultaneous use of the NPV (or EAV) and one of the internal rates of return involves additional work; however, this seems justified when important investment decisions are to be made.

c. The modified IRR has all the virtues of the IRR. In addition, it incorporates the correct reinvestment rate assumption and avoids the multiple rate of return problem. Consequently, the use of MIRR is preferred to that of IRR.

The reader is reminded that the final decision about project selection may be based on the "relative" and "absolute" objectives (see Section 2); that is, the application of Rule 1 and 2 to pecuniary values, which relates to the examination of the relative objectives, may be supplemented by requirements stipulated by the absolute objectives. Naturally, we can also use the concept of shadow pricing when applying Rules 1 or 2 to decisions of project acceptance.

5. TREATMENT OF UNCERTAINTY AND RISK IN PROJECT APPRAISAL

Rules 1 and 2 of Section 4 deal with deterministic investment decisions, since uncertainty and risk are not explicitly considered. It is clear, however, that any of the procedures to deal with uncertainty discussed in Chapter 5 may be used in combination with these rules. For instance, uncertainty may be incorporated by uncertainty loading on the interest rate used to determine the NPV employed in Rule 1 or 2. Alternatively, these rules can first be applied to optimistic values of estimated costs and benefits and, next, to conservative values, if the approach of sensitivity analysis is followed. In other words, each possible outcome of an investment is treated as deterministic.

The maximin, minimax, maximax, Laplace, Hurwicz, and minimax regret rules of Chapter 5 may also be used in combination with Rules 1 and 2. In this case, we would employ the former rules to eliminate one or more projects from consideration before we apply the latter rules to the remaining project candidates. Naturally, the maximin, minimax, and other rules may also be considered as alternative solution procedures to the application of Rule 2, since all of these techniques apply to the selection of one project from a set of mutually exclusive projects. For important investment decisions, it may pay off to take the time for the examination of alternatives by a number of different solutions.

Before considering the treatment of risk in Rules 1 and 2, we review two useful concepts in problems involving decisions under risk, that is, expected value and standard deviation. These concepts have already been introduced in Chapter 5 when we discussed portfolio risk. Since they are important concepts, we elaborate on them.

Expected Value and Standard Deviation

The expected value of a random variable is the sum of the products of its values by their associated probabilities. Suppose X is a random variable that assumes the values $a_1, a_2, \cdots, a_N$ with probabilities $p_1, p_2, \cdots, p_N$; then

$$E(X) = \sum_{i=1}^{N} a_i p_i$$

where $E(X)$ is the expected value of X. The standard deviation is a measure of the relative dispersion of a probability distribution about its expected value. The standard deviation of X is defined as the square root of its variance:

$$\sigma_x = \sqrt{V(X)}$$

where

$$\sigma_x = \text{standard deviation of } X$$
$$V(X) = \text{variance of } X.$$

The variance of X is given by

$$V(X) = \sum_{i=1}^{N} [a_i - E(X)]^2 p_i.$$

Let us first consider an investment decision under risk which involves the evaluation of a project in which the probability distributions of net receipts for various future periods are independent of one another. In other words, the outcome in period t does not depend on what happened in period $t - 1$. The service life of the project is deterministic. The expected value of the probability distribution of net present value for the project is:

$$E(P) = -C + \sum_{t=0}^{n} \overline{B}_t / (1 + i)^t \tag{1}$$

where

$E(P)$ = expected net present value (in dollars)
C = initial capital outlay required at time 0 (in dollars)
n = service life in years
t = time in years
i = interest rate
$\overline{B}_t$ = expected value of net receipts in year t (in dollars).

The standard deviation of possible net receipts for year t, σ_t, is computed by:

$$\sigma_t = \sqrt{\sum_{j=1}^{m} (B_{j,t} - \overline{B}_t)^2 p_{j,t}} \tag{2}$$

where

$\overline{B}_t$ = as defined above
j = index denoting a possible net receipt
m = number of possible net receipts considered
$B_{j,t}$ = the jth possible net receipt for year t (in dollars)
$p_{j,t}$ = probability of occurrence of $B_{j,t}$.

Given the assumption of mutual independence of net receipts for various future years, the standard deviation of the probability distribution of net present values is:

$$\sigma = \sqrt{\sum_{t=0}^{n} \sigma_t^2 / (1 + i)^{2,t}} \tag{3}$$

where the symbols are defined as above.

Let us elucidate the above symbols and formulas with the following example. Suppose a project costing $10,000.00 at time 0 is expected to generate the net receipts of Table 6.4 during its service life of three years. The table clearly shows the concept of risk; that is, we do not estimate deterministic values of net receipts in years 1,2, and 3, but rather indicate five probabilistic values for the net receipts in each year. Notice that the sum of the probabilities in each year amounts to 1 (for instance, in year 1 we have: 0.10 + 0.25 + 0.30 + 0.25 + 0.10 = 1). Assuming an interest rate of 10%, the expected values of net receipts during years 1,2, and 3 are:

Table 6.4
Expected Net Receipts for Example Problem

Year 1		Year 2		Year 3	
Proba-bility	Net Receipt	Proba-bility	Net Receipt	Proba-bility	Net Receipt
0.10	$4,000	0.15	$3,000	0.10	$2,000
0.25	5,000	0.20	4,000	0.20	3,000
0.30	6,000	0.30	5,000	0.40	4,000
0.25	7,000	0.20	6,000	0.20	5,000
0.10	8,000	0.15	7,000	0.10	6,000

$$\bar{B}_1 = 0.10(4,000) + 0.25(5,000) + 0.30(6,000) + 0.25(7,000)$$
$$+ 0.10(8,000) = \$6,000$$
$$\bar{B}_2 = 0.15(3,000) + 0.20(4,000) + 0.30(5,000) + 0.20(6,000)$$
$$+ 0.15(7,000) = \$5,000$$
$$\bar{B}_3 = 0.10(2,000) + 0.20(3,000) + 0.40(4,000) + 0.20(5,000)$$
$$+ 0.10(6,000) = \$4,000$$

We now use expression (1) to calculate the expected value of net present value for the project:

$$E(P) = -10,000 + 6,000/(1.10) + 5,000/(1.10)^2$$
$$+ 4,000/(1.10)^3 = \$2,592$$

Next, we use expression (2) to compute the standard deviation of the possible net receipts for year 1:

$$\sigma_1 = [0.10(4,000 - 6,000)^2 + 0.25(5,000 - 6,000)^2$$
$$+ 0.30(6,000 - 6,000)^2 + 0.25(7,000 - 6,000)^2 + 0.10(8,000$$
$$- 6,000)^2]^{1/2}$$
$$= \$1,140$$

The standard deviations of the possible net receipts for years 2 and 3 are also computed with expression (2) and amount to $\sigma_2 = \$1,183.00$ and $\sigma_3 = \$1,095.00$, respectively. Using equation (3), under the assumption of mutual independence of net receipts over time, the standard deviation about the expected value is as follows:

$$\sigma = \sqrt{(1,140)^2/(1.10)^2 + (1,183)^2/(1.10)^4 + (1,095)^2/(1.10)^6} = \$1,718$$

The value of $1,718.00 is a way for management to express the risk associated with the project costing $10,000.00 and with the net receipts of Table 6.4. The higher the value of the standard deviation σ, the more risk is involved.

The standard deviation of the probability distribution of possible net present values may also be used to obtain additional information for the evaluation of risk of a proposed investment project. This information consists of determining the probability of a project providing an NPV of less or more than a specified amount. Assuming that the probability distribution of possible NPVs is approximately normal, we are able to determine this probability by using the table of Appendix 4. This table presents probabilities of a value of Z being greater than the values tabulated in the margins.

The Z value is defined as follows:

$$Z = [P - E(P)]/\sigma \qquad (4)$$

where P = the net present value considered for the use of Appendix 4; $E(P)$ and σ are as defined in equations (1) and (3), respectively.

To illustrate the use of expression (4) and Appendix 4, let us determine the probability that the net present value of the above example will be equal to or less than zero. Thus, in expression (4), we fill out $P = 0$, $E(P) = \$2,592.00$ and $\sigma = \$1,718.00$, and find:

$$Z = [0 - 2,592]/1,718 = -1.509$$

Looking in Appendix 4, we find that there is a 0.0559 probability that the NPV of our project will be zero or less. Notice that the digits 1.5 and 09 of $Z = -1.509$ are read from the left and upper margins of Appendix 4, respectively.

As mentioned earlier, we can only use the Z table of Appendix 4 if we are willing to assume that the probability distribution of possible NPVs is approximately normal. In view of the Central Limit Theorem of mathematical statistics, there is a good chance that this approximation is reasonable. The theorem informs us that, when summing random variables having distributions other than normal, the distribution of this sum still approaches a normal distribution under certain conditions. The conditions required are not very stringent. Although the most common version of the Central Limit Theorem requires that the random variables be independent and identically distributed, various other versions also exist where one or both of these assumptions can be replaced by much weaker conditions. With reference to expression (1), we notice that each $\overline{B}_t$ value represents the sum of the random variables referred to in the above theorem.

Chebyshev's Inequality Theorem rather than Appendix 4 may be used to make reasonably strong probability statements if the normal distribution assumption cannot be made. A discussion of this theorem requires an advanced knowledge of mathematical statistics and is, therefore, not presented here. Readers with such a knowledge will most likely be able to use Chebyshev's Inequality Theorem, since the approach is similar to the one used in Appendix 4.

The assumption of mutual independence of net receipts from one year to another has been made in the above use of expected values and standard deviations for the evaluation of risky investments. Frequently the net receipt in one future period depends upon the net receipts in previous periods. For instance, if an investment project turns bad in the early years, the probability is high that net receipts in later years also will be lower than originally expected. The consequence of autocorrelation of annual net receipts over time is that the standard deviation of the probability distribution of possible net present values is larger than it would be under the assumption of mutual independence of net receipts. The greater the degree of correlation, the greater the dispersion of the probability distribution. Thus, expression (3) can no longer be used. The expected value of net present value—see expression (1)—however, is the same, regardless of correlation over time. The examination of autocorrelated cash flows (that is, a situation where one or more net receipts in one or more future periods depend upon the net receipts in one or more previous periods) requires knowledge of applied statistics, which is beyond the scope of this book.

Simulation

Simulation (sometimes called stochastic simulation or Monte Carlo simulation) is a method used to estimate the probability distribution of a variable, such as a project's expected net present value, on the basis of a simulated sample. Thus, simulation should be viewed as a technique for the determination of probability distributions necessary for the computations of standard deviations and expected values, rather than an approach to measure the economic desirability of a project like the expected value and standard deviation.

To illustrate the simulation method, let us consider the third year net receipts of the example problem of Table 6.4 and a simulated sample of 50. We use the last digits of the telephone numbers in a directory as a randomization device. Thus, a sample of size 50 is obtained by drawing the appropriate number of observations for each possible outcome in the third year. To obtain the values of the third year net receipts, we let the last digit (0) represent a third year net receipt of $2,000.00; (1) and (2) represent a net receipt of $3,000.00; (3), (4), (5), and (6) represent a net receipt of $4,000.00; (7) and (8) represent a net receipt of $5,000.00; and (9) represents a net receipt of $6,000.00. Thus, the number of digits representing a net receipt is indicative of the probability of occurrence of that net receipt. Upon termination of the sampling procedure, we can draw the frequency distribution of third year annual receipts.

Frequently, a computer is used for the application of simulation techniques. Thus, all possible outcomes of the variables affecting the net present value of a project and their probabilities are fed into a computer. The computer then selects at random one outcome of each of the variables, allowing for realistic restrictions for interdependencies in the variables. Given the selected outcomes of all the variables, the corresponding net present values of the investment are calculated. This process is repeated until a large enough sample is obtained for a close approximation to the actual probability distribution of the net present values. There are a number of random selection "packages" on the market which select (at random) values from various kinds of probability distributions.

An advantage of simulation is that it requires no mathematical skills on the part of investment appraisers. It is a helpful technique whenever a fairly complete probability picture (probability distribution) is desired. However, simulation is not very well suited for deriving generalizations for the following reasons.

a. It is an imprecise technique providing only statistical estimates rather than exact results.

b. It is highly specific to the postulated inputs, requiring a new simulation process if any variations in the assumptions or in the investment itself are to be examined.

In addition, the following disadvantages relate to the use of simulation.

c. Simulation yields only numerical data about the predicted performance of investments, but it does not yield additional insight into cause-and-effect relationships.

d. An unresolved issue is the determination of the optimal simulation sample size.

e. Other than a comparison of frequency distributions, simulation provides no guidance on how to use the estimates obtained with it in order to select the investments to be approved.

Rules 1 and 2

Let us now consider the approaches toward the treatment of risk as described earlier in relation to the application of Rules 1 and 2. We will consider the use of the NPV index in these rules.

The traditional method of handling decisions under risk amounts to reducing the estimates of possible values of a project's prospective cash flow during each year to a single expected value as given by expression (1). Next, the problem is analyzed as if this expected value were certain to occur. Naturally, this traditional method is rather crude, since standard deviations are ignored. Its attractiveness is that the economic desirability of an investment is expressed in a single measure.

It is clear that because of the above single measure, both Rules 1 and 2 can be easily used in combination with expected monetary values; that is, we simply use these measures of a project's NPV in Rules 1 and 2.

The standard deviation [see expression (3)] and expected value [see expression (1)] are used in combination with Rule 1 by adding a provision pertaining to the maximal allowable value of the standard deviation of the probability distribution of net present values of project j'. ("No project with a standard deviation larger than x units should be accepted.") This maximal value depends entirely on management's assessment of risk. Large, diversified firms are generally less averse to risk than small firms, and are, therefore, willing to accept higher values of the standard deviation.

The principle of dominance is used if Rule 2 is applied to the selection of one project from two mutually exclusive projects in combination with the concepts of standard deviation and expected value. The principle of dominance states that if the investor is faced with the problem of choosing between two projects with equal expected net present values, he or she will choose the one with the smaller risk. Similarly, when choosing between projects with equal risks but unequal net present values, the investor will select the project with the largest expected net present value. This project is said to dominate the other one. In a more formal way, the principle of dominance is stated as follows:

> In making a decision between two projects, $\{E(P), \sigma\}$ and $\{E'(P), \sigma'\}$, if either $E(P) < E'(P)$ and $\sigma \geq \sigma'$, or $E(P) \leq E'(P)$ and $\sigma > \sigma'$, the investor will select the second project, $\{E'(P), \sigma'\}$.

Repetitive application of the above principle to a pairwise examination of projects is suggested if Rule 2 is applied to the selection of one project from more than two mutually exclusive projects.

It is clear that the principle of dominance may not always result in a selection. For instance, what will the investor decide if he/she finds that $E(P) > E'(P)$ and $\sigma > \sigma'$? In this case, we replace Rule 2 by the following algorithm or step-by-step procedure. This algorithm may be applied to the selection of one project from two or more mutually exclusive projects.

Step 1. Calculate the expected value and standard deviation of the net present value for each project considered. The expected value and standard deviation of the net present value of a project i are called $E(P)_i$, and σ_i, respectively.

Step 2. Check for dominance by using the principle of dominance, and eliminate the projects which are dominated by one or more other projects. The remaining set of projects is called the efficient set. Proceed to Steps 3 through 7 with the efficient set.

Step 3. For the two projects with the largest positive $E(P)$, calculate the expected difference $E(P)_d$ and the standard deviation of the difference, σ_d, as follows:

$$E(P)_d = E(P_i) - E(P_j)$$

and

Table 6.5
E(P) and σ **Values for Example Problem**

Project	E(P)	σ	σ²
A	+$3,000	25,000	625,000,000
B	+ 2,500	12,000	144,000,000
C	+ 200	1,000	1,000,000
D	+ 100	8,000	64,000,000

$$\sigma_d = \sqrt{\sigma_i^2 + \sigma_j^2}.$$

Step 4. With the information obtained in Step 3, determine the "probability of reversal." This probability is defined as the probability that between two projects the one with the greater *E(P)* will turn out to be less desirable than the other. Thus, the probability of reversal is the probability that the difference in net present values of projects i and j, or $(P_i - P_j)$, is smaller than zero.

Step 5. Select the more preferable of the two projects considered in Step 4 based on management's preferences with respect to expected net present values and probabilities of reversal.

Step 6. Repeat Steps 3, 4, and 5 to compare the project selected in Step 5 to the project having the next largest *E(P)*. Select the more preferable of these two projects.

Step 7. Repeat Steps 3 though 6 as long as alternative projects exist and it seems that, based on the considerations of Step 5, the project having the next smallest *E(P)* may be sufficiently competitive to the current most desirable project. The final selection is the project which has the most positive *E(P)* and which has not been judged to be less desirable than some other project due to consideration of the probability of reversal.

To illustrate the use of this algorthim, consider the four mutually exclusive projects with *E(P)* and σ values as given in Table 6.5. It is assumed that the net present value for each project is normally distributed so that the distribution of differences between any two of the projects is normal.

Step 2 of the algorithm calls for elimination of Project D. Step 3 calls for the following comparison of projects A and B:

$$E(P)_d = \$3,000 - \$2,500 = \$500.00$$

and

$$\sigma_d = \sqrt{625,000,000 + 144,000,000} = \$27,730.00$$

Step 4 calls for the calculation of the probability of reversal. Appendix 4 can be used since the distribution of the differences is normal. The Z value is:

$$[0 - E(P)_d]/\sigma_d = -500/27,730 = -0.018$$

Appendix 4 indicates that the probability of reversal is 0.49. Carrying out Step 5, management decides that this probability of reversal is too high a risk to take. Therefore, Project B is selected. Next, Step 6 calls for the following comparison of Project B to Project C.

$$E(P)_d = \$2,500 - \$200 = \$2,300.00$$

and

$$\sigma_d = \sqrt{144,000,000 + 1,000,000} = \$12,020.00$$

The associated probability of reversal is now 0.42. Carrying out Step 5, management decides that this probability of reversal is small enough to take the risk. Consequently, the final selection is Project B. Note that the application of Rule 2 without considering the information about standard deviations would result in the selection of Project A.

It should be noted that the concepts of standard deviation and expected value may also be employed in combination with the use of the internal rate of return or its modified version in Rules 1 and 2. The internal rate of return R under considerations of risk may be computed with equation (1) by substituting 0 and R for $E(P)$ and i, respectively. Expression (2) remains the same, while i in expression (3) is replaced by R.

SUGGESTIONS FOR FURTHER READING

Adler, H. A. *Economic Appraisal of Transport Projects: A Manual with Case Studies.* Baltimore, MD: The Johns Hopkins University Press, 1987.

Bussey, L. E., and G. T. Stevens. "Formulating Correlated Cash Flow Streams." *Engineering Economist* (Fall 1972).

Chance, C. *Project Finance.* London: IFR Publishing, 1994.

Hillier, F. S. *The Evaluation of Risky Interrelated Investments.* Amsterdam, Holland: North Holland Publishing Co., 1969.

CHAPTER 7

Programming and Planning

He who has no taste for order, will be often wrong in his judgement, and seldom considerate or conscientious in his actions.

—John C. Lavater

Chapter 5 developed the concept of the weighted average cost of capital (WACOC), while Chapter 6 demonstrated how the cost of capital is used in project evaluations. In this chapter, we introduce the concept of capital budgeting. Capital budgeting and the cost of capital are actually interrelated, that is, we cannot determine the cost of capital until we determine the size of the capital budget; and we cannot establish the size of the capital budget until we determine the cost of capital. Section 2 shows how the cost of capital and the capital budget must be determined simultaneously.

Next, we introduce capital rationing which arises when a firm places an absolute limit on the size of its capital budget. In other words, capital rationing is a situation in which a firm either will not or cannot raise capital beyond a certain limit. It is often self-imposed due to the restrictive conditions lenders impose on a firm, and/or reluctance on the part of the board of directors to raise more equity capital for fear they will lose control of the firm, or simple preference for not growing too fast. Capital rationing can also be caused by the fact that a firm is passing through a period of relatively low profitability due to exceptionally severe competition. This competition, while reducing profits available for reinvestment, may make it extremely costly or difficult to raise further equity capital and to obtain additional debt capital. In public organizations, capital rationing may occur if the capital budget is fixed by political determination, by the high costs of raising additional funds through taxation, and the public authority cannot borrow or otherwise procure more investment funds.

It can be argued that capital rationing does not exist in the public sector if the interest rate represents the true opportunity cost of capital. That is, the opportunity cost of capital is too low if the rate of return of the most attractive project which, in view of a budget constraint, is not adopted, is higher. The return on the marginal public project represents the true opportunity cost of capital if it exceeds the rate of return on comparable investments in the private sector. The return on private investment represents the real opportunity cost of capital if it is anticipated that public investment funds are large enough so that the return on the marginal public project would be below the return on private investment. The result of this situation would be that some of the budgeted funds are withheld from investment in the public sector. As we have seen in Chapter 5, the establishment of the true opportunity cost of capital in the public sector is by no means a simple matter; capital rationing is, therefore, likely to occur.

Section 4 discusses a heuristic procedure for dealing with capital rationing. Other techniques available for capital rationing are integer programming and dynamic programming; however, their presentation is beyond the scope of this book due to their mathematical complexity.

The simplex method, which is an algorithm or step-by-step procedure for solving linear optimization problems, is the subject of Section 5. It has widespread application both in investment analysis as well as in economic and engineering problems. Since we are primarily interested in the application of the simplex method, we will not discuss its mathematical deriviation; the reader is referred to any standard linear programming text for the deriviation (see, for instance, *Finite Mathematics with Applications* under "Suggestions for Further Reading").

Section 6 demonstrates that deductive reasoning should be the base for the preparation of policies and strategies of a nation's economic development plan. Deductive reasoning should be followed by an examination of the interrelationships and organizational implications.

Finally, the use of the word "programming" in this chapter has no relation to the computer connotation of this word, which means the preparation of a logical sequence of operations to be performed by a digital computer in solving a problem or in processing data. We use the word "programming" to refer to the procedures for dealing with the planning of capital investments. The step-by-step development of these programming techniques facilitates, however, the preparation of a computer program for them. Thus, it should be a simple matter for a computer programmer to develop computer programs for any of the techniques presented in this chapter. In fact, a computer program for the simplex method is available on the market.

1. USING THE MCC IN CAPITAL BUDGETING

As a company tries to attract more new dollars, the cost of each dollar will at some point rise. In other words, the weighted average cost of capital (WACOC) depends on the amount of new capital raised; the WACOC will, at some point, rise if more and more capital is raised during a given period. This is because (a) flotation costs cause the cost of new equity to be higher than the cost of retained earnings; and (b) higher rates of return on debt, preferred stock, and common stock may be required to induce investors to supply additional capital to the company. The marginal cost of capital (MCC) is defined as the cost of the last dollar of new capital that the company raises; the marginal cost rises as more and more capital is raised during a given period.

A graph which shows how the WACOC changes as more and more new capital is raised during a given period is called the marginal cost of capital schedule. Figure 7.1 shows how the WACOC changes for the following example. From $0 to $150 million of new capital the WACOC is 10%, whereas just beyond $150 million the WACOC rises to 11% since cost of debt rises. This may be due to the fact that a bank is willing to lend a company at a given interest rate up to a given limit; beyond this limit the interest rate will be higher due to the additional risk exposure the bank is taking. At $200 million, the WACOC rises again to 12% since, at this point, external equity is required and the cost of external equity is higher than the cost of retained earnings (Section 2 of Chapter 5). There could, of course, be still more break points or points at which the WACOC would increase; they would occur if the interest rate continued to rise, or if the cost of stock of preferred and/or common stock rose.

A part of the capital budgeting process involves assessing the riskiness of each project, and assigning it a capital cost based on its relative risk. The cost of capital assigned to an average risk project should be the MCC. Less risky projects should be evaluated with a lower cost of capital, while more risky projects should be assigned higher costs of capital. In other words, firms first measure the MCC and then scale it up or down to reflect an individual project's riskiness. Unfortunately, because risk cannot be measured precisely, there is no good way of specifying exactly how much higher or lower than the MCC the costs of capital of non-average risk projects should be; given the present state of the art, risk adjustments are necessarily judgmental and somewhat arbitrary.

Since the cost of capital depends on how much capital a firm raises, the question of which WACOC it should use arises. Specifically, in the example of Figure 7.1, should we use a WACOC of 10, 11, or 12%? The answer is based on the concept of marginal analysis which tells us that firms should expand output to the point where marginal revenue equals marginal cost. At that point, the last unit of output exactly covers its cost—further expansion would reduce

Figure 7.1
Combining the MCC and IOS Schedules to Determine the Optimal Capital Budget

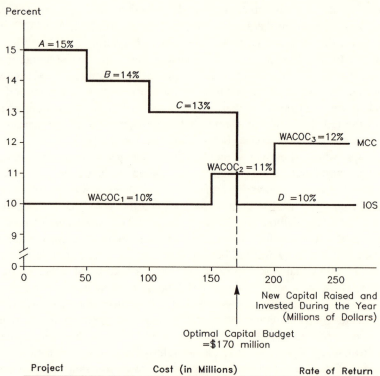

Project	Cost (in Millions)	Rate of Return
A	$50	15%
B	$50	14%
C	$70	13%
D	$80	12%

profits and the firm would forego profits at any lower production rate. Section 3 of Chapter 8 presents examples of the concept of marginal analysis.

To apply the concept of marginal analysis, we introduce a schedule that is analogous to the MCC schedule. This is the investment opportunity schedule (IOS), which shows the rate of return that is expected on each potential investment opportunity. Figure 7.1 shows an IOS for projects A, B, C, and D. The first three projects all have expected rates of return which exceed the cost of capital that will be used to finance them; but the expected return on Project D is less than its cost of capital. Consequently, projects A, B, and C should be accepted, and Project D should be rejected. The WACOC at the point where the IOS intersects the MCC curve is defined as the corporate cost of capital—this point reflects the marginal cost of capital to the corporation.

2. THE OPTIMAL CAPITAL BUDGET

As mentioned in the introduction to this chapter, capital budgeting consists of (a) identification of the set of investment opportunities, (b) estimation of the future cash inflows associated with each project, (c) determination of the present value (PV) of cash inflows of each project, and (d) comparison of each project's PV with its cost, and accepting a project if the PV of its future cash inflows exceeds its cost. To obtain the optimal capital budget we should use in step (c) a firm's marginal cost of capital; however, at this point in our capital budgeting process, we do not yet know this cost of capital. Therefore, we compute the internal rate of return (IRR) of each project to develop a graph like Figure 7.1. Specifically, the rates of return of projects A, B, C, and D in this figure are the internal rates of return, and based on these returns we accept projects A, B, and C, and reject Project D. The firm's marginal cost of capital is the WACOC where the IOS intersects the MCC curve, which in the example of Figure 7.1 is 11%. We can now proceed with carrying out the aforementioned step (c) by using the weighted average cost of capital equal to the firm's marginal cost of capital. Thus, if the costs of projects A, B, and C amount to $50 million, $50 million, and $70 million, respectively (as indicated in Figure 7.1), and assuming that carrying out the aforementioned step (d) also results in the selection of projects A, B, and C, then the optimal capital budget is $170 million.

In Chapter 6 we learned that the use of the IRR in project selection does not always guarantee a correct decision, whereas the use of the NPV (or EAV) index does guarantee a correct decision. It is, therefore, recommended to check whether the use of the NPV (or AEV) with a WACOC equal to the firm's marginal cost of capital would result in the same selection—in case of the example of Figure 7.1, this means the selection of projects A, B, and C, and the rejection of Project D. If the selection is not the same, we should develop a graph like Figure 7.1 for projects selected with the NPV rather than the IRR index. Next, we would use the IRR of these selected projects to plot the IOS and MCC curves. Fortunately, a situation where the IRR and NPV indices do not result in the same selection of projects does not happen often.

Up to this point, we have not considered the determination of the optimal capital budget when there are some mutually exclusive projects among the identified set of investment opportunities. Consider, for example, that we have identified projects A, B, C, D, and E, and that projects B and C are mutually exclusive, and each has an IRR larger than the marginal cost of capital. In this case, we develop two graphs like Figure 7.1—one for projects A, B, D, and E, and one for projects A, C, D, and E. Next, we determine the marginal cost of capital related to each graph and the corresponding sum of net present values of projects with an IRR larger than the marginal cost of capital. Project B is selected if the sum of net present values of the projects including Project B is larger than the sum of net present values including Project C. Naturally, if the former sum is smaller than the latter one, we select Project C.

It is noted that the aforementioned discussion of establishing the optimal capital budget was given for a rather small set of identified investment opportunities in order to keep the presentation simple. However, the methodology can be applied to any number of identified investment opportunities.

Although the procedures set forth in the preceding paragraphs are conceptually correct, and understanding of their underlying logic is important, management often uses a more judgmental, less quantitative process for establishing the final capital budget. Typically, the financial vice-president of a company acquires reasonably good estimates of the MCC schedule and the IOS from the treasurer and director of capital budgeting, respectively. These two schedules are then combined, as in Figure 7.1, to get a reasonably good approximation of the company's marginal cost of capital (the cost of capital at the intersection of the IOS and MCC schedules). The corporate MCC is then scaled up or down for each division to reflect the division's risk characteristics and capital structure, which is included if a company finances different assets in different ways. For instance, one division may have most of its capital tied up in special-purpose machinery, which is not very well suited as collateral for loans, while another division may have a lot of real estate which is good collateral. As a result, the division with the real estate has a higher debt capacity than the division with the machinery and, consequently, an optimal capital structure which contains a higher percentage of debt.

Suppose, for instance, that the corporate MCC is 11.0%. The financial vice-president may then decide to assign a factor 0.9 to a stable and low-risk division, but a factor of 1.1 to a more risky division. Therefore, the cost of capital of the low-risk division is 0.9(11.0%) = 9.9%, while that for the more risky division is 1.1(11.0%) = 12.1%. Next, each project within each division is classified into one of three groups—high risk, average risk, and low risk—and the same 0.9 and 1.1 factors are used to adjust the divisional MCCs. For example, a low-risk project in the low-risk division would have a cost of capital of 0.9(9.9%) = 8.9%, and a low-risk project in the more risky division would have a cost of capital of 0.9(12.1%) = 10.9%. A high-risk project in the low-risk division would have a cost of capital of 1.1(9.9%) = 10.9%, and a high-risk project in the more risky division would have a cost of capital of 1.1(12.1%) = 13.3%. Naturally, the corporate MCC of 11.0% is not adjusted for an average-risk project in an average-risk division.

After having established the adjusted cost of capital for each project in each division, we determine the net present value (NPV) for each project by using its risk-adjusted cost of capital. The optimal capital budget consists of all independent projects with risk-adjusted positive NPVs plus those mutually exclusive projects with the risk-adjusted highest positive NPVs among their mutual exclusive ones.

The above-described approach toward establishing the final capital budget has the advantage that it forces a company to think carefully about each division's relative risk, about the risk of each project in each division, and about the relationship between the total amount of capital raised and the cost of that capital. In addition, the company's capital budget is adjusted to reflect capital market conditions—the cost of capital to evaluate projects will increase if the cost of debt and equity rises; and projects that are marginally acceptable when capital costs are low will be ruled unacceptable when capital costs are high.

3. CAPITAL RATIONING

As discussed above, under ordinary circumstances, a company should expand to the point where its marginal return is just equal to its marginal cost. However, some firms set an absolute limit on the size of their capital budgets so that the size of the budget is less than the level of investment called for by the NPV criterion. This is called capital rationing.

The main reason for capital rationing is that some firms are reluctant to engage in external financing through either borrowing or selling stock. One management may not wish to sell equity capital for fear of losing some measure of voting control. Another management may refuse to use any form of outside financing on the basis of safety and control being more important than additional profits. Still others may set a limit on capital expenditures because of limitations of available managerial talent, although it is difficult to believe that additional managerial talent cannot be hired if not available within the firm. These are all cases of capital rationing resulting in a slower rate of expansion than would be dictated by purely rational wealth-maximizing behavior.

If a firm faces capital rationing, what can the financial manager do? The objective should be to select projects, subject to the capital rationing constraint, such that the sum of the projects' NPV is maximized.

Both in the literature and in practice, there appears to be considerable confusion as to how to choose projects from a given number of proposed capital investment projects, if a given capital constraint does not permit the undertaking of all proposed projects. Some authors recommend ranking projects requiring the same capital outlay in descending order of their net present values. The investor then goes down the list, constructing as many projects as the present budget permits. However, ranking in descending order of net present values cannot be applied if projects do not require the same capital outlay. Consider, for instance, three projects with B_1, B_2, and B_3 equal to \$800, \$600, and \$250, respectively; C_1, C_2, and C_3 equal to \$500, \$400, and \$100, respectively; and a budget constraint equal to \$500 (all symbols are as defined in Section 4 of Chapter 6). Ranking in descending order of net present values would result in selection of Project 1 with $B_1 - C_1 = 300, while selection of projects 2 and 3 results in higher total net benefit of \$350.

The following example elucidates why employment of the internal rate of return may lead to incorrect decisions. Consider the following three projects and suppose that the available budget is \$200:

| Projects | C_j | $b_{t,j}$ | | R_j | $B_j - C_j$ at $i=3\%$ |
		t=1	t=2		
$j = 1$	$100	$110	0	10.0%	$ 7
$j = 2$	$100	0	$120	7.1%	$11
$j = 3$	$100	0	$115	7.0%	$ 8

Using the net present value index, it picks projects 2 and 3, which results in a maximum of total net benefits. But using the internal rate of return index, it incorrectly picks projects 1 and 2.

How do we develop a procedure for the selection of a number of projects from the proposed capital investment projects to be used if a given budget constraint does not permit the undertaking of all proposed projects? The program of the most productive investments is determined by a combination of projects j such that $\Sigma_j(B_j - C_j)$ of this combination is larger than this expression for any other combination of projects with a sum of initial investment outlays less than or equal to the budget constraint. Examination of each possible combination in order to select the one with the largest sum of net benefits is only feasible if the number of proposed investment projects is small. The number of permissible combinations is likely to be astronomical if the number of proposed investments is not small, and the total of their associated capital outlays is significantly in excess of the given budget.

We have already seen that ranking of the proposed projects in descending order of their net present values, $B_j - C_j$, or internal rates of return, R_j, and going down this list, implementing as many projects as the present budget permits, may lead to incorrect decisions. Should we, therefore, follow the recommendation of the B/C advocates—that is, rank the proposed projects in descending order of the B_j/C_j ratios and go down the list, implementing as many projects as the budget permits? It is particularly this question which is subject to much controversy and confusion. It can be shown mathematically, however, that a procedure based on ranking of benefit-cost ratios may lead to incorrect selections.

Will one obtain a maximum sum of net benefits of projects selected if one chooses them based on a ranking of benefit-cost ratios, and if one does some "reshuffling" when the "last" project more than exhausts the budget? The problem is that in order to ensure the selection of projects with a maximum sum of net benefits, the examination of *which projects* to reshuffle may be time consuming. In addition, the reshuffling may not only be required when the "last" project more than exhausts the budget, but at other stages of the selection procedure as well. In fact, the analysis of which projects to reshuffle may be as time consuming as the aforementioned examination of each possible combination of projects j in order to arrive at the combination with the largest sum of net benefits and a sum of initial investment outlays smaller than or equal to the budget constraint.

The following heuristic procedure is recommended for capital rationing problems since it is relatively simple and sufficiently accurate for most practical situations. It is developed for those policy makers who are continually faced with the tradeoff between elaborate methods, on the one hand, and cursory approximations, on the other. The step-by-step procedure could be easily programmed for use with a computer.

4. HEURISTIC PROCEDURE

The procedure consists of the following nine steps.

Step 1. Determine $B_j - C_j$ for all projects j ($j = 1,2, \cdots, n$).

Step 2. Rank the projects in descending order of $B_j - C_j$, and assign the indices $i = 1,2, \cdots, n$, accordingly.

Step 3. Using the ranking of Step 2, go down the list, collecting as many projects as the budget permits. Call the project collected with the lowest $B_j - C_j$ value project $i = i^*$. Determine $\sum_{i=1}^{i^*} (B_i - C_i)$ and $\sum_{i=1}^{i^*} C_i$ for the projects collected.

Step 4. Collect projects with $i < i^*$ not included in Step 3, and project $i = i^* + 1$. Reassign indices $q = 1, 2, \cdots$, to these projects in accordance with the descending order of their $B_i - C_i$ values.

Step 5. Determine for each of the projects $q = 1,2, \cdots$, which of the projects collected in Step 3 will have to be deleted in order to include a project q without exhausting the budget. The deletion process starts with $i = i^*$ and is performed according to ascending order of $B_i - C_i$ values.

Step 6. Step 5 results in the following groups of projects:

project $q = 1$ + (projects not deleted in Step 5 under $q = 1$)
project $q = 2$ + (projects not deleted in Step 5 under $q = 2$)

.
.
.

Determine ΣC_i and (Budget $- \Sigma C_i$) for each of the above groups.

Step 7. For each of the groupings formed in Step 5, collect all projects eliminated in that step, along with all q-labeled projects (except the q project used in forming the group) and all projects i where $i > i^* + 1$. For each of these collections, rank the projects in descending order of their $B_i - C_i$ values.

Step 8. For each collection formed in Step 7, go down the list, adding projects to the corresponding groups of projects of Step 6 until no further projects can be added without making the total costs of these additional projects larger than the (Budget $- \Sigma C_i$) value computed for that particular group in Step 6.

Step 9. Compute $\Sigma (B_i - C_i)$ for each group formed by combining corresponding groups from steps 6 and 8. Select the group of projects with the highest $\Sigma (B_i - C_i)$ value from the above groups and the group of projects collected in Step 3.

Table 7.1 presents an application of the heuristic procedure to ten proposed projects and an available budget of $750,000.00.

Under capital rationing, the objective is, as mentioned earlier, to select the combination of proposed projects that provides the highest net present value, subject to the budget constraint. If this constraint is strictly enforced, it may be better to accept several smaller, less profitable projects that allow full utilization of the budget than to accept a small number of large projects that results in part of the budget being unused. The following oversimplified example illustrates this—suppose four investment opportunities exist:

Project	B_j	C_j	$B_j - C_j$
$j = 1$	$142,500	$125,000	$17,500
$j = 2$	196,000	175,000	21,000
$j = 3$	230,000	200,000	30,000
$j = 4$	165,000	150,000	15,000

If the budget constraint were $300,000, we should select projects 1 and 2 rather than Project 3 despite the fact that $B_j - C_j$ (and B_j/C_j) values are lower for the first two proposed projects. This is evident since the total net present value of projects 1 and 2 is $38,500, whereas the net present value of Project 3 is $30,000. Application of Step 4 of the heuristic procedure would indeed result in the selection of projects 1 and 2.

It is noted, however, that application of the heuristic procedure to the example of Table 7.1 results in the selection of projects 1, 5, and 6, with a total cost of $710,000 and total net present value of $840,000, rather than the choice of projects 4, 5, 6, 7, 8, and 9 with a total cost and net present value of $720,000 and $800,000, respectively.

The advantage of the heuristic procedure is that it reduces significantly the amount of effort required to examine the total number of possible combinations of the proposed projects with total costs smaller than or equal to the budget constraint, in order to determine the combination of projects such that $\Sigma_j (B_j - C_j)$ of this combination is larger than the corresponding expression for any other combination of projects. The evaluation of the above total number of possible combinations may be time consuming. If, for example, some 20 projects are considered and only 5 of them can be financed, the arithmetic of permutations and combinations tells us that 15,504 investment project combinations must be examined by the investor in order to find the most profitable among them. In the example of Table 7.1, this total number of combinations is 31.

Table 7.1
Application of Heuristic Procedure to Ten Proposed Projects

Benefits and Costs   *Step 1*
(in thousands of dollars)

Project	B_j	C_j		Project	$B_j - C_j$	Project	$B_j - C_j$
$j= 1$	1,000	600		$j= 1$	400	$j= 6$	160
$j= 2$	1,000	650		$j= 2$	350	$j= 7$	100
$j= 3$	1,000	500		$j= 3$	500	$j= 8$	40
$j= 4$	600	300		$j= 4$	300	$j= 9$	20
$j= 5$	300	120		$j= 5$	180	$j= 10$	10
$j= 6$	250	90					
$j= 7$	200	100					
$j= 8$	100	60					
$j= 9$	70	50					
$j= 10$	60	50					

	Step 2				*Step 3: $i^* = 6$*	
Project		$B_i - C_i$	C_i	Project	$B_i - C_i$	C_i
$i= 1$	$(j= 3)$	500	500	$i= 1$	500	500
$i= 2$	$(j= 1)$	400	600	$i= 5$	180	120
$i= 3$	$(j= 2)$	350	650	$i= 6$	160	90
$i= 4$	$(j= 4)$	300	300	Totals	840	710
$i= 5$	$(j= 5)$	180	120			
$i= 6$	$(j= 6)$	160	90		*Step 4*	
$i= 7$	$(j= 7)$	100	100		Project	
$i= 8$	$(j= 8)$	40	60			
$i= 9$	$(j= 9)$	20	50	$q= 1$ (or $i= 2$)		
$i= 10$	$(j= 10)$	10	50	$q= 2$ (or $i= 3$)		
				$q= 3$ (or $i= 4$)		
				$q= 4$ (or $i= 7$)		

Step 5

For $q = 1$:	For $q = 2$:	For $q = 3$:	For $q = 4$:
$i= 6$	$i= 6$	$i= 6$	$i= 6$
$i= 5$	$i= 5$	$i= 5$	
$i= 1$	$i= 1$	$i= 1$	

Step 6

For $q = 1$:		For $q = 2$:		For $q = 3$:		For $q = 4$:	
Project	C_i	Project	C_i	Project	C_i	Project	C_i
$i= 2$	600	$i= 3$	650	$i= 4$	300	$i= 7$	100
						$i= 5$	120
						$i= 1$	500
ΣC_i	600		650		300		720
Budget $-\Sigma C_i$	150		100		450		30

Table 7.1 (continued)

Step 7

For $q = 1$:	For $q = 2$:	For $q = 3$:	For $q = 4$:
$i= 1$	$i= 1$	$i= 1$	$i= 2$ (or $q= 1$)
$i= 3$ (or $q= 2$)	$i= 2$ (or $q= 1$)	$i= 2$ (or $q= 1$)	$i= 3$ (or $q= 2$)
$i= 4$ (or $q= 3$)	$i= 4$ (or $q= 3$)	$i= 3$ (or $q= 2$)	$i= 4$ (or $q= 3$)
$i= 5$	$i= 5$	$i= 5$	$i= 6$
$i= 6$	$i= 6$	$i= 6$	$i= 8$
$i= 7$ (or $q= 4$)	$i= 7$ (or $q= 4$)	$i= 7$ (or $q= 4$)	$i= 9$
$i= 8$	$i= 8$	$i= 8$	$i= 10$
$i= 9$	$i= 9$	$i= 9$	
$i= 10$	$i= 10$	$i= 10$	

Step 8

For $q = 1$:		For $q = 2$:		For $q = 3$:		For $q = 4$:	
Project	C_i	Project	C_i	Project	C_i	Project	C_i
$i= 5$	120	$i= 6$	90	$i= 5$	120	None	
				$i= 6$	90		
				$i= 7$	100		
				$i= 8$	60		
				$i= 9$	50		
Totals	120		90		420		0

Step 9

For $q = 1$:		For $q = 2$:		For $q = 3$:		For $q = 4$:	
Project	B_i-C_i	Project	B_i-C_i	Project	B_i-C_i	Project	B_i-C_i
$i= 2$	400	$i= 3$	350	$i= 4$	300	$i= 7$	100
$i= 5$	180	$i= 6$	160	$i= 5$	180	$i= 5$	180
				$i= 6$	160	$i= 1$	500
				$i= 7$	100		
				$i= 8$	40		
				$i= 9$	20		
Totals	580		510		800		780

Hence, select the projects collected in Step 3: $j= 3$ (or $i= 1$); $j= 5$ (or $i= 5$); and $j= 6$ (or $i= 6$).

It is noted that the number of projects considered in the example of Table 7.1 is relatively small; the efficiency of the heuristic procedure becomes more apparent if the number of proposed projects is large, which is often the case when governments or large corporations have to select projects for implementation. The amount of reduced effort obtained by applications of the procedure depends on the number of proposed projects, their capital requirements, including the variation in these requirements, and the available budget or the possible number of projects which can be financed.

In essence, the procedure results in a reduction of the amount of effort required to obtain the optimal combination of projects, since it concentrates on the examination of projects with the larger $B_j - C_j$ values. Mostly, these are the projects with a good likelihood of being included in the optimal combination. The heuristic procedure does not guarantee an optimal answer. Experience indicates, however, that the probability of arriving at a non-optimal selection is small (less than 10%).

The heuristic procedure applies to the selection of independent projects. How do we employ it if the list of proposed capital investment projects contains mutually exclusive projects? Rule 2 (Section 4, Chapter 6) may be applied before proceeding with the application of our selection procedure if mutually exclusive projects are to be considered. Naturally, a more correct manner to treat mutually exclusive projects is the application of our selection procedure to sets of proposed projects representing the various feasible combinations of mutually exclusive projects. Consider, for instance, six proposed projects—a, b, c, d, e, and f—and suppose that b and c as well as d and e are mutually exclusive. The aforementioned sets of proposed projects are (a, b, d, f), (a, c, d, f), (a, b, e, f), and (a, c, e, f) for this situation. It is clear that this approach may be time consuming. It is also noted that the application of the heuristic procedure to interdependent projects can best be handled by considering the interdependent projects as one investment project.

Probabilistic information can be used in the execution of the heuristic procedure by carrying out the following procedure prior to the application of the heuristic procedure.

Step 1. Calculate the expected value $E(P)$ and the standard deviation σ of the net present value for each project considered by using the methods of Section 5 of Chapter 6.

Step 2. Determine for each project the probability that the expected net present value will be less than zero. This is also done with one of the methods of the above Section 5 (use of Z table or Chebyshev's inequality).

Step 3. With the information obtained in Step 2, eliminate from further consideration those projects which have, in the judgment of management, too high a probability that the expected net present value will be less than zero ("probability of loss"). Using expected net present values, proceed with the application of the heuristic procedure.

Before moving on to the next section, it is noted that often there is a better method of handling the types of situations that give rise to capital rationing. Generally, capital rationing occurs when a company believes that it will have problems if it tries to raise capital beyond some specified amount. Such a situation can be rationally handled by increasing the company's weighted average cost of capital as the amount of capital raised increases. Next, we proceed as explained in sections 1 and 2 of this chapter.

5. SIMPLEX METHOD

The simplex method is an algorithm for solving linear optimization models; that is, a linear objective function is to be maximized (or minimized) subject to a number of linear constraints. Such problems are known as linear programming problems. A number of different algorithms have been proposed to solve these problems, but the one below has, in general, proved to be the most effective.

The simplex method for maximization problems is as follows.

Step 1. Rewrite the maximization problem by introducing $x_0 = $ the value of the objective function, and slack variables. The equations obtained in this manner are numbered 1, 2, 3, and so on. [The (1) is assigned to the equation for the objective function.]

Step 2. Select a starting feasible solution. A simple way for obtaining such a solution is to take $x_0 = 0$, the slack variables equal to the constraint levels, and all other variables equal to zero.

Step 3. Check the coefficients of the variables equal to zero in equation (1). An optimal solution exists if all these coefficients are non-negative. Select the variable with the largest negative coefficient if no optimal solution exists, and proceed to Step 4.

Step 4. Determine what the value of the variable selected in Step 3 has to be such that one of the variables in the current solution becomes zero. This is done in the following way.

a. Take the ratios of the right-hand side of the current equations to the coefficients of the selected variable (ignore ratios with zero or negative numbers in the denominator).
b. Select the minimal ratio—this ratio equals the value of the selected variable, which we call x_j, in the next trial solution.
c. Set the variable in the equation, for which the minimal ratio occurs in the current solution, equal to zero (in Step 5 we refer to this equation as equation k).

Step 5. Rewrite the equations of the current solution.

a. Divide the coefficients and the right-hand side of equation (k) by the coefficient of its variable x_j.
b. Multiply the coefficients and the right-hand side of the equation obtained above by [-coefficient of x_j in equation (g)] and add the thus obtained equation to equation (g); this is done for all equations, except equation (k). Thus, the equation index (g) refers to all equations except equation (k). Return to Step 3.

The following example illustrates the use of the simplex method in investment analysis. Suppose the total production costs for products A and B are $5.00 and $4.00 per unit, respectively. These production costs must be paid in cash at the end of the period in which they are incurred. All sales are on credit and are to be repaid by the end of the following period. A bank is willing to loan up to $300.00 for one period at an interest rate of 10% per period, provided a "quick asset ratio" of at least 3:1 is maintained while the loan is outstanding. A quick asset ratio is the ratio of cash, accounts receivable, and marketable securities to current liabilities. There are no marketable securities and current liabilities, while cash and accounts receivable amount to $600.00. The interest is payable when the loan is due one period later. The amount borrowed, if any, will be needed for one period only, since production costs are paid at the end of the current period and all collections on sales are made by the end of the following period. Unit selling prices are \$8.00 for both products A and B, which are processed in divisions 1 and 2. The maximal capacities of divisions 1 and 2 are 500 and 700 units per period, while the coefficients of capacity utilization for products A and B are, respectively, 2 and 3, in division 1, and, respectively, 4 and 2 in division 2. We are interested in the optimal production mix—that is, the number of units of production of products A and B to be financed from the opening cash balance (assumed to be \$600.00) and/or the bank loan.

To solve our problem, we formulate the profit function:

$$x_0 = (8 - 5)x_1 + (8 - 5 - 0.5)x_2 + (8 - 4)x_3 + (8 - 4 - 0.4)x_4$$
$$= 3x_1 + 2.5x_2 + 4x_3 + 3.6x_4$$

where

x_1 = number of units of Product A financed from the opening cash balance
x_2 = number of units of Product A financed from bank loan
x_3 = number of units of Product B financed from the opening cash balance
x_4 = number of units of Product B financed from bank loan.

The above function has to be maximized subject to the following constraints:

Division 1 capacity constraint: $2x_1 + 2x_2 + 3x_3 + 3x_4 \leqslant 500$
Division 2 capacity constraint: $4x_1 + 4x_2 + 2x_3 + 2x_4 \leqslant 700$
Quick asset ratio: $\dfrac{600 - 5x_1 - 4x_3}{5x_2 + 4x_4} \geqslant 3$ or

$$5x_1 + 15x_2 + 4x_3 + 12x_4 \leqslant 600$$

Loan limit: $5x_2 + 4x_4 \leqslant 300.$

Step 1 of the simplex method gives:

$$x_0 - 3x_1 - 2.5x_2 - 4x_3 - 3.6x_4 = 0. \qquad (1)$$
$$2x_1 + 2x_2 + 3x_3 + 3x_4 + x_5 = 500 \qquad (2)$$
$$4x_1 + 4x_2 + 2x_3 + 2x_4 + x_6 = 700 \qquad (3)$$
$$5x_1 + 15x_2 + 4x_3 + 12x_4 + x_7 = 600 \qquad (4)$$
$$5x_2 + 4x_4 + x_8 = 300. \qquad (5)$$

Step 2 calls for the selection of a feasible starting solution.

$$x_0 = 0, x_5 = 500, x_6 = 700, x_7 = 600, x_8 = 300, x_1 = x_2 = x_3 = x_4 = 0.$$

The check of Step 3 indicates that an optimal solution has not yet been obtained since the coefficients of x_1, x_2, x_3, and x_4 in equation (1) are negative. We select the variable with the largest negative coefficient or x_3.

Application of Step 4 gives the following ratios:

ratio related to equation (1) is ignored
ratio related to equation (2) is 500/3
ratio related to equation (3) is 700/2
ratio related to equation (4) is 600/4, which is the minimal
one; thus, $x_3 = 150$, $x_7 = 0$, and $k = 4$.

Application of Step 5 gives:

$$
\begin{aligned}
x_0 + \quad 2x_1 + 12.5x_2 \quad\quad + \quad 8.4x_4 \quad\quad\quad\quad + \quad x_7 \quad\quad &= 600 \quad (1)\\
-7/4x_1 - 37/4x_2 \quad\quad - \quad 6x_4 + x_5 \quad\quad - 3/4x_7 \quad\quad &= 50 \quad (2)\\
3/2x_1 - \quad 7/2x_2 \quad\quad - \quad 4x_4 \quad + x_6 - 1/2x_7 \quad\quad &= 400 \quad (3)\\
5/4x_1 + 15/4x_2 + x_3 + 12/4x_4 \quad\quad\quad + 1/4x_7 \quad\quad &= 150 \quad (4)\\
x_2 \quad\quad + \quad 4x_4 \quad\quad\quad\quad\quad\quad + x_8 &= 300. \quad (5)
\end{aligned}
$$

Application of Step 3 indicates that we have obtained the following optimal solution: $x_0 = 600$, $x_3 = 150$; and the slack variables x_5, x_6, and x_8 and 50, 400, and 300, respectively (all other variables are zero). Thus, the optimal course of action is the production of 150 units of Product B financed exclusively from the opening cash balance. At first, this result may appear astonishing since the profit function shows a profit for the production financed from the opening cash balance as well as that financed from a bank loan. We recall, however, that the quick asset ratio is a barrier to a higher output.

The above simplex method applies to maximization problems. Only Step 3 has to be modified in order to be able to use the algorithm for minimization problems. Step 3 reads, in this case, as follows:

Check the coefficients of the variables equal to zero in equation (1). An optimal solution exists if all these coefficients are non-positive. Select the variable with the largest positive coefficient if no optimal solution exists and proceed to Step 4.

The computer has made linear programming a practical computational technique for problems having a large number of variables and constraints. Almost any computer center will have an operational linear programming software package.

The above application to the choice of manufacturing Product A or Product B, with financing from the opening cash balance or a bank loan, is an example of the usefulness of the simplex method. Other examples of useful applications include the determination of the profitability of a particular line of business, the establishment of appropriate capacity dimensions of a new piece of heavy equipment, the establishment of cash flow requirements, the purchasing of the optimal mix of raw materials, the production scheduling of a series of underground oil reservoirs, and the development of an annual plan to integrate the major decisions of an entire organization. Since the formulation of a linear objective function and the related linear constraints is often the most difficult part in the use of a linear programming model, we present two more examples without the actual application of the simplex method. After all, programming software packages are available for finding solutions with this method.

Example 1. The Knox Mix Company has the option of using one or more of four different types of production processes. The first and second yield items of Product A, and the third and fourth yield items of Product B. The inputs for each process are labor measured in man-weeks, pounds of Material Y and boxes of Material Z. Since each process varies in its input requirements, the profitabilities of the processes differ, even for the processes producing the same item. The manufacturer, deciding on a week's production schedule, is limited in the range of possibilities by the available amounts of manpower and both kinds of raw materials. Total availabilities of man-weeks, pounds of Material Y, and pounds of Material Z for the different processes are 15, 120, and 100 units, respectively. Input requirements for one item of Product A and one item of Product B are as follows:

Item	One Item of Product A		One Item of Product B	
	Process 1	Process 2	Process 3	Process 4
Labor	1	1	1	1
Material Y	6	5	3	2
Material Z	3	5	10	14

Unit profits of the production of A with processes 1 and 2 are \$4 and \$5, respectively; those of the production of B with processes 3 and 4 are \$10 and \$11, respectively. The decision problem formulated as a linear programming model is as follows:

Maximize $(4x_1 + 5x_2 + 10x_3 + 11x_4)$
subject to the following constraints:
$1x_1 + 1x_2 + 1x_3 + 1x_4 \le 15$ (man-weeks)
$6x_1 + 5x_2 + 3x_3 + 2x_4 \le 120$ (Material Y)
$3x_1 + 5x_2 + 10x_3 + 14x_4 \le 100$ (Material Z)
$x_1 \ge 0; x_2 \ge 0; x_3 \ge 0; x_4 \ge 0$

where

x_1 = items of Product A produced with Process 1
x_2 = items of Product A produced with Process 2
x_3 = items of Product B produced with Process 3
x_4 = items of Product B produced with Process 4.

Example 2. The Fly-By-Night Airline must decide on the amounts of jet fuel to purchase from three possible vendors. The airline refuels its aircraft regularly at the four airports it serves.

The oil companies have said that they can furnish up to the following amounts of fuel during the coming month: 250,000 gallons for Oil Company 1; 500,000 gallons for Oil Company 2; and 600,000 gallons for Oil Company 3. The required amount of jet fuel is 100,000 gallons at Airport 1; 200,000 gallons at Airport 2; 300,000 gallons at Airport 3; and 400,000 gallons at Airport 4.

When transportation costs are added to the bid price per gallon supplied, the combined cost per gallon (in dollars) for jet fuel from each vendor furnishing a specific airport is as follows:

	Company 1	Company 2	Company 3
Airport 1	12	5	5
Airport 2	10	11	14
Airport 3	8	11	13
Airport 4	11	13	9

The decision problem formulated as a linear programming model is as follows:

Minimize $(12x_1 + 10x_2 + 8x_3 + 11x_4 + 5x_5 + 11x_6$
$+ 11x_7 + 13x_8 + 5x_9 + 14x_{10} + 13x_{11} + 9x_{12})$
Subject to the following constraints:
$x_1 + x_2 + x_3 + x_4 \leqslant 250,000$
$x_5 + x_6 + x_7 + x_8 \leqslant 500,000$
$x_9 + x_{10} + x_{11} + x_{12} \leqslant 600,000$
$x_1 + x_5 + x_9 \geqslant 100,000$
$x_2 + x_6 + x_{10} \geqslant 200,000$
$x_3 + x_7 + x_{11} \geqslant 300,000$
$x_4 + x_8 + x_{12} \geqslant 400,000$
$x_1 \geqslant 0; x_2 \geqslant 0; x_3 \geqslant 0; x_4 \geqslant 0; x_5 \geqslant 0; x_6 \geqslant 0; x_7 \geqslant 0; x_8 \geqslant 0;$
$x_9 \geqslant 0; x_{10} \geqslant 0; x_{11} \geqslant 0; x_{12} \geqslant 0$

where

x_1 = gallons of fuel from Company 1 to Airport 1
x_2 = gallons of fuel from Company 1 to Airport 2
x_3 = gallons of fuel from Company 1 to Airport 3
x_4 = gallons of fuel from Company 1 to Airport 4
x_5 = gallons of fuel from Company 2 to Airport 1
x_6 = gallons of fuel from Company 2 to Airport 2
x_7 = gallons of fuel from Company 2 to Airport 3
x_8 = gallons of fuel from Company 2 to Airport 4
x_9 = gallons of fuel from Company 3 to Airport 1
x_{10} = gallons of fuel from Company 3 to Airport 2
x_{11} = gallons of fuel from Company 3 to Airport 3
x_{12} = gallons of fuel from Company 3 to Airport 4

6. ECONOMIC DEVELOPMENT PLANS

Most developing countries realize that the process of development is very costly. To ensure optimal use of the resources available, the governments frequently prepare economic development plans covering periods of anywhere between three and ten years. The methodology of the preparation of such a plan does not depend much on the time span covered. The time span is generally based on considerations of the extent to which investment commitments are made; the country's dependence upon economies of other countries; the availability of, and the need for, infrastructural facilities; and the degree of detail incorporated in the plan.

Economic development plans are not only prepared by developing countries. The extent to which a plan is fully comprehensive and obligatory on the whole economy depends on a country's state of development as well as its institutions and ideology. For instance, the Indian plans have related only to the public sector (including nationalized industries and factories), while the French plans have been extended to the private sector by discussion–persuasion. In the United States, no formal public sector plan is made since, in view of the availability of exceptionally good statistics, the federal government expects that the information provided suffices for sensible planning by private and state planners.

Naturally, the preparation of an economic development plan depends on a large number of aspects. Although the establishment of development guidelines applicable to a large variety of countries appears to be a formidable task, some general guidelines can be formulated. We will discuss these for "mixed" economies where some responsibility is left to the private enterprise.

Rules 1 and 2 of Section 4 of Chapter 6—rules dealing with the acceptance of an independent project or the selection of a project from a group of mutually exclusive projects—can be used in combination with the concepts of shadow pricing and social or accounting rates of discount. However, these rules should, in this case, use the NPV index rather than the internal rate of return. It is clear that Rules 1 and 2 (and the NPV index) can be used in combination with the aforementioned concepts since they only deal with the requirement of a specified non-negative NPV and the examination of the greatest NPV of a group of mutually exclusive projects. In the following discussion of the preparation of economic development plans, we will indicate at which stage of the preparation these rules are to be used.

The preparation of economic development plans may be divided into the following phases:

a. Determination of the opportunities and constraints for further progress.

b. Listing of national objectives.

c. Formulation of national policies and strategies to accomplish the national objectives.

d. Listing of sectoral objectives.

e. Formulation of sectoral policies and strategies to accomplish both the national and sectoral objectives.

Determination of the Opportunities and Constraints

This determination is based on the following ten components.

1. A geographical inventory of the total resources of the country, reflecting the characteristics of the country.
2. Cognition of the utilization of capacity for the existing projects and programs.
3. An investigation of the existing internal trade routes, the external trade relationships, and the geographical identification of major markets.
4. A comprehension of the effectiveness of the various units in the administrative structure.
5. A complete understanding of the allocation of authority between the legislative and executive departments of the government.
6. A cognitive awareness of both the attitudes and the status of vested authority among those who are concerned with decision making and implementation of economic development.
7. A survey of both the needs and the potential development involvement of the commonality or the majority of the people whose standard of living is expected to be raised with the economic development plan.
8. An understanding of the role of the political structure as a vehicle to express needs and desires from the people, to mobilize potentially available internal resources, and to influence decisions with respect to economic development.
9. A respectful awareness and understanding of a country's religious and cultural developments.
10. An appraisal of the past performance and current level of development of the economy.

Item 10 is usually based on trend analysis of national accounts data such as national income, imports, exports, savings, and per capital income. Perhaps a reason that economic development plans of the past decade have frequently not resulted in the anticipated raising of the standard of living of the commonality is that too little attention was paid to the first nine items and too much to item 10. This is particularly dangerous in view of the existing reality of emerging economies—that is, the unavailability of reliable national accounts data as a result of lack of statistics and/or shortage of skilled manpower to prepare the data (and consequent futility of preparing totals without understanding their composition or the method of collocation). Items 2, 3, and 4, together with profound observations about symptoms of dietary deficiencies and conditions of housing and hygiene, may under such conditions provide better means of appraisal of past performance.

Problems remain even if reliable national accounts data are available. For instance, national income frequently reflects influences of all kinds which should be eliminated in order to appraise "real" past performance. Examples of such influences are: the valuation of government output at factor cost by assuming a benefit-cost ratio of 1.0 and thereby actually defining away the problems of evaluating government output; the absence of the effects of buyer and seller surpluses in the national income; and the absence of increased leisure, which increases welfare if it is chosen freely, in the national accounts to be included in the real national income.

The foregoing ten components determine the opportunities and limitations of a country's absorptive capacity with respect to further progress. These are now used for the tentative listing of national objectives.

Listing of National Objectives

These objectives should be based on the recognition of two important aspects inherent in planning. These are the maintenance and improvement of existing works and services, and the construction of new works and the introduction of new ways of producing goods and services. The former aspect frequently tends to be neglected, although a central government of a country has a general responsibility for seeing that development is making optimal use of resources. In addition, it has to bear most of the costs of providing the physical infrastructure.

It should be stressed that maintenance and improvement of only physical infrastructure is not sufficient. Allowance must also be made for normal pay increments for civil servants in view of their aging and a possible rise in local living costs. Consequently, forward thinking should not be limited to the construction of new works and the introduction of new ways of producing goods and services.

Examples of national objectives which may be derived from the ten components of the previous section are as follows.

1. *Diversification of sources of national income.* For instance, the first development plan of the Kingdom of Saudi Arabia had as one of its main objectives the diversification of sources of national income and the reduction of dependence on oil through increasing the share of other productive sectors in gross domestic product. This objective of the Saudi government was based on the belief that sole reliance on exports of petroleum products for the supply of foreign exchange and growth in per capita income is dangerous in the long term. Subterranean water resources that can be exploited at varying costs for irrigation, higher yields on existing cultivated land, and the production of higher value crops have enabled Saudi Arabia to partially substitute domestic production for imports of food stuffs. In addition, growing world demand, particularly in the nearby markets of Africa and Asia, offers increasing opportunities for the export of petrochemicals and fertilizers.

In another country, for example, one with a local agrarian economy, considerations of a growing labor surplus in the agricultural sector and an impending diminishing viability of export markets may lead to diversification. The establishment of agro-based industries often has the additional advantage of favorably utilizing the financial resources of a vested interest in land ownership.

2. *Maximization of output.* This objective may be based on observations of

underutilization of existing infrastructure, a large portion of the populace living at the subsistence level, and/or a populace disinterested in the development process. It indicates the desirability of policies pertaining to quick yielding investments as well as complementary investments that will reinforce the success of formerly implemented projects.

Activities with high returns over short gestation periods mean, in the sphere of small industries, that equal emphasis is to be placed on the full use of existing capacity and its orderly expansion as on the creation of carefully selected new capacity. Maximization of output in the transportation and communications sectors means that the allocation of resources for repair and maintenance should, in general, receive higher priority than those for new construction, while the social services sector should concentrate on projects with field level reinforcing effects.

Naturally, maximization of output should not be carried out to such an extreme that the requirements of physical infrastructure and institution building in subsequent plans are completely ignored.

3. *Development of human resources.* An objective of developing human resources pertains to a more effective contribution to production and increased participation in the development process by several elements of society. It may be based on considerations of a deterioration in the population to resources ratio, urban unemployment, rural underemployment, and unequal distribution of the benefits of development by social groups and economic classes of the populace.

Translation of the fruits of economic gains into social improvements does not only lead to a more equal distribution of the benefits but also to a populace better equipped to contribute to the development process themselves.

A more equal distribution of benefits may also be obtained by a revision of the tax system. Perhaps a major reason why redistribution of income is so difficult to obtain in many developing countries is that in such countries taxes on outgoings are very much more important as revenue raisers than in advanced countries. This largely reflects the difficulties of collecting taxes on incomings.

4. *Elimination of dependence on foreign assistance.* Two main aspects of inflow of foreign resources are the augmentation of domestic savings and the addition to the pool of foreign exchange which is often needed for the increasing import requirements of a growing economy. Contrary to normal belief, the supply of financial resources is often not the most serious bottleneck in economic development. Once a country has adopted a sensible development plan which seems to be within its powers, it frequently does not have too many difficulties in borrowing the balance that cannot be met from home resources.

Elimination of dependence on foreign assistance is commendable in view of a country's concern for its future generation to be faced with the problem of debt service. In addition, foreign assistance may not be desirable—even a grant or soft loan—due to the motives which lie behind the preferred gift. For instance, some advanced countries have presented gifts primarily to help some particular pocket of unemployment at home rather than the beneficiary. Acceptance of gifts should particularly be carefully examined if the donor stipulates that the beneficiary must also accept the type of equipment offered and the timing of the gift, even if the one is expensive to maintain and the other inconvenient in relation to other plans.

Elimination of grants and soft loans may also be desirable if they require complementary expenditures on land, site, maintenance, or cooperating labor, which impose a continuing drain on the country's development finances. In brief, gifts should be politely refused if they are not consistent with a country's development plan.

The above four national objectives only serve as illustrations. Other examples of national objectives include a more equal distribution of the benefits of development by geographical areas; the economic, social, and political integration of a country; promotion and maintenance of social justice; preservation of national security; economic stability; and the establishment of preconditions for sustained and long-term growth.

It is clear that some national objectives may be contradictory. For instance, an implication of emphasizing maximization of output is the simultaneous deemphasis of other matters such as the development of human resources or a more equal distribution of benefits by region. In addition, the simultaneous pursuit of diverse objectives is often difficult in the light of the constraints that are imposed by the scarcity of resources. A tentative ranking of mutually consistent national objectives in descending order of their relative importance serves as the basis for the formulation of national policies and strategies. In addition, this ranking may be used to reduce the total number of initially selected objectives in order to allow for flexibility of planning at the sectoral level. The ranking is subject to modifications upon termination of the formulation of sectoral objectives.

Formulation of National Policies and Strategies

The principal guideline for the formulation of national policies and strategies is whether, with the given limitations of a country's absorptive capacity, they can result in the realization of the national objectives. Examples of national policies are a policy of individual economic freedom; a fiscal policy; a foreign exchange policy; an employment creation policy; a policy to increase the rate of domestic savings; a policy of strengthening various new institutions; a decentralization policy; a subsidy policy; a full-cost pricing policy; a price stability policy; and a policy pertaining to the role of the private sector.

Deductive reasoning is the base for the preparation of policies and strategies. This should be followed by an analysis of the interrelationships and organizational implications. An understanding of the potential problems in various departmental areas is crucial for the successful and timely implementation of interrelated policy measures. Examples of interrelated policy measures are fuel taxes and vehicle purchase taxes; taxes pertaining to capital assets and a policy involving the command over resources by the private or public sector; excise taxes and a policy pertaining to the role of the private sector in industrial development; and income redistribution policies and policies pertaining to regional development.

Our discussion of maximization of output as a national objective already illustrated the concept of deductive reasoning for the preparation of policies and strategies; that is, such an objective leads to a policy stressing maintenance and repair and economizing measures for construction. Consequently, sectoral allocations—allocations to the various economic sectors (agricultural, forestry, trade, power, transportation, communications, and social services)—are based on the need for maintenance and repair. The strategy for the composition of investments has an emphasis on quick yielding investments and complementary investments which will reinforce the success of formerly implemented projects. Complementary investments are determined by the demand for correlative and intermediate products and services, the supply of identified excess capacity, and the by-products of existing activities. It should be noted here that countries with "diversification of sources of national income" as a national objective would do well to also scrutinize projects with feasible linkage effects, since these have generally high rates of return.

Other examples of deductive reasoning are: a national objective of economic stability leading to a policy of price stability and certain fiscal measures; the spectrum of special skills available at a given time; and consequently, educational policies with a clear-cut growth effect in addition to a welfare effect.

Operational policy formulation should not be based on common beliefs (for example, that rural and agricultural development should receive high priority) since this will effectively improve the income distribution of a country—in other words, provide a higher standard of living for the commonality. Naturally, such strategy may well apply to quite a number of developing countries. However, it is doomed to failure if the existing reality is a labor surplus in the agricultural sector and an impending diminishing viability of export markets or other constraints such as the non-feasibility of exploiting additional water resources, increasing the yields, or producing higher value crops. Solutions to unequal income distributions should in such situations be sought by other policies such as one pertaining to taxes on incomings.

The distribution of sectoral allocations should reflect the plan objectives. These allocations as well as the national policies and strategies are subject to modifications upon termination of the formulation of sectoral policies and strategies.

The deductive reasoning for the preparation of policies and strategies can be supplemented with the building of long-term development models in countries with easy access to reliable statistics. For instance, the World Bank has developed models which require inputs such as (1) a series of projected levels of output for certain key sectors; (2) a series of sector incremental capital output ratios, estimated from the data for the preceding period; (3) a series of investment assumptions for certain sectors where investment and output cannot be tied directly or where output is functionally linked to investment; and (4) assumptions concerning the prices of a country's main exports and imports. With these inputs, the models determine the output levels for the remaining sectors, total gross domestic product, total fixed investment, sector exports, imports by end use, consumption, savings, resource gaps, and changes in stocks. Some models also project employment by sector, using fixed incremental labor-output ratios, and incorporate detailed balance of payments projections. The introduction of assumptions concerning factor payments, transfers, and other balance of payments flows, as well as terms and amounts of foreign aid, further enables the models to project debt-service payments and to calculate the level of exchange reserves necessary to ensure equilibrium between the balance of payments and national account projections.

The main advantage of these models is that a number of different combinations of assumptions can be examined. For instance, the effect of different assumptions about factor payments and transfers on projected debt-service payments and exchange reserves can be analyzed. Sound models are based on a process of deductive reasoning and an analysis of interrelationships.

Listing of Sectoral Objectives

The formulation of sectoral objectives calls for a more detailed analysis of the opportunities and constraints of each sector. The examination of the limitations of a country's absorptive capacity takes place primarily at the macro level; this analysis is now extended to the micro level. Thus, we acquire additional information about present conditions, existing successful sectoral programs, demand for goods and/or services, institutions, and organizational and administrative constraints pertaining to each sector. The process of collecting additional data is guided by the tentatively formulated national objectives and policies as well as the country's absorptive capacity at macro level.

The formulation of sectoral objectives may best be described as the translation of national objectives into sectoral ones. The translation serves to make the national objectives more practicable to deal with, as well as to indicate the mutual dependence of the functions of national and sectoral planning and consequent coordination between and among the various governmental units in charge of planning.

Additional information at the sectoral level is required since complete information on a particular situation in each sector can never be expected to be available at the national level. It is, however, only in as far as such information is relevant for the national planning and sectoral allocations that it should be used at the national level. The listing of sectoral goals requires a study covering a good deal of sectoral and regional detail, based on interviews, local observation, measurement, and so on.

Planners involved with the formulation of sectoral objectives should not rigidly adopt the national objectives and strategies since this would produce a Cournot solution with a global result inferior to that resulting from collusion. A Cournot solution takes the policies of other parties for granted, and the second best result obtained from this philosophy is due to the passivity of each planner with respect to the objectives of fellow planners. Thus, the more detailed information may necessitate adjustments and modifications in national objectives, policies, and strategies.

The final formulation of the national objectives should, however, be consistent with that of the sectoral objectives, while both should be based on existing limitations in order for development planning to transpire in an orderly manner. Erratic and inconsistent changes after such final formulation should be avoided since the probability of success of planning depends largely on the sustained ability to remain faithful to the national and sectoral objectives. Naturally, some degree of flexibility is appropriate since the nature of the planning process implies constant changes in the socioeconomic environment.

An example of consistency among national and sectoral objectives and existing limitations is the following. If a national objective pertains to the increase of the economy's absorptive capacity, and if farmers could produce more if they were better trained and additional credit were available, sectoral objectives would relate to the establishment of extension services and the development of credit.

From our discussion of sectoral objectives, it is evident that freelance planning in the various sectors inevitably leads to a number of bottlenecks. In addition, freelance planning results in duplication of efforts. An example of such duplication relates to agricultural planners and transport planners who do basically the same thing. That is, the former planners make forecasts of domestic demand for different products, imports, possible developments of agricultural processing industries, needs for feeder-road systems, irrigation schemes, and so on, on the basis of their own assumptions about long-term developments in population, incomes, and so on. The latter planners commence their studies with their own long-term projections, sectoral developments, regional developments, and so on, in order to be able to design their networks. Naturally, it would be much better if the agricultural and transport planners jointly prepare their forecasts.

Formulation of Sectoral Policies and Strategies

The principle guideline for the formulation of sectoral policies and strategies is whether, with the given limitations of the absorptive capacity of the various sectors, they can result in the realization of both national and sectoral objectives. The following example illustrates the process of establishing sectoral policies.

Suppose a country has as its national objective the maximization of output. In the sphere of industrial development, this means that industries are to be classified according to the needs for further economic development and linkage effects. The relative importance of each industry to the development process then provides insight into the desirable incentives and facilities. Next, the gamut of possible policies, such as tax holidays, protective tariffs, possible exemption of customs duties on imported raw materials and equipment, must be analyzed.

Thus, the formation of sectoral policies is done in much more detail (more alternatives are examined) than that of national policies.

Other examples indicative of the difference in detail required for the formulation of national and sectoral policies pertain to a national high-tension electricity network versus regional electricity networks; specialized hospitals versus regional and local health centers; national parks versus local parks and sports fields.

It is clear that the examination of interrelationships plays a major role in the planning at the sectoral level. For instance, an addition to the transportation network of a country, created as a consequence of the planning of new industries in a given area, will eventually affect the distribution of other activities and population through the increased accessibility of certain regions. This secondary development will depend on the layout of the infrastructure constructed which, in turn, will create the need for new additions to the technical infrastructure.

Sound planning calls for the integration of economic and physical planning as well as insight into the interrelationships themselves. Let us consider, for example, the analysis of the expansion of port capacity in a region that has two ports. Questions to be answered during this analysis include the following. Is it necessary to extend both ports in order to obtain more capacity, or only one of them? Or is it better to build a new one? If more capacity is desirable, does this mean more quay length or can the same goal be reached by more efficient utilization of the existing facilities? Answers to these questions call for the examination of available and planned hinterland activities and connections, topographical considerations, and considerations of a purely technical nature. What is the stimulating effect of better port facilities on the region's agricultural production? Will new production only be induced if projects and measures of a more direct agricultural nature are designed simultaneously? This depends on parameters such as quality of the soil, possibilities for irrigation, and the capabilities of the local farming population. Together with the analysis of possible other facets, final recommendations are made. It is hoped that they are not only beneficial to the region, but also will conform to national and sectoral objectives.

The establishment of sectoral strategies includes the determination of guidelines for allocating resources to specific sectoral investment projects and programs. Rules 1 and 2 of Section 4 of Chapter 6 can be applied for this purpose. A disadvantage of Rule 2, however, is that it is not very effective in identifying differences in returns during the early or later years of a project's expected life. That is, Project A may have a higher net present value (NPV) or internal rate of return than Project B, but an advantage of Project B over Project A is that high returns are anticipated during the early years of its life. The latter aspect, which is important if a country's national objectives include maximization of output, can only be considered by examining the cash flows of individual projects.

The allocation of resources to specific projects may also be performed by ranking the sectoral objectives in order of importance, followed by a project ranking in order of importance under each objective. Thus, the most important objective is assigned the highest number, and the project which maximizes a particular objective is assigned the highest number under that objective. The method supposes that intangible benefits are more easily considered by ranking them and costs in preference order rather than assigning an absolute value to intangible benefits. The method may be extended by attempting to assign a probability of implementation to each alternative.

The ranking of objectives and projects in the above manner has been applied to a number of urban development and urban transportation projects. There is, however, no specific reason why it cannot be used in other sectors of the economy.

The allocation of resources to specific projects may also be done with the goals achievement evaluation, which uses various methods to weigh the objectives and the contributions of the groups of people directly affected by the projects to the alternatives under each objective. Relative weights may be obtained by (1) sampling persons in affected groups, (2) holding a general community referendum, (3) obtaining views of community power structure, (4) holding public hearings, (5) analyzing the pattern of previous public hearings, and (6) asking the decision makers.

The choice of the aforementioned methods for allocating resources to specific projects depends primarily on a country's limitations and national objectives. For instance, a country with limited financial resources may wish to apply Rules 1 and 2. However, the goals achievement evaluation may be more appropriate for a member of the Organization of Petroleum Exporting Countries, since these countries have a lower cost of capital than most other nations. Naturally, the methods can also be used in sequence; differences in final selections obtained by them may then be resolved by considering all aspects—NPVs, internal rates of return, costs, importance of objectives, and contributions to the realization of objectives.

The best way to examine projects that are strongly dependent on each other is to consider them as a single investment. Two projects are interdependent if, for example, they share common costs or are mutually reinforcing in generating income.

In our discussion of sectoral objectives, we observed that adjustments and modifications in national objectives, policies, and strategies are likely to be introduced after the formulation of sectoral objectives. Likewise, the formulation of national policies and strategies and the formulation of sectoral policies and strategies are an iterative procedure. That is, after the formulation of sectoral policies and strategies, we should check whether these call for modifications in national policies and strategies.

The described preparation of economic development plans is based on the planning-in-stages approach that was originally developed by Tinbergen (see "Suggestions for Further Reading"). There are, however, slight differences in Tinbergen's approach and the one discussed above. Tinbergen distinguishes a macro phase, a sectoral phase, and a project phase. Thus, he does not explicitly mention the determination of the opportunities and constraints for further progress as a separate phase. In addition, the project phase is, in the approach described here, considered as a part of the formulation of sectoral strategies.

Finally, in the macro phase, Tinbergen emphasizes the choice of a growth target for the national income in view of a nation's savings potential, the possibilities of obtaining foreign capital, the implications for the balance of payments, and so on. In the sectoral phase, the expansion of production by sector and by region is determined, based on the increase in national income determined in the macro phase, the corresponding increase in demand within the country, the comparative advantage of the country with regard to the international sectors, the differences in production costs among regions, the transportation costs between the regions within the country as well as to and from abroad, and finally the regional income targets which are among the targets of economic policy. In the project phase, Tinbergen selects projects in accordance with the planned expansion and location of their corresponding sectors. Generally, Tinbergen's approach requires more detailed statistics than our approach. Naturally, requirements regarding reliable statistics may pose problems in developing countries.

Both Tinbergen's approach and the one described here are the top-down approach—that is, we start with the formulation of national objectives and, via the formulation of national policies and strategies and sectoral objectives, policies, and strategies, we allocate resources to individual projects. Alternatively, we could follow the bottom-up approach by which we start our planning at the local and regional level, with projects and plans which are then coordinated and possibly adjusted at the national level.

The difference between the top-down and bottom-up approaches is basically one of philosophy about the structure of society and the way it should be developed. In the former approach, the planners are primarily concerned about the consistency of the national model and wish to induce all lower levels to follow in such a manner that the national objectives are served best. The national planners act as the masters, while all others are executives. In the bottom-up approach, the planners are primarily concerned about building up their localities and regions, the need for local employment, housing, transportation, education, and medical care. This should not be construed, however, as suggesting that the planners of the top-down approach do not have these aspects in mind. It is merely a difference of emphasizing different aspects of the planning process.

An advantage of the bottom-up approach is that planners are likely to be closer to the reality of the world in which specific things are needed to improve the well-being of their area. However, there is no reason for the top-down approach to neglect careful project preparation, taking into account all relevant and specific regional, local, and sectoral aspects, and to neglect the regional and local authorities' participation in the detailed planning of their own area. These authorities should be encouraged to bring in the specific factors that are frequently not considered at the national planning level.

A disadvantage of the bottom-up approach is the danger of ending up with a national development plan with many inconsistencies since local and regional planners are likely to be only concerned with the well-being of their area. It should also be noted that the bottom-up approach may not be feasible in a country with a shortage of well-trained economic and physical planners.

The aggregational treatment of the planning-in-stages scheme sometimes leads to unsatisfactory results, regardless whether it follows the top-down or bottom-up approach. This may particularly be the case if in one region the problems have completely different characteristics than in another region. Consequently, it would be hazardous to consider only aggregate differences in the structures of regions. Regional planning may be preferred in such situations.

Regional planning emphasizes where an addition should be made to capacity, in which sector, and at what time. Two regional planning approaches may be distinguished. One approach considers simultaneously the allocation of resources to sectors and regions. It indicates the timing of such allocations together with preferences for certain regions, but it does not indicate the exact location of new production capacities. The other approach consists of models for a single industry for multiple regions. Thus, spatial location is considered in much greater detail than sectoral interdependencies. The main difference between regional planning and the planning-in-stages is that the former form of planning explicitly takes into account interregional and regional flows of commodities and transportation costs, which is normally not done in the latter form.

Regional planning can also be effective in countries with a large migration from rural areas to the cities. This migration may result from the introduction of compulsory education in rural areas which largely promotes demand for jobs in which the acquired knowledge can be profitably employed, but which are scarcely available in these areas. A disadvantage of regional planning is that there is a tendency for concentration of growth in highly developed regions, which will tend to increase differences in the level of development between regions.

SUGGESTIONS FOR FURTHER READING

Beenhakker, A. *A Kaleidoscopic Circumspection of Development Planning*. Rotterdam, Holland: Rotterdam University Press, 1973.

Beenhakker, H. L. *Capital Investment Planning for Management and Engineering*. Rotterdam, Holland: Rotterdam University Press, 1975.

Beenhakker, H. L., S. Carapetis, L. Crowther, and S. Hertel. *Rural Transport Services: A Guide to Their Planning and Implementation*. Boulder, CO: Westview Press, 1987.

Friedman, L. S. *Microeconomic Policy Analysis*. New York: McGraw-Hill Publishing Company, 1984.

Fruhunan, W., W. C. Kester, S. P. Mason, T. R. Piper, and R. S. Ruback. *Case Problems in Finance*. Boston: Richard D. Irwin, 1992.

Mennes, L. B. M., J. Tinbergen, and J. G. Waardenburg. *The Element of Space in Development Planning*. Amsterdam, Holland: North-Holland Publishing Co., 1969.

Zitarelli, D. E., and R. F. Coughlin. *Finite Mathematics with Applications*. New York: Saunders College Publishing, 1992.

CHAPTER 8

Cost Minimization Problems

Take care of the pence, and the pounds will take care of themselves.
                                                    —Benjamin Franklin

This chapter considers cost minimization problems related to leasing decisions, replacement and expansion investments, sequential decision problems, and costs of transportation. These problems have one feature in common, namely, that the economic justification for maintaining the function of a capital asset or obtaining the function of a potential asset has already been shown.

In the case of leasing decisions, the question is whether the effective ownership of an asset should be obtained by leasing or outright purchase. The concept of replacement implies that one wishes to maintain the function of an existing capital asset, most probably the physical capacity of a facility or machine. The question is whether we should replace the existing facility or machine in view of more modern and efficient models available on the market and/or high operating and maintenance costs of the present equipment due to old age. Expansion investments call for the analysis of optimal expansion policies for an anticipated growth in demand. Thus, the economic objective is the minimization of the present value of the total costs to meet this growing demand. Sequential decision problems are analyzed with the help of decision trees. The transportation algorithm is introduced to select routes so as to allocate the production of various plants to a number of terminal points with a minimal total cost.

Lease-or-buy and allied problems are relatively simple. Because these problems frequently occur, they are likely to be of interest to many readers. The discussion of leasing and purchasing in Section 1 shows the interrelationship between the economic analysis of projects and financing problems.

The main purpose of Section 2 is to compare advantages and disadvantages of various replacement methods available both in the literature and in practice. Many businesses are faced with the problem of deciding which method to use. This problem is aggravated by the fact that most of the replacement methods are treated in isolation in the literature, while underlying assumptions are frequently not clearly stated.

Section 3 focuses on the problem of deciding when to undertake a major expansion of production, marketing, or other facilities. It does so by applying the concept of marginal analysis.

Section 4 demonstrates the use of decision trees in sequential decision problems. We will argue that if today's decisions affect tomorrow's decisions, then tomorrow's decisions have to be examined before we can act rationally today.

Section 5 discusses the problem of how to ship quantities from supply to demand centers such that the total cost of transport is minimized.

As mentioned elsewhere in this book, the type of analysis used in this chapter may be labeled cost-effectiveness analysis rather than cost-benefit analysis. The ensuing presentation is not an exhaustive treatment of cost minimization problems associated with capital investments. In fact, the simplex method of Chapter 7 is an example of a procedure applicable to other cost minimization problems. The sections of this chapter, which can be read independently, deserve a separate treatment in view of their frequent occurrence in the private or public sectors.

1. LEASING AND PURCHASING

The basic idea of leasing is to avoid tying up capital in equipment if it can be used more profitably in other ways. Office space, warehouses, transportation equipment such as trucks and railroad cars, automatic data processing systems, and other pieces of equipment may be either leased or purchased.

In our discussion of leasing versus purchasing, we will assume that an organization has already shown the economic justification for obtaining effective use of an asset by one of these two means. Most lease-or-buy decisions concern unequal periods of lease and of ownership. For instance, a firm may purchase a warehouse with an economically useful life of 50 years, or it may be offered a lease of the warehouse for only 15 years. These alternatives can be compared by reducing them to a common time period. Either the lease period or the economic life can be used for the common time period. In the former case we estimate the value of ownership of the asset after the lease period (15 years in the above example), while in the latter case we consider the likely costs of leasing the asset for the period of its economic life. Both approaches should result in the same decision.

Except for differences in the lease period and economic life and effects of taxation, there is no significant difference between owning and leasing the same asset over the same period. That is, the resale value of both lease and freehold are closely related over time. The advantage of avoiding risk associated with the residual value of an asset at the end of the lease is usually negligible for lease periods of more than 15 to 20 years. Naturally, this residual value may be affected by the asset's suitability in later years compared to more modern assets then possibly existing, but the discounted value of this change in suitability is likely to be small. The examples of problems involving decisions of leasing and purchasing, which are presented later in this section, indicate that effects of taxation can be significant. These effects relate to tax deductible lease expenses and tax allowances for depreciation on an asset which is owned rather than leased.

It is important to emphasize that the difference in risk between leasing and buying is negligible since lessors frequently overemphasize the advantage of reduced risk to a potential lessee. Normally, a lessor company will not be able to accept the risks of obsolescence at a cost lower than that incurred by a lessee. In fact, in many circumstances it can be assumed that this cost is higher for the lessor since the assets in question reflect a proportion of his capital employed, which is much larger than the corresponding proportion of the lessee who only uses these assets for normal business purposes. Consequently, the lessor is likely to require a higher risk premium per asset for obsolescence. The cost of accepting risk of obsolescence will only be lower for the lessor than the lessee, if the former has an advantage of economics-of-scale or skill and/or cheaper finance, or if he has lower profitability requirements. For instance, a dealer who has an agency with a large manufacturer, and obtains his equipment 20% cheaper than the public, may be able to also hire out this equipment on favorable terms.

Leasing may affect a company's ability to raise capital in a different way than buying. Companies sometimes sell a specific asset and subsequently lease it in order to free capital for other investment purposes. Leasing itself puts less burden on long-term debt limitations. On the other hand, the assets of many lease-or-buy alternatives are often of a highly marketable nature and, if purchased, can be used to raise substantial amounts of debt capital in the form of mortgage debentures secured on these assets. We should note, however, that in many cases the securing of debt capital on specific assets does not mean that a firm can raise more loan capital than with other forms of debt financing (Chapter 5, Section 2). This is clear since an additional debt secured on specific assets and occurring on a firm's balance sheet is likely to reduce the amount of debt the firm can raise with other forms of financing. In other words, a specific debt affects financial ratios (Chapter 1, Section 5) in the same manner as any other long-term debt.

In some situations, it is possible, however, to raise additional debt capital with the purchase of an asset, rather than its leasing. For instance, debt capital raised as a specific charge on assets may be the main source of debt capital to a specific firm that has inadequate financial standing for other forms of debt financing.

It is of interest to note that the attitude to lease commitments differs from one country to another. In the United States, where summary statements of lease commitments must be disclosed to the Securities and Exchange Commission, the security analysts tend to consider a firm leasing an asset as one in the joint operation of buying it and raising capital to pay for it. Thus, leasing in the United States does not necessarily mean the release of capital for other investment purposes. In fact, the existence of extensive lease commitments may have adverse effects on a firm's credit status, since the fixed nature of lease obligations may be held to be an impairment of the security which the firm can offer to other direct lenders.

Leasing may, however, offer a means of increasing the debt of a company beyond what would normally be possible by means of direct debt raising in a country like England, where companies are under no legal obligation to reveal their lease commitments. Naturally, we should recall that particulars other than summary statements of lease commitments and financial ratios, namely, a firm's past record and future prospects, play a role in a firm's ability to raise debt capital.

Our discussion of the possible effects of leasing or purchasing on debt financing illustrates the importance of recognizing the connection between the financing and the economic evaluation of some capital investments. Let us now consider the economic aspects in more detail. The cost savings associated with purchasing are principally the lease commitments saved. Cash flows related to the leasing and buying alternatives are usually known with a high degree of certainty. The following example illustrates these points.

Suppose a firm, which owns a warehouse, is considering selling it and leasing it back from the potential purchaser. This type of transaction, which is a means of raising capital for the firm in question, is common in the United States. The lease is for 30 years, after which the residual value of the warehouse will be negligible. The potential purchaser has a long-term development plan for the site of the warehouse, and plans to demolish it after 30 years. He offers a price of $1,120,000 and a flat rent of $174,000 per year during the 30 years. The lease-back arrangement stipulates that the firm will be responsible for repairs and maintenance.

To examine whether the offer of the potential purchaser is attractive to the firm, we note that the retaining of the warehouse by the firm essentially means that it is foregoing the sale price of $1,120,000 in order to "save" rents of $174,000 per year (after tax). For simplicity of exposition, we first assume that the present value of the tax allowances that arise with the specific depreciation method applicable to the warehouse is negligible.

Computation of the internal rate of return of the "investment" of $1,120,000 to make annual savings of $174,000 (after tax) poses no new problems. Assuming a corporation tax of 48%, paid 12 months in arrears, the internal rate of return R is found with the following equation:

$$1,120,000 = [1 - 0.48 \text{ sppwf } (R\%, 1)] \text{ pwf } (R\%, 30) (174,000)$$

Note that the pwf ($R\%$, 30) is the present worth factor used to transform the annual payments of $174,000 over a period of 30 years into an equivalent present value (Appendix 1). We assume that the annual payments are made at the end of each year. The expression within the square brackets is the effective net of tax factor. A corporation tax of 48% amounts to an effective tax rate of sppwf ($R\%$, 1) if the average delay in tax payments is one year. The delay in tax payments is taken into account simply by multiplying the pre-tax flows by [1 − 0.48 sppwf ($R\%$, 1)] to convert them to their net of tax amounts.

The internal rate of return R is the only unknown in the above equation and can, therefore, be computed. It is about 7%. This is the return from the "investment" (foregoing the sale price) of $1,120,000 resulting in lease commitments saved if the firm retains the warehouse. The firm should sell the warehouse if its weighted average cost of capital is below 7%. Another way of looking at the offer of the potential purchaser is by observing that the firm could afford to pay up to 7% to raise the capital from another source. It is noted that the transaction can also be evaluated on the basis of equity cash flows. In fact, this may be preferable since the cost savings associated with the purchasing alternative are principally the lease commitments saved, which are known with certainty for a relatively long period from the terms being offered by the potential purchaser.

For simplicity of exposition, we assumed that the present value of the tax allowances that arise with the specific depreciation method applicable to the warehouse is negligible. Inclusion of tax allowances can be done with the help of present value expressions like expressions (3) or (4) of Appendix 5. That is, if the firm forfeits significant tax allowances for depreciation on the warehouse by selling it, then we should deduct their present value from the purchasing price of $1,120,000. The following example illustrates the use of expressions like the aforementioned ones in the evaluation of leasing and purchasing alternatives.

Suppose a firm has a choice of buying a small store for $400,000 or leasing it for 20 years at a rent of $60,000, payable annually in arrears. The lease arrangement stipulates that the firm will be responsible for repairs and maintenance. Annual rent payments are a deductible expense for tax purposes, while the tax allowance for depreciation on the store is according to the straight-line depreciation method. A corporation tax is assumed to be 48%, paid one year in arrears. The firm expects that with normal expansion activities in the future, the store will be too small after 20 years and, therefore, will be sold. The sales price of the store 20 years hence is estimated at $300,000, while tax consequences of this sale are negligible. The firm is unable to raise a significant amount of debt capital on the building; consequently, the purchase is to be entirely financed by equity capital with a cost of 8% after tax. Should the firm lease or buy the store?

The purchase price of $400,000 is considered as a cost-saving investment which saves annual lease payments of $60,000 (after tax) for 20 years and gives rise to a final capital gain of $300,000 at the end of the twentieth year from the sale of the building. The internal rate of return R of this investment can be established from the following equation:

$$400,000 = [1 - 0.48 \text{ sppwf}(R\%, 1)] \text{ pwf}(R\%, 20)(60,000) \\ + (300,000) \text{ sppwf}(R\%, 20) + P''$$

where P'' = the present value of tax allowances that arise with the straight-line depreciation method (see expression (4) of Appendix 5). The firm should buy the store if the value of R is larger than 8%.

Naturally, the net present value (NPV) index rather than the internal rate of return can also be used. The present value of the after-tax cash savings related to the purchasing route is:

$$\text{NPV} = [1 - 0.48 \text{ sppwf}(8\%, 1)] \text{ pwf}(8\%, 20)(60,000) \\ + (300,000) \text{ sppwf}(8\%, 20) + P'' - 400,000$$

where P'' is as defined above (the interest rate i of the expression for P'' in Appendix 5 is now 8%). The purchasing alternative is preferable if this expression results in a positive value.

2. REPLACEMENT INVESTMENTS

The equipment replacement situation involves comparing an existing or "defender" piece of equipment to one or several "challenger" pieces of equipment. Naturally, the concepts of replacement investments are not necessarily limited to equipment or machinery, but may also include capital assets such as warehouses or office buildings.

In replacement situations, it is preferable to think of the function of an asset rather than the asset as the entity which is replaced. That is, milling machines are not replaced by milling machines, but rather milling capacity is replaced by milling capacity. For instance, three new machines may replace six old machines with no change in normal output since technical changes in equipment frequently impinge upon the capacity of equipment to do work. Depending on the setting, the replacement decision has been framed with deterministic or stochastic inputs. For reasons of brevity, the replacement models of this section are only discussed for deterministic inputs. It is noted, however, that the various procedures for treatment of uncertainties and risks, which have been discussed in Section 5 of Chapter 6, are also applicable to investment decisions involving the minimization of costs.

In this section we will analyze in detail the assumptions underlying each replacement method, and compare the accuracy and simplicity of the methods. In the absence of such an evaluation, a prospective user of a replacement method has little basis for judging the relative desirability of using one method over another under various circumstances. Table 8.1 summarizes the assumptions made in the replacement models to be discussed in this section. As we will see, the models are

Table 8.1
Assumptions of Various Replacement Models

1. Expected service lives and salvage values of both defender and challenger are ignored.	6. The salvage values of defender and challenger are constant.
2. Current market value of the defender is ignored.	7. The expected service lives of defender and challenger are constant.
3. Cost of capital is ignored.	8. The choice of the expected remaining service life of the defender has no influence on the purchasing price, salvage value and service life of the challenger.
4. The effects of technological changes on demand for the challenger's output are ignored.	
5. The equipment decreases in value at a uniform rate.	

not based on all of the eight assumptions of this table, but rather on some combinations of them. Generally, a specific model is easier to work with if the number of assumptions is large and/or the degree of deviation from real-world situations implied by each assumption is higher. Alternatively, the more assumptions we relax, the more we approach an optimal situation. We will discuss these assumptions before reviewing the various replacement methods.

Assumptions

The assumption related to ignoring expected service lives and salvage values of defender and challenger should be avoided since two investment proposals that generate the same income over an arbitrarily preselected period of time will appear to be equally attractive, even though the life of one may significantly exceed the life of the other. It is also not desirable to ignore the current market value of the defender, if it is significant.

The assumption of ignoring the cost of capital facilitates the computations, since it avoids the use of the discounting formulas of Appendix 1. Approximate solutions based on this assumption can only be regarded as valid ones if there is not much of a disparity between the expected service lives and annual costs of the two alternatives considered—defender and challenger.

It is difficult to incorporate the effects of technological changes on demand for the challenger's output in a replacement model. An explicit analysis of demand would be required to include such effects. In addition, workable methods can only be obtained by introducing a large number of other assumptions associated with both the demand analysis and the replacement evaluation.

The assumption of a uniform rate of decrease in equipment value is frequently made in replacement models that ignore the cost of capital. These two assumptions enable us to say that if the purchasing price and the salvage value of the challenger are $\$P$ and $\$S$, respectively, then the average investment is $\frac{1}{2}(\$P + \$S)$. Such a crude approach should only be followed if there is not much difference in the expected service lives and the percentages of the purchasing prices which represent the salvage values of the challenger and defender.

The assumptions of constant salvage values and service lives are often made in replacement models and are likely to have little effect on the choice indicated by them. Assuming that the choice of the expected remaining service life of the defender has no influence on the purchasing price, salvage value, and service life of the challenger is reasonable unless significant technological changes and/or price changes other then those due to general inflation are expected in the near future.

The same example problem will be used in the discussion of the replacement methods in order to facilitate a comparison of them. The information about the defender and challenger of the example problem is given in Table 8.2. It is noted that, due to the specific assumptions made, we do not need all of the information of this table for each replacement method.

Payback Method

As explained in Section 4 of Chapter 6, the payback method is based upon the estimation of the payback period of an investment. The underlying assumptions are assumptions 1 through 4 of Table 8.1. Applied to replacement investments, the payback period is equal to the quotient of the challenger's purchasing price divided by its annual savings over the defender's use.

Item 6 of Table 8.2 indicates that the annual savings of the challenger amount to $800. With a challenger's purchasing price of $17,000 of Table 8.2, we obtain a payback period of 21 years. The proposed replacement is accepted if this payback period is less than a predetermined number.

It is of interest to note that some authors suggest that payback be used as a constraint in all capital budgeting decisions. Their suggestion is primarily based on the method's ease of application. However, simplicity alone does not justify application as the errors inherent in the payback method are substantial. Payback's continued use, even as a constraint in capital budgeting decisions, cannot be recommended. It is unfortunate that several studies indicate that this method is the most widely used equipment replacement technique.

Equivalent Annual Cost and Present Worth Methods

These methods are based on the principles of Appendix 1, and their underlying assumptions are assumptions 4, 6, and 7 of Table 8.1. Thus, in the case of the equivalent annual cost method, we express all relevant costs and salvage values (that is, negative costs) of challenger and defender in uniform annual equivalents. Next, these equivalents are compared. That is, if the annual equivalent cost of the challenger is higher than that of the defender, we should keep the old equipment. We should discard it if the challenger's annual equivalent cost is lower than that of the defender.

Using the information of items 1 through 7 of Table 8.2, we compute the following.

Table 8.2
Defender and Challenger Information of Example Problem[1]

Item No.	Description of Information	Information Defender	Information Challenger
1.	Expected service life (n)	10 years	12 years
2.	Present age[2]	9 years	-
3.	Purchasing price (P)	-	$17,000
4.	Current market value	$2,700	-
5.	Salvage value at end of service life (S)	$2,300	$ 2,444
6.	Constant net annual operating costs (D)	$5,900	$ 5,100
7.	Effective interest rate (i)	10%	10%
8.	Decline in defender's salvage value, $s(t)$, in year 9	$ 100	
	year 10	$ 200	
	year 11	$ 400	
9.	Defender's cost of operation, $D_0(t)$, in year 9	$5,900	
	year 10	$6,000	
	year 11	$6,200	

[1] Notice that the data of items 6 and 9 pertain to different assumptions about annual operating costs. Similarly, the data of item 8 cannot be considered simultaneously with the defender's data of items 1 and 5.
[2] Remaining expected service life of defender is one per year (= $10 - 9$).

Challenger's equivalent annual cost:

annual equivalent of purchasing price = $17,000 crf(10%, 12) = $17,000 (0.14676)		$2,495
constant net annual operation costs		$5,100
	Total	$7,595
annual equivalent of salvage value = $2,444 sff(10%, 12) = $2,444 (0.04676)		$ 114
Challenger's equivalent annual cost		$7,481

Defender's equivalent annual cost:

annual equivalent of defender's current market price = $2,700 crf(10%, 1) = $2,700 (1.100)		$2,970
constant net annual operating costs		$5,900
	Total	$8,870
annual equivalent of salvage value = $2,300 sff(10%, 1) = $2,300 (1.00000)		$2,300
Defender's equivalent annual cost		$6,570

We conclude that the old equipment should not yet be replaced, since $7,481 exceeds $6,570.

Naturally, the equivalent annual cost method can also be used if the annual operating costs are not constant. In this case, we calculate first the total present value of all the annual operating costs by multiplying each annual cost by its respective single payment present worth factor; next, the sum of these present values is obtained. This sum is now converted in an equivalent annual cost.

The present worth method converts all relevant costs and salvage values (that is, negative costs) of challenger and defender in present values. These values are then compared; the old piece of equipment is kept if the present value of costs of the challenger is higher than that of the defender.

Compromise Method

This method, which is based on assumptions 3, 4, 5, 6, and 7 of Table 8.1, is a compromise between the payback method and the equivalent annual cost or present worth method. It avoids much of the inaccuracy of the former method, while the computations are easier and less time consuming than those of the latter two methods.

According to the compromise method, we approximate the components of equipment costs (depreciation, interest, and operating expenses) by averages over the expected or remaining expected life of the equipment. With the information of items 1 through 7 of Table 8.2, we have the following.

Challenger's average annual costs:

depreciation = 1/12 ($17,000 − $2,444)	$1,213
interest expense = (0.10)½($17,000 + $2,444)	$ 972
constant net annual operating costs	$5,100
Challenger's average annual costs	$7,285

Defender's average annual costs:

depreciation = $2,700 − $2,300	$ 400
interest expense = (0.10)½($2,700 + $2,300)	$ 250
constant net annual operating costs	$5,900
Defender's average annual costs	$6,550

Thus, the defender's replacement would be premature.

Note that the interest expense is computed by multiplying the average investment cost by the annual interest rate. The average investment cost is the sum of the initial cost and salvage value divided by two. The computation of this average is based on the simplifying assumption that equipment decreases in value at a uniform rate.

An average annual operating cost is to be computed if the annual operating costs are not constant. For instance, if the annual operating costs of a defender are \$5,800 and \$6,000 during its remaining life of two years, then its average annual operating cost is ½ (\$5,800 + \$6,000) = \$5,900.

The equivalent annual cost and compromise methods do not always identify the same most attractive course of action. A different identification can particularly be expected if there is a great disparity in the expected service lives of challenger and defender, and if their respective total annual costs do not differ very much.

Incremental Cost Method

The replacement methods just described consist of a comparison of costs of challenger and defender and a subsequent decision about the replacement in question. The incremental cost method, which is based on assumptions 2, 3, 4, 6, 7, and 8 of Table 8.1, consists of the determination of the optimal year of replacement. It is noted that assumptions 6 and 7 only apply to the challenger since the replacement decision is based on the defender's incremental costs. The optimal year is established with the help of the following expression.

$$C(n_0) = \sum_{t=1}^{t=n_0} [s(t)+D_0(t)]+(T-n_0)(P-S+E)/n \tag{1}$$

$$0 \le n_0 \le T$$

where

C = cost of maintaining capacity during the entire planning horizon (function of n_0)
n_0 = the number of additional years the defender is kept
n = expected service life of the challenger (in years)
T = planning horizon in years
$s(t)$ = decline in the salvage value of the defender in year t
$D_0(t)$ = defender's cost of operation in year t
P = challenger's purchasing price
S = salvage value of the challenger
E = total costs of challenger's operation over its service life of n years.

According to expression (1), the defender contributes to the total cost during the first n_0 years of the planning horizon. Notice that $n_0 = 0$ indicates an immediate replacement, while $n_0 = T$ indicates no replacement during the planning horizon. The defender's salvage value depends on the replacement year and is most likely a decreasing function of time. We only consider the decline of this salvage value, or $s(t)$, since expression (1) is based on the incremental costs pertaining to the replacement decision. The defender's cost in year t is $[s(t) + D_0(t)]$. This expression must be summed for the first n_0 years if the defender is kept for that long a period.

The expression $(P - S + E)/n$ represents the average annual cost of the challenger over its expected life of n years. The choice of n_0 determines which portion of this life will fall inside the planning horizon of T years. It is, therefore, reasonable to include the same portion of the challenger's lifetime costs in the cost criterion.

Expression (1) represents the cost of maintaining capacity during the planning horizon. The optimal year of replacement is the year for which the defender's incremental annual cost $s(t) + D_0(t)$ exceeds for the first time the average annual cost of the challenger. The optimal value of n_0, which is indicative for the optimal year of replacement, may be found by inspection. The following example illustrates this.

With the challenger's information of items 1, 3, 5, and 6 of Table 8.2, we compute $(P - S + E)/n$, or [\$17,000 − \$2,444 + 12(\$5,100)]/12 = \$6,313. The defender's information of items 8 and 9 of Table 8.2 indicates that the value of $[s(t) + D_0(t)]$ exceeds for the first time the challenger's average annual cost of \$6,313 for $n_0 = 3$ since $[s(t = 2) + D_0(t = 2)] = \$6,200$ and $[s(t = 3) + D_0(t = 3)] = \$6,600$. Consequently, the optimal value of n_0 is 3 years.

Discussion

There is no single answer to the question "Which of the reviewed replacement methods should we use?" The answer depends on the number and type of assumptions we can make in a particular situation without diverting too much from real-world conditions; the availability of parameters required for a specific replacement model; and the required manpower and time available to pursue the more complicated and accurate methods. It should be emphasized, however, that a prerequisite to the use of any of the methods to guide replacement decisions is a clear understanding of the assumptions of the particular method by the person who makes or recommends the decision.

The payback and compromise methods offer the same computational ease, but the latter one avoids much of the inaccuracy of the former one. Consequently, we cannot recommend the use of the payback method.

The equivalent annual cost and present worth methods are equivalent in terms of accuracy and simplicity. The compromise method has computational advantages over these methods, since it avoids the use of compound interest factors. The use of the compromise method is only recommended if there is no great disparity in the expected lives of challenger and defender, and if a significant difference between their respective total annual costs exists.

The incremental cost method differs from the aforementioned methods in that its use results in the establishment of the optimal year for the defender's replacement, rather than a comparison of the defender's and challenger's costs, and a subsequent decision whether replacement should, or should not, take place now.

3. EXPANSION INVESTMENTS

To explain the concept of expansion investments, we will first consider a simple example. Suppose a beer company is approaching the limit of capacity in its existing plant. As sales expand, consideration must be given to establishing a new plant nearer to distant markets. We have a choice of (a) establishing a new plant away from the existing one, and (b) continuing output at the existing plant without increasing its capacity through overtime and shift working. We do not consider increasing the capacity of the existing plant because alternative (a) has a significant advantage of lower cost of transportation.

The annual costs of the old plant resulting from output X for the area to be covered by the new plant can be represented by:

$$aX + b \qquad (2)$$

where

a = incremental cost of producing and transporting the beer to sales centers, in dollars per thousand gallons
b = a fixed cost per year, in dollars
X = annual output for the area to be covered by the new plant, in thousands of gallons.

Similarly, the annual cost for output X of the new plant can be given by:

$$cX + d \qquad (3)$$

where

c = incremental cost of producing and transporting the beer to sales centers, in dollars per thousand gallons
d = a fixed cost per year, in dollars
X = as defined above.

Notice that the difference in a and b, on the one hand, and c and d, on the other, is that the former notation applies to beer produced in the old plant (with overtime and shift work), while the latter notation refers to beer produced in the new plant.

If the production of beer by the new plant is postponed by one year, the firm will be involved in the same capital outlays but all postponed one year. Let us call the present capital outlay net of tax reliefs of the new plant C (see Appendix 5 for the computation of tax reliefs). The savings from postponed erection of the new plant for one year is $C - C/(1 + i) = Ci/(1 + i)$, where i is the firm's weighted average cost of capital. The expression $Ci/(1 + i)$ is simply the interest savings arising one year hence on the present cost of all future capital outlays involved in establishing the new plant. The total cost savings from postponing establishment of the new plant for one year is then:

$$cX + d + Ci/(1 + i). \qquad (4)$$

From the concept of marginal analysis (Section 1 of Chapter 7), we know that the minimal cost occurs where the costs incurred by continuing production on the existing plant are just offset by the cost savings from postponing the new plant for one more year. Consequently, the minimal cost occurs when:

$$aX + b - [cX + d + Ci/(1 + i)] = 0. \qquad (5)$$

Note that the first two terms of equation (5) represent expression (2), the third and fourth terms represent expression (3), while the expression between the square brackets is the one given by expression (4). The only unknown variable in equation (5) is X, the volume of output produced for the year that gives the minimal cost. Solving the equation for X, we obtain:

$$X = [d - b + Ci/(1 + i)]/(a - c). \qquad (6)$$

If the new plant has an appreciable gestation period, this can be allowed for by compounding the capital cost C forward to the date at which the plant comes into effective operation. Thus, if the capital outlays required for the new plant are undertaken over a period of two years before the plant comes into operation, and amount to C_1 and C_2 at the end of the first and second year, respectively, the capital cost is taken as $C_1 (1 + i) + C_2$ instead of C.

It is noted that under the conditions assumed, the optimal output X is in no way affected by time. The new plant should be installed whenever the optimal output is reached, whether it is next year or ten years hence. If inflation is small or affects the various costs of expression (6) in approximately the same manner ("general inflation"), and the timing of the optimal output is not too far into the future (say, 4 or 5 years hence), the margin of error is likely to be small. If these conditions are not satisfied, we could easily expand equation (6) by making a, b, c, d, and C a function of time (similar to making the defender's salvage value and costs of operation a function of time in equation (1) of the incremental cost replacement method discussed in Section 2).

An example of the application of expression (6) is as follows. Suppose the incremental costs a and c in the above given example of our beer company amount to $100.00 and $50.00 per thousand gallons, respectively, and the annual fixed costs b and d are $10,000.00 and $6000.00, respectively. The required capital cost, C, amounts to $2,000,000.00, and the weighted average cost of capital is 10%. The optimal output X is according to expression (6):

$$X = [6000.00 - 10,000.00 + 2,000,000.00(0.10)/1.10]/(100 - 50)$$
$$= 3,556 \text{ thousand gallons.}$$

Future costs of both the old and new plant together will be minimized if the new plant is installed just prior to annual future sales in the area to be covered by the new plant rising to 3,556 thousand gallons. If sales forecasts in this market indicate such a rise in three years' time, this would be the optimal time for having the new plant ready. As sales forecasts are constantly being revised, the estimated optimal date will vary, but no final decision is necessary until sales can be forecast to reach the critical time reduced by whatever period it takes to install the new plant, hire and transfer personnel, and so on. Such a period is typically 12 to 18 months. It is recommended that the calculation of when to expand is not a once-and-for-all calculation indicating a future date at which plans should be put into operation without further consideration in the interim since future sales forecasts do change over time.

Let us now consider a second example in which we determine the optimal date on which to undertake a major expansion of a head office accommodation. Suppose a company owns a mortgaged head office which accommodates 1,500 of its 2,000 staff, while the remaining 500 are scattered in variously located, leased accommodations. Since staff is growing fairly rapidly, the firm has previously acquired a suitable site on which to build an entirely new head office. This new site has a planning permission for an office accommodating 3,000 staff. As the company expects its staff to grow to this number sometime over the next ten years, there appears to be fairly conclusive grounds for building to the maximum permitted size. If this is done prior to the staff expanding to 3,000 people, the company can make arrangements for a suitable proportion of the surplus accommodation to be let out on short-term leases to allow for the building being more fully occupied by the company's existing staff as its numbers grow. The basic data of the problem are summarized in Table 8.3. Given these facts, we will determine the optimal date at which to sell the old building and to build and occupy the new one.

We note that the cost of the site for the new building is not considered in our calculations, since the site has already been acquired and paid for. Its cost is a sunk cost, and sunk costs are normally not to be included in an economic evaluation.

The old office (with a fixed staff of 1,500) has a total annual cost of $190,000, but the remaining 500 staff are maintained elsewhere at a cost of $82,500 or $165 per head. The general formulation of the costs of continuing with the old building is:

$$a(X - Z) + b = aX + b - aZ \qquad (7)$$

where

a = cost per person of leased accommodation (dollars)
b = total annual operating costs (fixed and variable) of the old building (dollars)
X = total number of staff when the new office will be opened
Z = staff in the existing building.

Filling out the values of a, b, and Z in expression (7) gives:

$$aX + b - aZ = 165X + 190,000 - 165(1,500) = 165X - 57,500.$$

Table 8.3
Basic Data Pertaining to the Expansion of Office Accommodation

Description	Costs in dollars (net of tax)	Symbol
Old Building		
Equity funds that will be realized from resale after repaying the outstanding mortgage	2,500,000	
Total operating costs (fixed and variable) with 1,500 staff	190,000	*b*
Cost per person of maintaining 500 additional staff in leased accommodation	165	*a*
New Building		
Total cost (excluding the cost of the site already acquired)	7,000,000	
Mortgage at 6½% before (3½% after) tax repayable in 25 years (assume 50% renewed on same terms at end of first 25 years, making 50 years in all)	6,000,000	
Estimated value at end of 50 years, including site	3,000,000	
Annual costs		
Variable costs per person	20	*c*
Fixed costs	260,000	*d*
Annual rent from leasing of surplus accommodation (average) per person	110	*p*

For the new building, it is assumed that the assets will enable the company to obtain all the debt capital indicated in Table 8.3 as specific debt finance additional to the company's normal debt financing. The weighted average cost of capital is 8%. The net present value of the equity capital cost is as follows:

Total capital outlay	$7,000,000
Plus net present value of future interest and debt repayments	2,844,000
Less	
Total debt inflow from mortgage	− 6,000,000
Net equity realization from sale of old building	− 2,500,000
Net present value of equity cost	$1,344,000

It is noted that the above given value of $2,844,000 represents the present value (at 8%) of 3½% after tax interest on $6,000,000 for 25 years followed by a net debt repayment of $3,000,000, and 3½% after tax interest on $3,000,000 for a further 25 years, concluded by a debt repayment of $3,000,000 which is assumed to be exactly offset by the residual value of the building at that time. Thus, we have:

—present value of 3½% of $6,000,000 per year for first 25 years is 10.675($210,000) = $2,242,000, where the factor 10.675 is the series present worth factor of Appendix 2 (for $i = 8\%$ and $n = 25$);

—present value of the debt repayment of $3,000,000 is 0.146 ($3,000,000) = $438,000, where 0.146 is the single payment present worth factor of Appendix 2 (for $i = 8\%$ and $n = 25$);

—present value of 3½% of $3,000,000 per year for second 25 years, computed as of the end of year 25 is 10.675($105,000) = $1,121,000, and computed as of the beginning of year 1 the present value is 0.146($1,121,000) = $164,000, where 10.675 and 0.146 are as defined above; and

—net present value of future interest and debt repayments is $2,242,000 + $438,000 + $164,000 = $2,844,000.

As we did in the first example, we note that the savings from postponed erection of the new office building is $C - C/(1 + i) = Ci/(1 + i)$, where C is the net present value of equity cost, and i is the weighted average cost of capital. In the above calculation, we established a value of $1,344,000 for C, and the $i = 8\%$, thus, $Ci/(1 + i) = \$1,344,000(0.08)/1.08 = \$99,556$.

The total cost savings from postponing establishment of the new office building for one year can be written as:

$$cX + d + Ci/(1 + i) - p(K - X) = (c + p)X + d + Ci/(1 + i) - pK \qquad (8)$$

where

c = annual variable cost per person of the new building (dollars)
d = fixed costs of the new building (dollars)
p = the average, annual rent (net of tax and allowing for vacancies) from letting surplus accommodation in the new building (dollars per person)
K = capacity of the new building
C, X, i = as defined above.

It is of interest to compare expression (4) of the first example to the above expression (8); the difference is "$- p(K - X)$," which is needed in expression (8) since we do not receive rental income from surplus accommodation in the new building if we postpone its erection by one year.

We note again that from the concept of marginal analysis, we know that the minimal cost occurs when the costs incurred by continued use of the old office are just offset by the cost savings from postponing the new office for one more year. Hence, the minimal cost occurs when:

$$aX + b - aZ - [(c + p)X + d + Ci/(1 + i) - pK] = 0. \qquad (9)$$

We already know that the first three terms of equation (9) are equal to $165X - 57,500$, that $Ci/(1 + i) = 99,556$, and that $K = 3,000$; using $c = 20$, $p = 110$, and $d = 260,000$ as indicated in Table 8.3 results in:

$$165X - 57,500 - 130X - 260,000 - 99,556 + 330,000 = 35X - 87,056$$
$$= 0, \text{ or } X = 2,487 \text{ (say 2,500).}$$

The personnel department predicts that the staff will reach 2,500 four years from now, so that is when the new building will be occupied and the old one sold. The aforementioned discussion does not consider intangibles such as ease of communications, staff morale, and company's prestige, which may be better with the new office building. In order to assess whether the opening of the new office should be advanced in the light of these non-financial considerations, it is important to establish the cost to the company of such departures from the financial optimum. Suppose, for instance, that the personnel department predicts that three years hence staff will reach 2,350. In this case, we can establish the cost of departing from the financial optimum by filling out $X = 2,350$ in expression (9) and keeping the values of the other parameters the same.

4. DECISION TREES

A fundamental problem in the analysis of a net present value (NPV) is dealing with uncertain outcomes. This section introduces the device of decision trees for identifying uncertain cash flows.

Imagine you are considering a new consulting service. You estimate that there is a 60% chance that the demand will be high in the first year. If demand is high in the first year, there is an 80% chance that it will continue to be high over the next six years. If demand is low in the first year, there is a 70% chance that it will continue to be low for the next six years.

Forecast revenue is $90,000 a year during the first two years, and $95,000 a year thereafter if demand is high; if it is low, forecast revenue is $65,000 a year during the first two years, and $70,000 a year thereafter. You have the option to terminate to offer the service in any year, in which case, of course, revenues are zero. Costs other than those of computer hardware and software are forecast at $50,000 a year during the first two years, and $55,000 a year thereafter regardless of demand. These costs can also be terminated in any year. You have a choice on costs of computer hardware and software. That is, one possibility is to buy your own, which involves an initial outlay of $100,000 and no subsequent expenditure while the equipment has an economic life of seven years and no salvage value. The alternative is to rent the hardware and software as

Figure 8.1
Decision Tree for Providing Consulting Service (Thousands of Dollars)

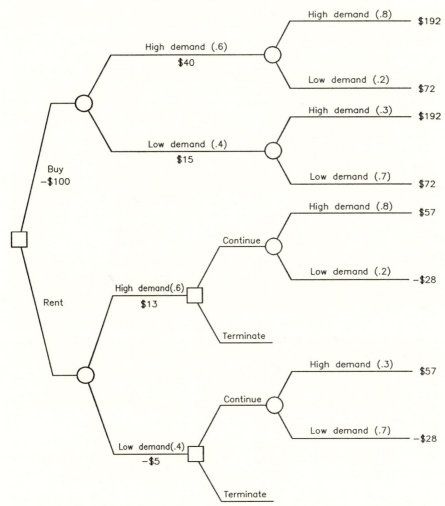

necessary; you estimate that the rental costs amount to 30% of revenues. To keep the presentation simple, we assume that if you do not buy the computer equipment today, you cannot do so later, and if you buy it you cannot resell it. In addition, we assume that there are no taxes. The weighted average cost of capital is 10%. Should you buy the computer equipment or rent it?

In a situation like this one, it helps to draw a decision tree as is done in Figure 8.1. Note that in this figure the various choices are displayed and that a square indicates a decision point or a point in time where a decision has to be made.

For instance, the square on the left side represents the initial decision to buy or rent the computer equipment. Figure 8.1 also indicates whether demand will be high or low, while the probability of a high or low demand is given in parentheses.

We note the following.

a. The probabilities in the second year depend on the first year outcome; for instance, if demand is high in the first year, then there is an 80% chance that it will also be high in the second year, and the chance of high demand in both the first and second years is $0.6 \times 0.8 = 0.48$.

b. If demand is high, income at the end of the first year is $90,000 - $50,000 = $40,000 for the buy-option (not taking into account the initial capital outlay for the time being), and $90,000 - $50,000 - 0.30($90,000) = $13,000 for the rent-option (see Figure 8.1).

c. If demand is low, income at the end of the first year is $65,000 - $50,000 = $15,000 for the buy-option (not taking into account the initial capital outlay for the time being), and $65,000 - $50,000 - 0.30($65,000) = -$5,000 (rounded off) for the rent-option.

d. Since annual costs and revenues remain constant during the last five years of the economic life of the computer equipment, Figure 8.1 gives the decision tree only for the first two years; the figures at the end of the second-year branches represent the NPVs as of the end of the second year.

e. The amount at the end of the second-year branch of Figure 8.1 and related to the high demand occurring during the first two years for the buy-option is computed as follows: $90,000 - $50,000 + 3.791($95,000 - $55,000) = $192,000 (rounded off), where 3.791 = the present worth factor defined in Appendix 1 (given A, find P for $n = 5$ and $i = 10\%$).

f. The other amounts at the end of the second-year branches of Figure 8.1 are computed as follows:

$$\$15,000 \quad + 3.791(\$70,000 - \$55,000) = \$72,000,$$
$$\$13,000 \quad + 3.791(\$40,000 - 0.30 \times \$95,000) = \$57,000, \text{ and}$$
$$-\$5,000 \quad + 3.791(\$15,000 - 0.30 \times \$70,000) = -\$28,000.$$

g. Since the decision of buying the computer equipment is assumed to be irreversible, and the amounts at the end of the second-year branches for the buy-option of Figure 8.1 are all positive, no decision points to either continue or terminate the consulting service is given in the figure.

In the analysis of decision trees, we start at the right side of Figure 8.1 and work our way back to the left side. Thus, in order to decide what to do today, we first decide what to do next year. The only decision to be made next year is whether to terminate the consulting service when following the rent-option for two possible situations, that is, high demand in the first year and low demand in the first year. In the case of high demand, the expected payoff for continuing the service is (probability of high demand × payoff with high demand) + (probability of low demand × payoff with low demand) = (0.8)($57,000) + (0.2)(− $28,000) = $40,000. Thus, it pays to continue the service. In case of low demand in the first year, the expected payoff for continuing the service is (0.3)($57,000) + (0.7)(−$28,000) = −$2,500. Consequently, we should terminate the consulting service in the rent-option if demand is low in the first year.

Having made the decision what to do next year, we determine the NPV of the rent-option as follows:

$$[(0.6)\$13,000 - (0.4)\$5,000]/1.10 + (0.6)[(0.8)\$57,000$$
$$- (0.2)\$28,000]/(1.10)^2 = \$5,300 + \$19,800 = \$25,100.$$

The NPV for the buy-option is:

$$-\$100,000 + [(0.6)\$40,000 + (0.4)\$15,000]/1.10$$
$$+ (0.6)[(0.8)\$192,000 + (0.2)\$72,000]/(1.10)^2$$
$$+ (0.4)[(0.3)\$192,000 + (0.7)\$72,000](1.10)^2 = -\$100,000$$
$$+ \$27,300 + \$83,300 + \$35,700 = \$46,300.$$

Thus, it pays to buy the computer equipment.

The above example is a simplification of the sequential decision problems that financial managers face. The important points it makes, however, is that (a) decision trees are helpful for identifying uncertain cash flows; and (b) if today's decisions affect subsequent decisions, then subsequent decisions have to be examined before one can rationally examine today's. By displaying the links between subsequent decisions, decision trees assist the financial manager in finding the strategy with the highest NPV. There is, however, a problem with decision trees, and that is that they can get complex quickly. For instance, what will you do in the above example if demand is neither high or low but just middling? Or what if there is uncertainty about revenues and costs in the last five years of the above example? We could draw a decision tree covering this expanded set of events and decisions but it would be a large one. Naturally, computers can help to deal with more complex situations.

5. TRANSPORTATION ALGORITHM

As the name indicates, this algorithm, which is a special case of the simplex method (Chapter 7), has been developed to solve transportation problems. It involves the selection of transportation routes so as to allocate the production of various plants to a number of terminal points with a minimal total cost.

In a more formal way, the transportation problem is defined as:

$$\text{Minimize} \sum_{i=1}^{m} \sum_{j=1}^{n} C_{ij} x_{ij} \tag{10}$$

Subject to

$$\sum_{j=1}^{n} x_{i,j} = S_i \qquad \text{for } i = 1, 2, \cdots, m \tag{11}$$

$$\sum_{i=1}^{m} x_{i,j} = D_j \qquad \text{for } j = 1, 2, \cdots, n \tag{12}$$

$$x_{i,j} = 0, 1, 2, \cdots, \qquad \text{for all } i \text{ and } j \tag{13}$$

where

i = index denoting a supply center
j = index denoting a terminal point
m = number of plants or supply centers
n = number of terminal points
$x_{i,j}$ = integer indicating the quantity to be shipped from i to j
$C_{i,j}$ = cost to ship a unit quantity from i to j
S_i = supply of plant i
D_j = demand of terminal point j.

Note that the constraints (11) and (12) ensure that each of the m plants i cannot ship more than their available supply S_i, and that the demands D_j in each of the n terminal points j are to be satisfied, respectively. One plant can ship to one or more terminal points, while one such point can be supplied by one or more plants. The algorithm assumes that all the S_i and D_j are positive integers satisfying the condition that total supply equals total demand.

The transportation algorithm is as follows.

Step 1. Construct a cost-quantity matrix with the typical element $C_{i,j}$ given in the upper left corner of each cell i, j. The matrix also gives the total supply of each plant i and the total demand of each terminal point j in the last column and last row, respectively.

Step 2. Select a feasible initial solution.

Step 3. Check whether the feasible solution can be improved by employing some of the unused routes. This check is performed by considering a simple "loop" for each unused cell; a simple loop has precisely two unit costs in a row and two unit costs in a column and starts with a used cell. Moreover, it contains only one unused cell. The feasible solution cannot be improved if the alternate addition and subtraction of the unit costs corresponding to each loop result in non-positive values. Proceed to Step 4 if the feasible solution can be improved.

Step 4. Improve the feasible solution by entering the largest possible quantity in the empty cell corresponding to the simple loop with the largest positive value. The largest possible quantity is equal to the smallest quantity in the two-element row or two-element column of the simple loop in which the unused cell is located. This entering calls for the adjustment of other cells of the loop; all variables not in the loop remain unchanged. Return to Step 3 after these adjustments have been made.

The following example elucidates the application of the transportation algorithm. Suppose there are three supply centers A, B, and C, with a supply of 6, 1, and 10 tons, respectively. There are four demand centers D, E, F, and G, with a demand of 7, 5, 3, and 2 tons, respectively. We are interested in minimizing the total cost of supplying the demand centers from the supply centers. Table 8.4 shows the costs per unit quantity (per ton) transported from a supply to a demand center and the solution to our transportation problem. Note that the transport cost for shipments from B to E is zero; this is possible if an organization is using excess truck capacity available for such shipments.

Any feasible solution may be selected in Step 2. A simple way to obtain a feasible solution is by application of the northwest rule or an allocation of quantities in the matrix of Step 1 which starts in the northwest corner and proceeds accordingly. Thus, a maximal quantity of 6 is allocated to cell (A, D); next, a maximal quantity of 1 is allocated to cell (B, E); next, a maximal quantity of 3 is allocated to cell (C, F); next, a quantity of 2 is allocated to cell (C, G); finally, to satisfy the total demand in D and E, we allocate quantities of 1 and 4 to cells (C, D) and (C, E), respectively. Note that these maximal quantities are determined by either total supply or total demand constraints.

In Step 3 it does not matter whether we go clockwise or counterclockwise in our alternate additions and subtractions. For example, going counterclockwise in the first loop of the first application of Step 3 would also give 2 (that is, 2 − 3 + 8 − 5). Consideration of a loop starts with a used cell. For instance, in the first application of Step 3, the loop corresponding to cell (A, F), which is the loop through cells (A, D), (C, D), (C, F), and (A, F) starts with cell (A, D), to which a quantity of 6 has been allocated in Step 2. Starting with cell (A, F) would have produced the wrong result ($11 − 2 + 5 − 15 = −1$, instead of $+ 1$). Note that, in the example, each loop has only one unused cell.

Table 8.4 shows that the first application of Step 4 consists of filling out a quantity of 4 in the empty cell corresponding to the loop with the largest positive value (the first loop). This quantity is the largest possible value, since the two-element row and two-element column of the loop in which the empty cell (A, E) is located [the row consisting of cells (A, D) and (A, E) and the column consisting of cells (A, E) and (C, E)] contain the quantities 6 and 4, respectively. The adjustment of other cells consists of subtracting 4 from cell (C, E), adding 4 to cell (C, D), and subtracting 4 from cell (A, D).

The optimal solution of Table 8.4 calls for the shipment of 7, 1, and 2 tons from supply center C to demand centers D, F, and G, respectively; the shipment of one ton from supply center B to demand center F; and the shipment of 5 and 1 tons from supply center A to demand centers E and F, respectively. The total cost of this routing amounts to $100,000 as compared to $112,000 related to the initial feasible solution of Step 2.

Table 8.4
Example of Transportation Algorithm

Unit Costs of Transportation (in thousand dollars):

To From	D	E	F	G
A	2	3	11	7
B	1	0	6	1
C	5	8	15	9

Application of Step 1 results in:

Column Row	D	E	F	G	Total Supply
A	2	3	11	7	6
B	1	0	6	1	1
C	5	8	15	9	10
Total Demand	7	5	3	2	

Application of Step 2 gives:

Column Row	D	E	F	G	Total Supply
A	2 6	3	11	7	6
B	1	0 1	6	1	1
C	5 1	8 4	15 3	9 2	10
Total Demand	7	5	3	2	

Application of Step 3 calls for the consideration of simple loops for each unused cell or cells (A, E), (A, F), (A, G), (B, D), (B, F), and (B, G). The six loops are:

Cell (A, E): 2 - 5 + 8 - 3 = 2
Cell (A, F): 2 - 5 + 15 - 11 = 1
Cell (A, G): 2 - 5 + 9 - 7 = -1
Cell (B, D): 0 - 8 + 5 - 1 = -4
Cell (B, F): 0 - 8 + 15 - 6 = 1

Table 8.4 (continued)

Cell (B, G): $0 - 8 + 9 - 1 = 0$

The values corresponding to the above six loops (2, 1, -1, -4, 1, and 0) are not all nonpositive; consequently, we proceed to Step 4:

Column Row	D		E		F		G		Total Supply
A	2	2	3	4	11		7		6
B	1		0	1	6		1		1
C	5	5	8		15	3	9	2	10
Total Demand		7		5		3		2	

Return to Step 3 to check whether the newly obtained solution can be improved:

Cell (A, F): $2 - 5 + 15 - 11 = 1$
Cell (A, G): $2 - 5 + 9 - 7 = -1$
Cell (B, D): $2 - 3 + 0 - 1 = -2$
Cell (B, F): $15 - 5 + 2 - 3 + 0 - 6 = 3$
Cell (B, G): $9 - 5 + 2 - 3 + 0 - 1 = 2$
Cell (C, E): $5 - 2 + 3 - 8 = -2$

The six values related to these six loops are not all nonpositive. Thus we proceed to Step 4:

Column Row	D		E		F		G		Total Supply
A	2	1	3	5	11		7		6
B	1		0		6	1	1		1
C	5	6	8		15	2	9	2	10
Total Demand		7		5		3		2	

Return again to Step 3 to check whether the previous solution can be improved:

Table 8.4 (continued)

Cell (A, F): 15 - 5 + 2 - 11 = 1
Cell (A, G): 9 - 5 + 2 - 7 = -1
Cell (B, D): 5 - 15 + 6 - 1 = -5
Cell (B, E): 6 - 15 + 5 - 2 + 3 - 0 = -3
Cell (C, E): 5 - 2 + 3 - 8 = -2
Cell (B, G): 9 - 15 + 6 - 1 = -1

These values indicate that we still do not have an optimal solution. Thus, we proceed to Step 4:

Column Row	D	E	F	G	Total Supply
A	²	³ 5	¹¹ 1	⁷	6
B	¹	⁰	⁶ 1	¹	1
C	⁵ 7	⁸	¹⁵ 1	⁹ 2	10
Total Demand	7	5	3	2	

Returning to Step 3 in order to check whether this solution can be improved gives:

Cell (A, D): 11 - 15 + 5 - 2 = -1
Cell (A, G): 9 - 15 + 11 - 7 = -2
Cell (B, D): 5 - 15 + 6 - 1 = -5
Cell (B, E): 3 - 11 + 6 - 0 = -2
Cell (B, G): 9 - 15 + 6 - 1 = -1
Cell (C, E): 3 - 11 + 15 - 8 = -1

All of these values are nonpositive. Consequently, our present solution is optimal.

SUGGESTIONS FOR FURTHER READING

Amling, F. *Investments: An Introduction to Analysis and Management*. Needham Heights, MA: Ginn Press, 1993.

Beenhakker, H. L. *Replacement and Expansion Investments*. Rotterdam, Holland: Rotterdam University Press, 1975.

Helfert, E. A. *Techniques of Financial Analysis*. Boston: Richard D. Irwin, 1994.

Higgens, R. C. *Analysis for Financial Management*. Boston: Richard D. Irwin, 1995.

APPENDIX 1

Discounting and Compounding

This appendix presents a review of discounting and compounding methods and the use of financial calculators. These methods are sine qua non for financial managers and professionals.

1. DISCOUNTING AND COMPOUNDING AT ANNUAL INTERVALS

A given sum of money now is normally worth more than an equal sum at some future date. The concept "money has a time value" is the basic assumption of discounting and compounding. Frequently one considers time in discrete units of one year.

We introduce the following definitions:

P = an amount of money at the present time
F = an amount of money at the end of n periods in the future
A = a constant amount paid or received at the end of each of n periods in the future ("uniform series")
n = the number of periods or times at which interest is calculated
i = the interest rate used for calculations of interest in any one of the n periods mentioned above.

The definitions refer to "periods of time," which are normally years. However, "period of time," rather than "year" is preferred to eliminate redefining the symbols when other units of time are considered.

Table A.1 presents six interest factors to use when specific data are given:

spcaf	when P is given and F is to be obtained
sppwf	when F is given and P is to be obtained

Table A.1
Interest Factors for Discrete Discounting and Compounding

Find Given	P	F	A
P	1	spcaf $= (1+i)^n$	crf $=$ $[1-(1+i)^{-n}-1]^{-1}i$
F	sppwf $= (1+i)^{-n}$	1	sff $=$ $[(1+i)^n-1]^{-1}i$
A	pwf $=$ $[1-(1+i)^{-n}]i^{-1}$	caf $=$ $[(1+i)^n-1]i^{-1}$	1

caf	when A is given and F is to be obtained
sff	when F is given and A is to be obtained
pwf	when A is given and P is to be obtained
crf	when P is given and A is to be obtained.

The interpretation of the above acronyms is as follows:

$$
\begin{aligned}
\text{spcaf} &= \text{single payment compound amount factor} \\
\text{sppwf} &= \text{single payment present worth factor} \\
\text{caf} &= \text{(series) compound amount factor} \\
\text{sff} &= \text{sinking fund factor} \\
\text{pwf} &= \text{(series) present worth factor} \\
\text{crf} &= \text{capital recovery factor.}
\end{aligned}
$$

The first of these six factors, spcaf, allows us to determine the value n periods hence of a present amount P if the interest rate is i. Thus, given P, i, and n it allows for the computation of F. Consider the following simple, arithmetic example of the use of spcaf.

Suppose it is desired to find the sum to which $1,000.00 would grow over three years when the appropriate annual interest rate is 10%. From the spcaf formula of Table A.1 we compute as follows:

$$
\begin{aligned}
F &= P(\text{given } P, \text{ find } F, i=10\%, n=3) \\
&= P \cdot \text{spcaf } (i=10\%, n=3) \\
&= P(1 + i)^n \text{ for } i = 10\% \text{ and } n=3 \\
&= \$1,000(1 + 0.10)^3 = \$1,000(1 + 0.10)(1 + 0.10)(1 + 0.10) \\
&= \$1,000(1.331) = \$1,331.00
\end{aligned}
$$

Appendix 2 gives values for sppwf, pwf, spcaf, and caf of Table A.1 for given values of i and n. The crf and sff are not included since their values may be obtained by taking the reciprocal of the values for caf and pwf, respectively. Alternatively, one can use a financial calculator (see Section 4 below).

The single payment present worth factor (sppwf) permits us to answer questions about the present value of capital available at some time in the future. Given F, i, and n, the P may be calculated from:

$$P = F \cdot \text{sppwf} = F(1 + i)^{-n}$$

where the expression $(1 + i)^{-n}$ is a convenient way of writing $1/(1 + i)^n$.

Suppose it is desired to know the present value of a sum of $150.00 arising two years hence when the appropriate annual interest rate is 10%. Using the sppwf formula we compute:

$$P = F \text{ (given } F, \text{ find } P, i=10\%, n=2)$$
$$= F \cdot \text{sppwf } (i=10\%, n=2)$$
$$= F(1 + i)^{-n} \text{ for } i=10\%, \text{ and } n=2$$
$$= \$150(1 + 0.10)^{-2} = \$150(0.8264)$$
$$= \$123.96$$

The (series) compound amount factor (or caf) permits the calculation of a future sum F given that an amount A is invested at $i\%$ at the end of each of n equal intervals. The series of constant annual cash flows is known as an annuity.

Suppose an investor has an annuity in which a payment of $500.00 is made at the end of each year. If interest is 6% compounded annually, what is the amount after 20 years? From the caf formula this amount is as follows:

$$F = A \cdot \text{caf}(i=6\%, n=20)$$
$$= \$500[(1 + 0.6)^{20} - 1](0.6)^{-1}$$
$$= \$500(36.786) = \$18,393.00$$

Note that the expression $(0.6)^{-1}$ is again a convenient way of writing $1/(0.6)$. The value 36.786 may be obtained from Appendix 2.

The reciprocal of the caf is the sinking fund factor (or sff), which allows us to calculate the constant amount A which must be invested at the end of each period to yield an amount F at the end of the nth period. In financial terminology, the terminal value of a constant annual investment or annuity is usually referred to as a "sinking fund." This is a fund to which periodic payments are made and then invested to accumulate to a given amount by a certain date. This is often done for the purpose of replacing a machine at the end of its expected life, or for the redeeming of a loan.

Consider, as an example, involving the use of sff, an asset with a value of $5,000.00, a service life of 5 years, and a salvage value of $1,000.00. Using the sinking-fund depreciation method we are asked to compute the required year-end sinking fund deposits if the interest rate is 5%. Using the sff formula of Table A.1 we compute as follows:

$$A = F \cdot \text{sff}(i=6\%, n=5)$$
$$= \$4,000i[(1 + i)^n - 1]^{-1}$$
$$= \$4,000(0.1774) = \$709.60$$

Note that for F a value of $4,000.00 rather than $5,000.00 is used, because the asset has a salvage value of $1,000.00.

The (series) present worth factor (or pwf) enables us to calculate the present value of a uniform series A. Let us consider the following problem to illustrate the application of the pwf formula.

A firm is offered the choice of a 5-year lease on a machine:

> *Alternative (a)*: $10,000.00 down and $3,000.00 per annum for 5 years.
> *Alternative (b)*: $13,000.00 down and $2,150.00 per annum for 5 years.

Annual payments are to be made at the year end, the relevant interest rate is 7%, while problems of risk, inflation, tax, and so on, are ignored. Alternative (b) requires the firm to pay down $3,000.00 more at the beginning of the lease than alternative (a), but results in an annual year-end saving of $850.00 for 5 years. From the pwf formula the present values of alternatives (a) and (b) are:

$$\text{(a)} \quad P = \$10,000 + \$3,000[1 - (1 + i)^{-n}]i^{-1}$$
$$= \$10,000 + \$3,000(4.100)$$
$$= \$22,300.00$$
$$\text{(b)} \quad P = \$13,000 + \$2,150 [1 - (1 + i)^{-n}]i^{-1}$$
$$= \$13,000 + \$2,150(4.100)$$
$$= \$21,815.00$$

There is a gain of net present value by taking alternative (b) equal to:

$$\$22,300.00 - \$21,815.00 = \$485.00$$

and this alternative is, therefore, preferred.

A perpetual annuity (or perpetuity) is a perpetual series of annual constant cash flows. An example of a perpetuity is a consol, which is an interest-bearing bond issued by the British government having no maturity date. When a regular annual series is expected to go on perpetually, or $n \to \infty$ (the symbol for n tending to infinity), then the pwf formula becomes simply $P = A \cdot i^{-1}$. This is because $(1 + i)^{-n}$ tends to zero when $n \to \infty$.

The capital recovery factor (or crf) permits us to calculate the equal end of period payment A for n periods, which is equivalent to a present sum P. The following example illustrates the use of pwf, sppwf, and crf.

A young economist has estimated that his annual earnings should average $10,000.00, $15,000.00, and $20,000.00 per year in succeeding decades after graduation. He hopes to graduate next month and wants an idea of the value of all his years of studying. Assuming an annual interest rate of 6%, he therefore decides to determine (a) the present worth (at graduation) in cash of the 30 years' earning, and (b) the equivalent uniform annual value of the 30 years' estimated income.

His present worth is:

[$10,000·pwf($i=6\%$, $n=10$] + [$15,000·pwf($i=6\%$, $n=10$)·sppwf($i=6\%$, $n=10$)]

+ [$20,000·pwf($i=6\%$, $n=10$)·sppwf($i=6\%$, $n=20$)] = $10,000(7.360)

+ $15,000(7,360)(0.5584) + 20,000(7,360)(0.3118) = $73,600 + $61,647

+ $45,897 = $181,144.00

The equivalent uniform annual value of the 30 years' estimated income is:

$181,144·crf($i=6\%$, $n=30$) = $181,144(0.07265) = $13,160.00

2. ISSUES RELATED TO DISCRETE DISCOUNTING AND COMPOUNDING

We will now analyze various issues related to the six interest factors of Table A.1. Care must be exercised when using the formulas that contain the parameter A—that is, A is defined as the constant amount paid or received *at the end* of each of n periods in the future. The following example illustrates that the expressions are still useful if a constant amount is paid or received *at the beginning* of each of n periods in the future.

Suppose that we are interested in determining the value of a savings account at the end of 15 years if $200.00 is deposited in this account at the beginning of each of 15 years, and that the account draws 7% interest compounded annually. The solution to this problem is obtained by first assuming that the $200.00 is deposited at the end of each of 15 years. In this case, we have:

$$F = A·caf(i=7\%, n=15)$$
$$= \$200(25.129)$$
$$= \$5,025.80$$

This amount has to be reduced by $200.00, since in reality no deposit is made at the end of 15 years. Consequently, we obtain $4,825.80. However, this is still not the solution, since we have to add to the amount of $4,825.80 the end of 15 years equivalent of the very first deposit of $200. Thus, we have to add $F = P·spcaf$ ($i = 7\%$, $n = 15$) = $200(2.759) = $551.80. The value of our savings account at the end of 15 years is, therefore, $5,377.60.

Heretofore we have adopted the convention of discounting for an annual period. Now to analyze the discounting for periods of less than a year, we introduce these following definitions:

m = the total number of years
k = the number of compounding or conversion periods per year
j = the nominal yearly interest rate to be converted n times per year.

Thus, $i = j/k$ and $n = m·k$, where i and n are as defined previously.

Suppose you want to determine the amount to which $10,000.00 would grow in one year at 8% interest compounded semiannually. Thus, the nominal yearly interest rate, sometimes simply called the nominal rate, is equal to $j = 8\%$ and $n = 2$, since the interest is calculated twice a year. Consequently, the interest rate per conversion period is $i = j/k = 8\%/2 = 4\%$ and the amount F to which $10,000.00 will grow in one year at $j = 8\%$ is:

$$F = \$10,000(1 + i)^2 = \$10,000(1.04)^2$$
$$= \$10,000 \text{ spcaf } (i=4\%, n=2)$$
$$= \$10,820.00$$

In the examples of Section 1 we used an annual interest. In fact, this was the effective yearly rate or the amount by which an amount of money would grow during a year, regardless of the number of conversion periods. For instance, in the aforementioned example of $10,820.00 at 8% compounded semiannually, the $10,000.00 increased to $10,820.00 (or by 8.2%). Thus, the interest rate used for calculations of interest (or i) is 4%, the nominal yearly interest rate is 8.0%, and the effective yearly interest rate is 8.2%.

Denoting the effective yearly interest rate by q, we conclude that, by definition, the following relations exist:

$$(1 + q) = (1 + j/k)^k = (1 + i)^k$$

or

$$q = (1 + j/k)^k - 1 = (1 + i)^k - 1 \tag{1}$$

and

$$j/k = i = \sqrt[k]{(1+q)} - 1. \tag{2}$$

The following example is an additional problem involving discounting for periods of less than one year.

What is the effective yearly interest rate q corresponding to 12% compounded monthly? Note that the nominal rate frequently states the compounding period as a percentage compounded semiannually, compounded quarterly, compounded weekly, and so on. In our example, the nominal rate is 12% compounded monthly. Thus, $j = 12\%$, $k = 12$, and $i = 12\%/12 = 1\%$. According to expression (1), the effective yearly interest q is:

$$(1 + 0.01)^{12} - 1 = 0.127 \text{ (or 12.7\%)}.$$

Adaption to cover situations in which amounts of money arise at intervals which are multiples of a year is also easy. For example, suppose $1,000.00 occurs every b years beginning b years hence and lasting for c years. It is clear that this is equivalent to an annuity of $1,000.00 lasting c/b periods with an interest rate of $[(1 + q)^b - 1)]$ per period of b years, where q is the effective yearly interest rate. Let us call this equivalent interest rate z, where $z = [(1 + q)^b - 1]$, and introduce $y = c/b$. Consequently, the present value of a regular series arising at intervals of b years, beginning b years hence and lasting c years, is simply the pwf expression of Table A.1 with z substituted for i and y substituted for n or pwf(z, y).

Suppose we are interested in computing the present value of \$1,000.00 arising two years hence and again four years hence, while the annual interest rate is 10%. First we calculate the value of z:

$$z = (1 + q)^b - 1 = (1.10)^2 - 1 = 0.21.$$

Next,

$$y = c/b = 4/2 = 2.$$

Consequently, the present value is:

$$1,000 \cdot \text{pwf}(z = 21\%, y = 2) = \$1,000(1.510) = \$1,510.00$$

Thus, the application of the Appendix 2 interest tables can be extended. Note that the same answer is obtained as follows:

$$P = \$1,000 \cdot \text{sppwf}(i = 10\%, n = 2) + \$1,000 \cdot \text{sppwf}(i = 10\%, n = 4) = \$1,510.00$$

3. CONTINUOUS DISCOUNTING AND COMPOUNDING

The concept of continuous compounding also assumes that cash payments (or receipts) occur once per each of n interest periods, which are usually years. However, the compounding is continuous throughout each such interest period. Thus, with a nominal rate of interest per each of the n interest periods equal to r and interest being compounded k times per such an interest period, the expression for spcaf (in Table A.1) becomes:

$$F = P(1 + r \cdot k^{-1})^{k \cdot n}. \tag{3}$$

Note that compounding continuously really means that the value of k is considered to be infinitely large. Therefore, expression (3) should be written as:

$$F = P[\lim_{k \to \infty}(1 + r \cdot k^{-1})^{k \cdot n}]$$

or

$$F = P[\lim_{k \to \infty}(1 + r \cdot k^{-1})^{k}]^{n}.$$

Relying on our freshman calculus knowledge, we recall that:

$$\lim_{k \to \infty}(1 + r \cdot k^{-1})^{k} = e^{r} \tag{4}$$

Table A.2
Interest Factors for Continuous Discounting and Compounding

Find Given	P	F	A
P	1	$\text{cspcaf} = e^{rn}$	$\text{ccrf} =$ $(e^r-1)(1-e^{-rn})^{-1}$
F	$\text{csppwf} = e^{-rn}$	1	$\text{csff} =$ $(e^r-1)(e^{rn}-1)^{-1}$
A	$\text{cpwf} =$ $(1-e^{-rn})(e^r-1)^{-1}$	$\text{ccaf} =$ $(e^{rn}-1(e^r-1)^{-1}$	1

where e = the conventional symbol for the number 2.71828 known as the basis of natural logarithms. Thus, expression (4) may be simply written as $F = Pe^{rn}$. The expression e^{rn} for continuous compounding corresponds to $(1 + i)^n$ for discrete compounding. Consequently, $e^r = (1 + i)$ or $i = (e^r - 1)$.

Table A.2 gives the six continuous compounding formulas that correspond to the six discrete compounding formulas of Table A.1. They are arrived at by replacing the i of the formulas of Table A.1 by $(e^r - 1)$.

The acronyms of Table A.2 have the following interpretation:

    cspcaf = continuous compounding, single payment compound amount factor
    csppwf = continuous compounding, single payment present worth factor
      ccaf = continuous compounding, discrete payment compound amount factor
      csff = continuous compounding, discrete payment sinking fund factor
      cpwf = continuous compounding, discrete payment present worth factor
      ccrf = continuous compounding, discrete payment capital recovery factor.

Appendix 3 gives values for the cspcaf, csppwf, ccaf, and cpwf, for various r and n values. Values of csff and ccrf are not included, since their use is infrequent. It is clear that csff and ccrf values may be obtained by taking the reciprocal of the values of ccaf and cpwf, respectively.

The relation $i = (e^r - 1)$ indicates that, if $i = 0.10$, then $r = 0.094$. Consequently, the difference in answers obtained with discrete and continuous discounting and compounding procedures is a small percentage of the present or final sums of money involved. In addition, we should not be overly concerned about a difference of 0.006 between $i = 0.10$ and $r = 0.094$, since it is seldom possible to define the interest rate of cost of capital to be used in investment analyses to the accuracy of the nearest half of a percent. The following example illustrates the difference in answers obtained with discrete and continuous compounding procedures.

Suppose a company procures a machine for $15,000.00, which it agrees to pay for in six equal payments, commencing one year after the date of purchase, at an interest rate of 10% per year. Immediately after the second payment, the terms of the agreement are changed to allow the balance to be paid off in a single payment the next year. We are interested in computing the annual payment for the first two years and the final payment with both the discrete and continuous compounding procedures.

Discrete compounding. The yearly payment for the first two years is:

$$A = P(\text{given } P, \text{ find } A, i=10\%, n=6)$$
$$= \$15,000 \text{ crf}(i=10\%, n=6)$$
$$= \$15,000(0.22961) = \$3,444.15$$

The final payment is:

$$F = \$3,444.15 + A(\text{given } A, \text{ find } P, i=10\%, n=3)$$
$$= \$3,444.15 + \$3,444.15 \text{ pwf}(i=10\%, n=3)$$
$$= \$3,444.15 + \$3,444.15(2.487) = \$12,009.75$$

Continuous compounding. The yearly payment for the first two years is:

$$A = P(\text{given } P, \text{ find } A, r=10\%, n=6)$$
$$= \$15,000 \text{ cpwf}(r=10\%, n=6)^{-1}$$
$$= \$15,000(4.2900)^{-1} = \$3,496.50$$

The final payment is:

$$F = \$3,496.50 + A(\text{given } A, \text{ find } P, r=10\%, n=3)$$
$$= \$3,496.50 + \$3,496.50 \text{ cpwf}(r=10\%, n=3)$$
$$= \$3,496.50 + \$3,496.50(2.4644) = \$12,113.27$$

The difference in the above F values is $\$12,113.27 - \$12,009.75 = \$103.52$ or 0.86% of $\$12,009.75$.

4. FINANCIAL CALCULATORS

The equations pertaining to the computation of sppwf, pwf, spcaf, caf, crf, and sff (see Table A.1) have been programmed directly into financial calculators. These calculators can, therefore, be used to determine the values of P, F, and A of Table A.1. The calculators have the following five keys pertaining to the variables of the time value of money:

N (or n) representing the number of time periods;

I (or i) representing the interest rate per period;

PV representing the present value (P);

FV representing the future value or the value at the end of N periods (F);

PMT indicating payment and representing a constant amount paid or received at the end of each of N periods in the future (A); and

CHS indicating change sign, which is the key for changing the sign of an input (a benefit has a positive sign and a cost has a negative sign).

Before starting with the following examples, we must always press the keys *f* and *CLEAR FIN* to clear the financial registers.

What is the value of $500.00 deposited in a savings account with a 7% annual interest rate at the end of 10 years? Enter 500, *CHS*, and *PV*; 7, *I*; and 10, *N*. Press *FV* and the calculator finds a value of $983.57. Note that with most financial calculators, you first enter the number and then *CHS*, *PV*, *I*, or *N*. Also note that, in the example, we used the *CHS* key since the $500.—represents a payment or cost. If, in our example, the value of $983.57 at the end of 10 years is given and we have to compute its present value, we enter 983.57, *CHS*, *FV*; 7, *I*; and 10, *N* and press *PV* to find the present value of $500.—. The sequence in which we enter the inputs does not matter. In other words, we could also have entered 7, *I*; 10, *N*; and 983.57, *CHS*, *FV*, or any other sequence. The following are other examples of the use of financial calculators.

—Suppose you buy a security at a price of $156.70 and that it will pay $200.00 after 5 years. What is the interest rate *I*? Enter 156.70, *CHS*, *PV*; 200, *FV*; 5, *N*. Press *I* and the calculator finds a value of 5% for the interest rate.

—A security provides a return of 5%, costs $156.70, while you will receive $200.00 at maturity. When does the security mature? Enter 156.70, *CHS*, *PV*; 200, *FV*; 5, *I*. Press *N* and the calculator finds that it takes 5 years for the security to mature.

—Suppose an investor has an annuity in which a payment of $800.00 is made at the end of each year. If interest is 7% compounded annually, what is the amount after 20 years? Enter 800, *CHS*, *PMT*; 20, *N*; 7, *I*, and press *FV* to find $32,796.39 for the amount after 20 years.

—What is the present value of an annuity in which a payment of $100.00 at the end of each year is made, after 3 years? The interest rate is 5%. Enter 3, *N*; 5, *I*; and 100, *CHS*, *PMT*, and press *PV* to find a present value of $272.32.

Financial calculators can also be used to determine the present or future values of uneven cash flow streams. In this case, we start with pressing *g* and *CLEAR REG* to clear the financial registers. Consider, for example, the computation of the present value of a stream of payments starting with $50.00 at the beginning of the first year and followed by $200.00, $300.00, $300.00, $300.00, $300.00, $0.00, and $1000.00 at the beginning of each subsequent year. The interest rate is 6%. Rather than working with the keys *PV* and *FV*, we now use the following keys:

g and *f*, which are prefix keys;

CFo representing the first amount of the cash flow stream;

CFj representing a subsequent amount of the cash flow stream;

Nj representing the number of time periods in the stream;

NPV representing the present value;

NFV representing the future value or the value at the end of *N* periods (since the computation of this value is not often required, not all financial calculators have this key); and

RCL indicating recall, and which is used to display a number stored in the financial register.

The solution to the above problem is as follows. Enter 50, *g*, *CFo*; 200, *g*, *CFj*; 300, *g*, *CFj*; 4, *g*, *Nj*; 0, *g*, *CFj*; 1000, *g*, *CFj*; *RCL*, *n*; 6, *I*, and press *f NPV* to obtain the present value of $1,884.43.

Interest Tables for Discrete Compounding

Given P, Find F (spcaf)

Period	1%	2%	3%	4%	5%	6%	7%	8%	10%	12%	15%	20%
1	1.0100	1.0200	1.0300	1.0400	1.0500	1.0600	1.0700	1.0800	1.1000	1.1200	1.1500	1.2000
2	1.0201	1.0404	1.0609	1.0816	1.1025	1.1236	1.1449	1.1664	1.2100	1.2544	1.3225	1.4400
3	1.0303	1.0612	1.0927	1.1249	1.1576	1.1910	1.2250	1.2597	1.3310	1.4049	1.5209	1.7280
4	1.0406	1.0824	1.1255	1.1699	1.2155	1.2625	1.3108	1.3605	1.4641	1.5735	1.7490	2.0736
5	1.0510	1.1041	1.1593	1.2167	1.2763	1.3382	1.4026	1.4693	1.6105	1.7623	2.0114	2.4883
6	1.0615	1.1262	1.1941	1.2653	1.3401	1.4185	1.5007	1.5869	1.7716	1.9738	2.3131	2.9860
7	1.0721	1.1487	1.2299	1.3159	1.4071	1.5036	1.6058	1.7138	1.9487	2.2107	2.6600	3.5832
8	1.0829	1.1717	1.2668	1.3686	1.4775	1.5938	1.7182	1.8509	2.1436	2.4760	3.0590	4.2998
9	1.0937	1.1951	1.3048	1.4233	1.5513	1.6895	1.8385	1.9990	2.3579	2.7731	3.5179	5.1598
10	1.1046	1.2190	1.3439	1.4802	1.6289	1.7908	1.9672	2.1589	2.5937	3.1058	4.0456	6.1917
11	1.1157	1.2434	1.3842	1.5395	1.7103	1.8983	2.1049	2.3316	2.8531	3.4785	4.6524	7.4301
12	1.1268	1.2682	1.4258	1.6010	1.7959	2.0122	2.2522	2.5182	3.1384	3.8960	5.3503	8.9161
13	1.1381	1.2936	1.4685	1.6651	1.8856	2.1329	2.4098	2.7196	3.4523	4.3635	6.1528	10.699
14	1.1495	1.3195	1.5126	1.7317	1.9799	2.2609	2.5785	2.9372	3.7975	4.8871	7.0757	12.839
15	1.1610	1.3459	1.5580	1.8009	2.0789	2.3966	2.7590	3.1722	4.1772	5.4736	8.1371	15.407
16	1.1726	1.3728	1.6047	1.8730	2.1829	2.5404	2.9522	3.4259	4.5950	6.1304	9.3576	18.488
17	1.1843	1.4002	1.6528	1.9479	2.2920	2.6928	3.1588	3.7000	5.0545	6.8660	10.761	22.186
18	1.1961	1.4282	1.7024	2.0258	2.4066	2.8543	3.3799	3.9960	5.5599	7.6900	12.375	26.623
19	1.2081	1.4568	1.7535	2.1068	2.5270	3.0256	3.6165	4.3157	6.1159	8.6128	14.232	31.948
20	1.2202	1.4859	1.8061	2.1911	2.6533	3.2071	3.8697	4.6610	6.7275	9.6463	16.367	38.338
21	1.2324	1.5157	1.8603	2.2788	2.7860	3.3996	4.1406	5.0338	7.4002	10.804	18.822	46.005
22	1.2447	1.5460	1.9161	2.3699	2.9253	3.6035	4.4304	5.4365	8.1403	12.100	21.645	55.206
23	1.2572	1.5769	1.9736	2.4647	3.0715	3.8197	4.7405	5.8715	8.9543	13.552	24.891	66.247
24	1.2697	1.6084	2.0328	2.5633	3.2251	4.0489	5.0724	6.3412	9.8497	15.179	28.625	79.497
25	1.2824	1.6406	2.0938	2.6658	3.3864	4.2919	5.4274	6.8485	10.835	17.000	32.919	95.396
26	1.2953	1.6734	2.1566	2.7725	3.5557	4.5494	5.8074	7.3964	11.918	19.040	37.857	114.48
27	1.3082	1.7069	2.2213	2.8834	3.7335	4.8223	6.2139	7.9881	13.110	21.325	43.535	137.37
28	1.3213	1.7410	2.2879	2.9987	3.9201	5.1117	6.6488	8.6271	14.421	23.884	50.066	164.84
29	1.3345	1.7758	2.3566	3.1187	4.1161	5.4184	7.1143	9.3173	15.863	26.750	57.575	197.81
30	1.3478	1.8114	2.4273	3.2434	4.3219	5.7435	7.6123	10.063	17.449	29.960	66.212	237.38
35	1.4166	1.9999	2.8139	3.9461	5.5160	7.6861	10.677	14.785	28.102	52.800	133.18	590.67
40	1.4889	2.2080	3.2620	4.8010	7.0400	10.286	14.974	21.725	45.259	93.051	267.86	1469.8
45	1.5648	2.4379	3.7816	5.8412	8.9850	13.765	21.002	31.920	72.890	163.99	538.77	3657.3
50	1.6446	2.6916	4.3839	7.1067	11.467	18.420	29.457	46.902	117.39	289.00	1083.7	9100.4
55	1.7285	2.9717	5.0821	8.6464	14.636	24.650	41.315	68.914	189.06	509.32	2179.6	22645
60	1.8167	3.2810	5.8916	10.520	18.679	32.988	57.946	101.26	304.48	897.60	4384.0	56348

The appendix only reports interest factors most commonly used in investment analyses. See J. R. Canada, *Intermediate Economic Analysis for Management and Engineering* (Englewood Cliffs, NJ: Prentice-Hall, 1971) for interest factors from 0.5% to 50%.

Given F, Find P (sppwf)

Period	1%	2%	3%	4%	5%	6%	7%	8%	10%	12%	15%	20%
1	.9901	.9804	.9709	.9615	.9524	.9434	.9346	.9259	.9091	.8929	.8696	.8333
2	.9803	.9612	.9426	.9246	.9070	.8900	.8734	.8573	.8264	.7972	.7561	.6944
3	.9706	.9423	.9151	.8890	.8638	.8396	.8163	.7938	.7513	.7118	.6575	.5787
4	.9610	.9238	.8885	.8548	.8227	.7921	.7629	.7350	.6830	.6355	.5718	.4823
5	.9515	.9057	.8626	.8219	.7835	.7473	.7130	.6806	.6209	.5674	.4972	.4019
6	.9420	.8880	.8375	.7903	.7462	.7050	.6663	.6302	.5645	.5066	.4323	.3349
7	.9327	.8706	.8131	.7599	.7107	.6651	.6227	.5835	.5132	.4523	.3759	.2791
8	.9235	.8535	.7894	.7307	.6768	.6274	.5820	.5403	.4665	.4039	.3269	.2326
9	.9143	.8368	.7664	.7026	.6446	.5919	.5439	.5002	.4241	.3606	.2843	.1938
10	.9053	.8203	.7441	.6756	.6139	.5584	.5083	.4632	.3855	.3220	.2472	.1615
11	.8963	.8043	.7224	.6496	.5847	.5268	.4751	.4289	.3505	.2875	.2149	.1346
12	.8874	.7885	.7014	.6246	.5568	.4970	.4440	.3971	.3186	.2567	.1869	.1122
13	.8787	.7730	.6810	.6006	.5303	.4688	.4150	.3677	.2897	.2292	.1625	.0935
14	.8700	.7579	.6611	.5775	.5051	.4423	.3878	.3405	.2633	.2046	.1413	.0779
15	.8613	.7430	.6419	.5553	.4810	.4173	.3624	.3152	.2394	.1827	.1229	.0649
16	.8528	.7284	.6232	.5339	.4581	.3936	.3387	.2919	.2176	.1631	.1069	.0541
17	.8444	.7142	.6050	.5134	.4363	.3714	.3166	.2703	.1978	.1456	.0929	.0451
18	.8360	.7002	.5874	.4936	.4155	.3503	.2959	.2502	.1799	.1300	.0808	.0376
19	.8277	.6864	.5703	.4746	.3957	.3305	.2765	.2317	.1635	.1161	.0703	.0313
20	.8195	.6730	.5537	.4564	.3769	.3118	.2584	.2145	.1486	.1037	.0611	.0261
21	.8114	.6598	.5375	.4388	.3589	.2942	.2415	.1987	.1351	.0926	.0531	.0217
22	.8034	.6468	.5219	.4220	.3418	.2775	.2257	.1839	.1228	.0826	.0462	.0181
23	.7954	.6342	.5067	.4057	.3256	.2618	.2109	.1703	.1117	.0738	.0402	.0151
24	.7876	.6217	.4919	.3901	.3101	.2470	.1971	.1577	.1015	.0659	.0349	.0126
25	.7798	.6095	.4776	.3751	.2953	.2330	.1842	.1460	.0923	.0588	.0304	.0105
26	.7720	.5976	.4637	.3607	.2812	.2198	.1722	.1352	.0839	.0525	.0264	.0087
27	.7644	.5859	.4502	.3468	.2678	.2074	.1609	.1252	.0763	.0469	.0230	.0073
28	.7568	.5744	.4371	.3335	.2551	.1956	.1504	.1159	.0693	.0419	.0200	.0061
29	.7493	.5631	.4243	.3207	.2429	.1846	.1406	.1073	.0630	.0374	.0174	.0051
30	.7419	.5521	.4120	.3083	.2314	.1741	.1314	.0994	.0573	.0334	.0151	.0042
35	.7059	.5000	.3554	.2534	.1813	.1301	.0937	.0676	.0356	.0189	.0075	.0017
40	.6717	.4529	.3066	.2083	.1420	.0972	.0668	.0460	.0221	.0107	.0037	.0007
45	.6391	.4102	.2644	.1712	.1113	.0727	.0476	.0313	.0137	.0061	.0019	.0003
50	.6080	.3715	.2281	.1407	.0872	.0543	.0339	.0213	.0085	.0035	.0009	.0001
55	.5785	.3365	.1968	.1157	.0683	.0406	.0242	.0145	.0053	.0020	.0005	.0000
60	.5504	.3048	.1697	.0951	.0535	.0303	.0173	.0099	.0033	.0011	.0002	.0000

Given A, find P (pwf)

Period	1%	2%	3%	4%	5%	6%	7%	8%	10%	12%	15%	20%
1	0.9901	0.9804	0.9709	0.9615	0.9524	0.9434	0.9346	0.9259	0.9091	0.8929	0.8696	0.8333
2	1.9704	1.9416	1.9135	1.8861	1.8594	1.8334	1.8080	1.7833	1.7355	1.6901	1.6257	1.5278
3	2.9410	2.8839	2.8286	2.7751	2.7232	2.6730	2.6243	2.5771	2.4869	2.4018	2.2832	2.1065
4	3.9020	3.8077	3.7171	3.6299	3.5460	3.4651	3.3872	3.3121	3.1699	3.0373	2.8550	2.5887
5	4.8534	4.7135	4.5797	4.4518	4.3295	4.2124	4.1002	3.9927	3.7908	3.6048	3.3522	2.9906
6	5.7955	5.6014	5.4172	5.2421	5.0757	4.9173	4.7665	4.6229	4.3553	4.1114	3.7845	3.3255
7	6.7282	6.4720	6.2303	6.0021	5.7864	5.5824	5.3893	5.2064	4.8684	4.5638	4.1604	3.6046
8	7.6517	7.3255	7.0197	6.7327	6.4632	6.2098	5.9713	5.7466	5.3349	4.9676	4.4873	3.8372
9	8.5660	8.1622	7.7861	7.4353	7.1078	6.8017	6.5152	6.2469	5.7590	5.3282	4.7716	4.0310
10	9.4713	8.9826	8.5302	8.1109	7.7217	7.3601	7.0236	6.7101	6.1446	5.6502	5.0188	4.1925
11	10.368	9.7868	9.2526	8.7605	8.3064	7.8869	7.4987	7.1390	6.4951	5.9377	5.2337	4.3271
12	11.255	10.575	9.9540	9.3851	8.8633	8.3838	7.9427	7.5361	6.8137	6.1944	5.4206	4.4392
13	12.134	11.348	10.635	9.9856	9.3936	8.8527	8.3577	7.9038	7.1034	6.4235	5.5831	4.5327
14	13.004	12.106	11.296	10.563	9.8986	9.2950	8.7455	8.2442	7.3667	6.6282	5.7245	4.6106
15	13.865	12.849	11.938	11.118	10.380	9.7122	9.1079	8.5595	7.6061	6.8109	5.8474	4.6755
16	14.718	13.578	12.561	11.652	10.838	10.106	9.4466	8.8514	7.8237	6.9740	5.9542	4.7296
17	15.562	14.292	13.166	12.166	11.274	10.477	9.7632	9.1216	8.0216	7.1196	6.0472	4.7746
18	16.398	14.992	13.754	12.659	11.690	10.828	10.059	9.3719	8.2014	7.2497	6.1280	4.8122
19	17.226	15.678	14.324	13.134	12.085	11.158	10.336	9.6036	8.3649	7.3658	6.1982	4.8435
20	18.046	16.351	14.877	13.590	12.462	11.470	10.594	9.8181	8.5136	7.4694	6.2593	4.8696
21	18.857	17.011	15.415	14.029	12.821	11.764	10.836	10.017	8.6487	7.5620	6.3125	4.8913
22	19.660	17.658	15.937	14.451	13.163	12.042	11.061	10.201	8.7715	7.6446	6.3587	4.9094
23	20.456	18.292	16.444	14.857	13.489	12.303	11.272	10.371	8.8832	7.7184	6.3988	4.9245
24	21.243	18.914	16.936	15.247	13.799	12.550	11.469	10.529	8.9847	7.7843	6.4338	4.9371
25	22.023	19.523	17.413	15.622	14.094	12.783	11.654	10.675	9.0770	7.8431	6.4641	4.9476
26	22.795	20.121	17.877	15.983	14.375	13.003	11.826	10.810	9.1609	7.8957	6.4906	4.9563
27	23.560	20.707	18.327	16.330	14.643	13.211	11.987	10.935	9.2372	7.9426	6.5135	4.9636
28	24.316	21.281	18.764	16.663	14.898	13.406	12.137	11.051	9.3066	7.9844	6.5335	4.9697
29	25.066	21.844	19.188	16.984	15.141	13.591	12.278	11.158	9.3696	8.0218	6.5509	4.9747
30	25.808	22.396	19.600	17.292	15.372	13.765	12.409	11.258	9.4269	8.0552	6.5660	4.9789
35	29.409	24.999	21.487	18.665	16.374	14.498	12.948	11.655	9.6442	8.1755	6.6166	4.9915
40	32.835	27.355	23.115	19.793	17.159	15.046	13.332	11.925	9.7791	8.2438	6.6418	4.9966
45	36.095	29.490	24.519	20.720	17.774	15.456	13.606	12.108	9.8628	8.2825	6.6543	4.9986
50	39.196	31.424	25.730	21.482	18.256	15.762	13.801	12.233	9.9148	8.3045	6.6605	4.9995
55	42.147	33.175	26.774	22.109	18.633	15.991	13.940	12.319	9.9471	8.3170	6.6636	4.9998
60	44.955	34.761	27.676	22.623	18.929	16.161	14.039	12.377	9.9672	8.3240	6.6651	4.9999

Given A, Find F (caf)

Period	1%	2%	3%	4%	5%	6%	7%	8%	10%	12%	15%	20%
1	1.0000	1.0000	1.0000	1.0000	1.0000	1.0000	1.0000	1.0000	1.0000	1.0000	1.0000	1.0000
2	2.0100	2.0200	2.0300	2.0400	2.0500	2.0600	2.0700	2.0800	2.1000	2.1200	2.1500	2.2000
3	3.0301	3.0604	3.0909	3.1216	3.1525	3.1836	3.2149	3.2464	3.3100	3.3744	3.4725	3.6400
4	4.0604	4.1216	4.1836	4.2465	4.3101	4.3746	4.4399	4.5061	4.6410	4.7793	4.9934	5.3680
5	5.1010	5.2040	5.3091	5.4163	5.5256	5.6371	5.7507	5.8666	6.1051	6.3528	6.7424	7.4416
6	6.1520	6.3081	6.4684	6.6330	6.8019	6.9753	7.1533	7.3359	7.7156	8.1152	8.7537	9.9299
7	7.2135	7.4343	7.6625	7.8983	8.1420	8.3938	8.6540	8.9228	9.4872	10.089	11.067	12.916
8	8.2857	8.5830	8.8923	9.2142	9.5491	9.8975	10.260	10.637	11.436	12.300	13.727	16.499
9	9.3685	9.7546	10.159	10.583	11.027	11.491	11.978	12.488	13.579	14.776	16.786	20.799
10	10.462	10.950	11.464	12.006	12.578	13.181	13.816	14.487	15.937	17.549	20.304	25.959
11	11.567	12.169	12.808	13.486	14.207	14.972	15.784	16.645	18.531	20.655	24.349	32.150
12	12.683	13.412	14.192	15.026	15.917	16.870	17.888	18.977	21.384	24.133	29.002	39.581
13	13.809	14.680	15.618	16.627	17.713	18.882	20.141	21.495	24.523	28.029	34.352	48.497
14	14.947	15.974	17.086	18.292	19.599	21.015	22.550	24.215	27.975	32.393	40.505	59.196
15	16.097	17.293	18.599	20.024	21.579	23.276	25.129	27.152	31.772	37.280	47.580	72.035
16	17.258	18.639	20.157	21.825	23.657	25.673	27.888	30.324	35.950	42.753	55.717	87.442
17	18.430	20.012	21.762	23.698	25.840	28.213	30.840	33.750	40.545	48.884	65.075	105.93
18	19.615	21.412	23.414	25.645	28.132	30.906	33.999	37.450	45.599	55.750	75.836	128.12
19	20.811	22.841	25.117	27.671	30.539	33.760	37.379	41.446	51.159	63.440	88.212	154.74
20	22.019	24.297	26.870	29.778	33.066	36.786	40.995	45.762	57.275	72.052	102.44	186.69
21	23.239	25.783	28.676	31.969	35.719	39.993	44.865	50.423	64.002	81.699	118.81	225.03
22	24.472	27.299	30.537	34.248	38.505	43.392	49.006	55.457	71.403	92.503	137.63	271.03
23	25.716	28.845	32.453	36.618	41.430	46.996	53.436	60.893	79.543	104.60	159.28	326.24
24	26.973	30.422	34.426	39.083	44.502	50.816	58.177	66.765	88.497	118.16	184.17	392.48
25	28.243	32.030	36.459	41.646	47.727	54.865	63.249	73.106	98.347	133.33	212.79	471.98
26	29.526	33.671	38.553	44.312	51.113	59.156	68.676	79.954	109.18	150.33	245.71	567.38
27	30.821	35.344	40.710	47.084	54.669	63.706	74.484	87.351	121.10	169.37	283.57	681.85
28	32.129	37.051	42.931	49.968	58.403	68.528	80.698	95.339	134.21	190.70	327.10	819.22
29	33.450	38.792	45.219	52.966	62.323	73.640	87.347	103.97	148.63	214.58	377.17	984.07
30	34.785	40.568	47.575	56.085	66.439	79.058	94.461	113.28	164.49	241.33	434.75	1181.9
35	41.660	49.994	60.462	73.652	90.320	111.43	138.24	172.32	271.02	431.66	881.17	2948.3
40	48.886	60.402	75.401	95.026	120.80	154.76	199.64	259.06	442.59	767.09	1779.1	7343.9
45	56.481	71.893	92.720	121.03	159.70	212.74	285.75	386.51	718.90	1358.2	3585.1	18281
50	64.463	84.579	112.80	152.67	209.35	290.34	406.53	573.77	1163.9	2400.0	7217.7	45497
55	72.852	98.587	136.07	191.16	272.71	394.17	575.93	848.92	1880.6	4236.0	14524.	113219
60	81.670	114.05	163.05	237.99	353.58	533.13	813.52	1253.2	3034.8	7471.6	29220.	281733

Interest Tables for
Continuous Compounding

Given P, Find F (cspcaf)

Period	1%	2%	3%	4%	5%	6%	7%	8%	10%	12%	15%	20%
¼	1.0025	1.0050	1.0075	1.0101	1.0126	1.0151	1.0177	1.0202	1.0253	1.0305	1.0382	1.0513
½	1.0050	1.0101	1.0151	1.0202	1.0253	1.0305	1.0356	1.0408	1.0513	1.0618	1.0779	1.1052
¾	1.0075	1.0151	1.0228	1.0305	1.0382	1.0460	1.0539	1.0618	1.0779	1.0942	1.1191	1.1618
1	1.0101	1.0202	1.0305	1.0408	1.0513	1.0618	1.0725	1.0833	1.1052	1.1275	1.1618	1.2214
2	1.0202	1.0408	1.0618	1.0833	1.1052	1.1275	1.1503	1.1735	1.2214	1.2712	1.3499	1.4918
3	1.0305	1.0618	1.0942	1.1275	1.1618	1.1972	1.2337	1.2712	1.3499	1.4333	1.5683	1.8221
4	1.0408	1.0833	1.1275	1.1735	1.2214	1.2712	1.3231	1.3771	1.4918	1.6161	1.8221	2.2255
5	1.0513	1.1052	1.1618	1.2214	1.2840	1.3499	1.4191	1.4918	1.6487	1.8221	2.1170	2.7183
6	1.0618	1.1275	1.1972	1.2712	1.3499	1.4333	1.5220	1.6161	1.8221	2.0544	2.4596	3.3201
7	1.0725	1.1503	1.2337	1.3231	1.4191	1.5220	1.6323	1.7507	2.0138	2.3164	2.8577	4.0552
8	1.0833	1.1735	1.2712	1.3771	1.4918	1.6161	1.7507	1.8965	2.2255	2.6117	3.3201	4.9530
9	1.0942	1.1972	1.3100	1.4333	1.5683	1.7160	1.8776	2.0544	2.4596	2.9447	3.8574	6.0496
10	1.1052	1.2214	1.3499	1.4918	1.6487	1.8221	2.0138	2.2255	2.7183	3.3201	4.4817	7.3891
11	1.1163	1.2461	1.3910	1.5527	1.7333	1.9348	2.1598	2.4109	3.0042	3.7434	5.2070	9.0250
12	1.1275	1.2712	1.4333	1.6161	1.8221	2.0544	2.3164	2.6117	3.3201	4.2207	6.0496	11.023
13	1.1388	1.2969	1.4770	1.6820	1.9155	2.1815	2.4843	2.8292	3.6693	4.7588	7.0287	13.464
14	1.1503	1.3231	1.5220	1.7507	2.0138	2.3164	2.6645	3.0649	4.0552	5.3656	8.1662	16.445
15	1.1618	1.3499	1.5683	1.8221	2.1170	2.4596	2.8577	3.3201	4.4817	6.0496	9.4877	20.086
16	1.1735	1.3771	1.6161	1.8965	2.2255	2.6117	3.0649	3.5966	4.9530	6.8210	11.023	24.533
17	1.1853	1.4049	1.6653	1.9739	2.3396	2.7732	3.2871	3.8962	5.4739	7.6906	12.807	29.964
18	1.1972	1.4333	1.7160	2.0544	2.4596	2.9447	3.5254	4.2207	6.0496	8.6711	14.880	36.598
19	1.2092	1.4623	1.7683	2.1383	2.5857	3.1268	3.7810	4.5722	6.6859	9.7767	17.288	44.701
20	1.2214	1.4918	1.8221	2.2255	2.7183	3.3201	4.0552	4.9530	7.3891	11.023	20.086	54.598
21	1.2337	1.5220	1.8776	2.3164	2.8577	3.5254	4.3492	5.3656	8.1662	12.429	23.336	66.686
22	1.2461	1.5527	1.9348	2.4109	3.0042	3.7434	4.6646	5.8124	9.0250	14.013	27.113	81.451
23	1.2586	1.5841	1.9937	2.5093	3.1582	3.9749	5.0028	6.2965	9.9742	15.800	31.500	99.484
24	1.2712	1.6161	2.0544	2.6117	3.3201	4.2207	5.3656	6.8210	11.023	17.814	36.598	121.51
25	1.2840	1.6487	2.1170	2.7183	3.4903	4.4817	5.7546	7.3891	12.182	20.086	42.521	148.41
26	1.2969	1.6820	2.1815	2.8292	3.6693	4.7588	6.1719	8.0045	13.464	22.646	49.402	181.27
27	1.3100	1.7160	2.2479	2.9447	3.8574	5.0531	6.6194	8.6711	14.880	25.534	57.397	221.41
28	1.3231	1.7507	2.3164	3.0649	4.0552	5.3656	7.0993	9.3933	16.445	28.789	66.686	270.43
29	1.3364	1.7860	2.3869	3.1899	4.2631	5.6973	7.6141	10.176	18.174	32.460	77.478	330.30
30	1.3499	1.8221	2.4596	3.3201	4.4817	6.0496	8.1662	11.023	20.086	36.598	90.017	403.43
35	1.4191	2.0138	2.8577	4.0552	5.7546	8.1662	11.588	16.445	33.115	66.686	190.57	1096.6
40	1.4918	2.2255	3.3201	4.9530	7.3891	11.023	16.445	24.533	54.598	121.51	403.43	2981.0
45	1.5683	2.4596	3.8574	6.0496	9.4877	14.880	23.336	36.598	90.017	221.41	854.06	8103.1
50	1.6487	2.7183	4.4817	7.3891	12.182	20.086	33.115	54.598	148.41	403.43	1808.0	22026
55	1.7333	3.0042	5.2070	9.0250	15.643	27.113	46.993	81.451	244.69	735.10	3827.6	59874
60	1.8221	3.3201	6.0496	11.023	20.086	36.598	66.686	121.51	403.43	1339.4	8103.1	162755

Given F, Find P (csppwf)

Period	1%	2%	3%	4%	5%	6%	7%	8%	10%	12%	15%	20%
¼	0.9975	0.9950	0.9925	0.9900	0.9876	0.9851	0.9827	0.9802	0.9753	0.9704	0.9632	0.9512
½	0.9950	0.9900	0.9851	0.9802	0.9753	0.9704	0.9656	0.9608	0.9512	0.9418	0.9277	0.9048
¾	0.9925	0.9851	0.9778	0.9704	0.9632	0.9560	0.9489	0.9418	0.9277	0.9139	0.8936	0.8607
1	0.9900	0.9802	0.9704	0.9608	0.9512	0.9418	0.9324	0.9231	0.9048	0.8869	0.8607	0.8187
2	0.9802	0.9608	0.9418	0.9231	0.9048	0.8869	0.8694	0.8521	0.8187	0.7866	0.7408	0.6703
3	0.9704	0.9418	0.9139	0.8869	0.8607	0.8353	0.8106	0.7866	0.7408	0.6977	0.6376	0.5488
4	0.9608	0.9231	0.8869	0.8521	0.8187	0.7866	0.7558	0.7261	0.6703	0.6188	0.5488	0.4493
5	0.9512	0.9048	0.8607	0.8187	0.7788	0.7408	0.7047	0.6703	0.6065	0.5488	0.4724	0.3679
6	0.9418	0.8869	0.8353	0.7866	0.7408	0.6977	0.6570	0.6188	0.5488	0.4868	0.4066	0.3012
7	0.9324	0.8694	0.8106	0.7558	0.7047	0.6570	0.6126	0.5712	0.4966	0.4317	0.3499	0.2466
8	0.9231	0.8521	0.7866	0.7261	0.6703	0.6188	0.5712	0.5273	0.4493	0.3829	0.3012	0.2019
9	0.9139	0.8353	0.7634	0.6977	0.6376	0.5827	0.5326	0.4868	0.4066	0.3396	0.2592	0.1653
10	0.9048	0.8187	0.7408	0.6703	0.6065	0.5488	0.4966	0.4493	0.3679	0.3012	0.2231	0.1353
11	0.8958	0.8025	0.7189	0.6440	0.5769	0.5169	0.4630	0.4148	0.3329	0.2671	0.1920	0.1108
12	0.8869	0.7866	0.6977	0.6188	0.5488	0.4868	0.4317	0.3829	0.3012	0.2369	0.1653	0.0907
13	0.8781	0.7711	0.6771	0.5945	0.5220	0.4584	0.4025	0.3535	0.2725	0.2101	0.1423	0.0743
14	0.8694	0.7558	0.6570	0.5712	0.4966	0.4317	0.3753	0.3263	0.2466	0.1864	0.1225	0.0608
15	0.8607	0.7408	0.6376	0.5488	0.4724	0.4066	0.3499	0.3012	0.2231	0.1653	0.1054	0.0498
16	0.8521	0.7261	0.6188	0.5273	0.4493	0.3829	0.3263	0.2780	0.2019	0.1466	0.0907	0.0408
17	0.8437	0.7118	0.6005	0.5066	0.4274	0.3606	0.3042	0.2567	0.1827	0.1300	0.0781	0.0334
18	0.8353	0.6977	0.5827	0.4868	0.4066	0.3396	0.2837	0.2369	0.1653	0.1153	0.0672	0.0273
19	0.8270	0.6839	0.5655	0.4677	0.3867	0.3198	0.2645	0.2187	0.1496	0.1023	0.0578	0.0224
20	0.8187	0.6703	0.5488	0.4493	0.3679	0.3012	0.2466	0.2019	0.1353	0.0907	0.0498	0.0183
21	0.8106	0.6570	0.5326	0.4317	0.3499	0.2837	0.2299	0.1864	0.1225	0.0805	0.0429	0.0150
22	0.8025	0.6440	0.5169	0.4148	0.3329	0.2671	0.2144	0.1720	0.1108	0.0714	0.0369	0.0123
23	0.7945	0.6313	0.5016	0.3985	0.3166	0.2516	0.1999	0.1588	0.1003	0.0633	0.0317	0.0101
24	0.7866	0.6188	0.4868	0.3829	0.3012	0.2369	0.1864	0.1466	0.0907	0.0561	0.0273	0.0082
25	0.7788	0.6065	0.4724	0.3679	0.2865	0.2231	0.1738	0.1353	0.0821	0.0498	0.0235	0.0067
26	0.7711	0.5945	0.4584	0.3535	0.2725	0.2101	0.1620	0.1249	0.0743	0.0442	0.0202	0.0055
27	0.7634	0.5827	0.4449	0.3396	0.2592	0.1979	0.1511	0.1153	0.0672	0.0392	0.0174	0.0045
28	0.7558	0.5712	0.4317	0.3263	0.2466	0.1864	0.1409	0.1065	0.0608	0.0347	0.0150	0.0037
29	0.7483	0.5599	0.4190	0.3135	0.2346	0.1755	0.1313	0.0983	0.0550	0.0308	0.0129	0.0030
30	0.7408	0.5488	0.4066	0.3012	0.2231	0.1653	0.1225	0.0907	0.0498	0.0273	0.0111	0.0025
35	0.7047	0.4966	0.3499	0.2466	0.1738	0.1225	0.0863	0.0608	0.0302	0.0150	0.0052	0.0009
40	0.6703	0.4493	0.3012	0.2019	0.1353	0.0907	0.0608	0.0408	0.0183	0.0082	0.0025	0.0003
45	0.6376	0.4066	0.2592	0.1653	0.1054	0.0672	0.0429	0.0273	0.0111	0.0045	0.0012	0.0001
50	0.6065	0.3679	0.2231	0.1353	0.0821	0.0498	0.0302	0.0183	0.0067	0.0025	0.0006	0.0000
55	0.5769	0.3329	0.1920	0.1108	0.0639	0.0369	0.0213	0.0123	0.0041	0.0014	0.0003	0.0000
60	0.5488	0.3012	0.1653	0.0907	0.0498	0.0273	0.0150	0.0082	0.0025	0.0007	0.0001	0.0000

Given A, Find P (cpwf)

Period	1%	2%	3%	4%	5%	6%	7%	8%	10%	12%	15%	20%
¼	0.2484	0.2469	0.2453	0.2438	0.2423	0.2408	0.2393	0.2377	0.2348	0.2318	0.2274	0.2203
½	0.4963	0.4925	0.4889	0.4852	0.4816	0.4779	0.4744	0.4708	0.4637	0.4568	0.4465	0.4298
¾	0.7435	0.7370	0.7306	0.7242	0.7179	0.7116	0.7054	0.6992	0.6870	0.6751	0.6575	0.6291
1	0.9900	0.9802	0.9704	0.9608	0.9512	0.9418	0.9324	0.9231	0.9048	0.8869	0.8607	0.8187
2	1.9702	1.9410	1.9122	1.8839	1.8561	1.8287	1.8018	1.7753	1.7236	1.6735	1.6015	1.4891
3	2.9407	2.8828	2.8261	2.7708	2.7168	2.6640	2.6123	2.5619	2.4644	2.3712	2.2392	2.0379
4	3.9015	3.8059	3.7131	3.6230	3.5355	3.4506	3.3681	3.2880	3.1347	2.9900	2.7880	2.4872
5	4.8527	4.7107	4.5738	4.4417	4.3143	4.1914	4.0728	3.9584	3.7412	3.5388	3.2603	2.8551
6	5.7945	5.5976	5.4090	5.2283	5.0551	4.8891	4.7299	4.5771	4.2900	4.0256	3.6669	3.1563
7	6.7269	6.4670	6.2196	5.9841	5.7598	5.5461	5.3425	5.1483	4.7866	4.4573	4.0168	3.4029
8	7.6500	7.3191	7.0063	6.7103	6.4301	6.1649	5.9137	5.6756	5.2360	4.8402	4.3180	3.6048
9	8.5639	8.1544	7.7696	7.4079	7.0678	6.7477	6.4463	6.1624	5.6425	5.1798	4.5773	3.7701
10	9.4688	8.9731	8.5104	8.0783	7.6743	7.2965	6.9429	6.6117	6.0104	5.4810	4.8004	3.9054
11	10.365	9.7756	9.2294	8.7223	8.2512	7.8133	7.4059	7.0265	6.3433	5.7481	4.9925	4.0162
12	11.252	10.562	9.9270	9.3411	8.8001	8.3001	7.8376	7.4094	6.6445	5.9850	5.1578	4.1069
13	12.130	11.333	10.604	9.9356	9.3221	8.7585	8.2401	7.7629	6.9170	6.1952	5.3000	4.1812
14	12.999	12.089	11.261	10.507	9.8187	9.1902	8.6154	8.0891	7.1636	6.3815	5.4225	4.2420
15	13.860	12.830	11.899	11.056	10.291	9.5968	8.9654	8.3903	7.3867	6.5468	5.5279	4.2918
16	14.712	13.556	12.518	11.583	10.740	9.9797	9.2916	8.6684	7.5886	6.6934	5.6186	4.3325
17	15.555	14.268	13.118	12.090	11.168	10.340	9.5959	8.9250	7.7713	6.8235	5.6967	4.3659
18	16.391	14.966	13.701	12.576	11.574	10.680	9.8795	9.1620	7.9366	6.9388	5.7639	4.3932
19	17.218	15.649	14.266	13.044	11.961	11.000	10.144	9.3807	8.0862	7.0411	5.8217	4.4156
20	18.036	16.320	14.815	13.493	12.329	11.301	10.391	9.5826	8.2215	7.1318	5.8715	4.4339
21	18.847	16.977	15.348	13.925	12.679	11.585	10.621	9.7689	8.3440	7.2123	5.9144	4.4489
22	19.650	17.621	15.865	14.340	13.012	11.852	10.835	9.9410	8.4548	7.2836	5.9513	4.4612
23	20.444	18.252	16.366	14.738	13.328	12.103	11.035	10.100	8.5550	7.3469	5.9830	4.4713
24	21.231	18.871	16.853	15.121	13.630	12.340	11.221	10.246	8.6458	7.4030	6.0103	4.4795
25	22.010	19.477	17.325	15.489	13.916	12.563	11.395	10.382	8.7278	7.4528	6.0338	4.4862
26	22.781	20.072	17.784	15.843	14.189	12.773	11.557	10.507	8.8021	7.4970	6.0541	4.4917
27	23.544	20.655	18.229	16.182	14.448	12.971	11.708	10.622	8.8693	7.5362	6.0715	4.4963
28	24.300	21.226	18.660	16.508	14.694	13.158	11.849	10.728	8.9301	7.5709	6.0865	4.5000
29	25.048	21.786	19.079	16.822	14.929	13.333	11.980	10.827	8.9852	7.6017	6.0994	4.5030
30	25.789	22.335	19.486	17.123	15.152	13.499	12.103	10.917	9.0349	7.6290	6.1105	4.5055
35	29.384	24.920	21.345	18.461	16.115	14.191	12.601	11.277	9.2212	7.7257	6.1467	4.5125
40	32.803	27.259	22.946	19.556	16.865	14.705	12.953	11.517	9.3342	7.7788	6.1638	4.5151
45	36.056	29.376	24.323	20.453	17.448	15.085	13.201	11.679	9.4027	7.8079	6.1719	4.5161
50	39.151	31.291	25.509	21.187	17.903	15.367	13.375	11.787	9.4443	7.8239	6.1757	4.5165
55	42.094	33.024	26.530	21.788	18.257	15.575	13.498	11.859	9.4695	7.8327	6.1775	4.5166
60	44.894	34.592	27.408	22.280	18.533	15.730	13.585	11.908	9.4848	7.8375	6.1784	4.5166

Given A, Find F (ccaf)

Period	1%	2%	3%	4%	5%	6%	7%	8%	10%	12%	15%	20%
¼	0.2491	0.2481	0.2472	0.2463	0.2453	0.2444	0.2435	0.2426	0.2407	0.2389	0.2361	0.2316
½	0.4988	0.4975	0.4963	0.4950	0.4938	0.4925	0.4913	0.4900	0.4875	0.4850	0.4813	0.4750
¾	0.7491	0.7481	0.7472	0.7462	0.7453	0.7443	0.7434	0.7425	0.7405	0.7386	0.7358	0.7309
1	1.0000	1.0000	1.0000	1.0000	1.0000	1.0000	1.0000	1.0000	1.0000	1.0000	1.0000	1.0000
2	2.0101	2.0202	2.0305	2.0408	2.0513	2.0618	2.0725	2.0833	2.1052	2.1275	2.1618	2.2214
3	3.0303	3.0610	3.0923	3.1241	3.1564	3.1893	3.2228	3.2568	3.3266	3.3987	3.5117	3.7132
4	4.0607	4.1228	4.1865	4.2516	4.3183	4.3866	4.4565	4.5280	4.6764	4.8321	5.0800	5.5353
5	5.1015	5.2061	5.3140	5.4251	5.5397	5.6578	5.7796	5.9052	6.1683	6.4481	6.9021	7.7609
6	6.1528	6.3113	6.4758	6.6465	6.8237	7.0077	7.1987	7.3970	7.8170	8.2703	9.0191	10.479
7	7.2146	7.4388	7.6730	7.9178	8.1736	8.4410	8.7206	9.0131	9.6391	10.325	11.479	13.799
8	8.2871	8.5891	8.9067	9.2409	9.5926	9.9629	10.353	10.764	11.653	12.641	14.336	17.854
9	9.3704	9.7626	10.178	10.618	11.084	11.579	12.104	12.660	13.878	15.253	17.656	22.808
10	10.465	10.960	11.488	12.051	12.653	13.295	13.981	14.715	16.338	18.197	21.514	28.857
11	11.570	12.181	12.838	13.543	14.301	15.117	15.995	16.940	19.056	21.518	25.996	36.246
12	12.686	13.427	14.229	15.096	16.035	17.052	18.155	19.351	22.060	25.261	31.203	45.271
13	13.814	14.699	15.662	16.712	17.857	19.106	20.471	21.963	25.381	29.482	37.252	56.294
14	14.952	15.995	17.139	18.394	19.772	21.288	22.955	24.792	29.050	34.241	44.281	69.758
15	16.103	17.319	18.661	20.145	21.786	23.604	25.620	27.857	33.105	39.606	52.447	86.203
16	17.264	18.668	20.229	21.967	23.903	26.064	28.478	31.177	37.587	45.656	61.935	106.29
17	18.438	20.046	21.845	23.863	26.129	28.676	31.542	34.774	42.540	52.477	72.958	130.82
18	19.623	21.451	23.511	25.837	28.468	31.449	34.829	38.670	48.014	60.167	85.765	160.78
19	20.821	22.884	25.227	27.892	30.928	34.393	38.355	42.891	54.063	68.838	100.64	197.38
20	22.030	24.346	26.995	30.030	33.514	37.520	42.136	47.463	60.749	78.615	117.93	242.08
21	23.251	25.838	28.817	32.255	36.232	40.840	46.191	52.416	68.138	89.638	138.02	296.68
22	24.485	27.360	30.695	34.572	39.090	44.366	50.540	57.781	76.304	102.07	161.35	363.37
23	25.731	28.913	32.629	36.983	42.094	48.109	55.205	63.594	85.330	116.08	188.47	444.82
24	26.990	30.497	34.623	39.492	45.252	52.084	60.208	69.890	95.304	131.88	219.97	544.30
25	28.261	32.113	36.678	42.104	48.572	56.305	65.573	76.711	106.33	149.69	256.57	665.81
26	29.545	33.762	38.795	44.822	52.062	60.786	71.328	84.100	118.51	169.78	299.09	814.23
27	30.842	35.444	40.976	47.651	55.732	65.545	77.500	92.105	131.97	192.43	348.49	995.50
28	32.152	37.160	43.224	50.596	59.589	70.598	84.119	100.78	146.85	217.96	405.89	1216.9
29	33.475	38.910	45.540	53.661	63.644	75.964	91.218	110.17	163.30	246.75	472.57	1487.3
30	34.811	40.696	47.927	56.851	67.907	81.661	98.833	120.34	181.47	279.21	550.05	1817.6
35	41.698	50.182	60.998	74.863	92.735	115.89	146.03	185.44	305.36	515.20	1171.4	4948.6
40	48.937	60.666	76.183	96.862	124.61	162.09	213.01	282.55	509.63	945.20	2486.7	13459
45	56.548	72.253	93.826	123.73	165.55	224.46	308.05	427.42	846.40	1728.7	5271.2	36594
50	64.548	85.058	114.32	156.55	218.11	308.64	442.92	643.54	1401.7	3156.4	11166.	99481
55	72.959	99.210	138.14	196.64	285.59	422.28	634.32	965.95	2317.1	5757.8	23645.	270426
60	81.802	114.85	165.81	245.60	372.25	575.68	905.92	1446.9	3826.4	10498.	50064.	735103

Probability of a Value of $Z = [P - E(P)]/\sigma$ Being Greater Than the Values Tabulated in the Margins

z	.00	.01	.02	.03	.04	.05	.06	.07	.08	.09
.0	.5000	.4960	.4920	.4880	.4840	.4801	.4761	.4721	.4681	.4641
.1	.4602	.4562	.4522	.4483	.4443	.4404	.4364	.4325	.4286	.4247
.2	.4207	.4168	.4129	.4090	.4052	.4013	.3974	.3936	.3897	.3859
.3	.3821	.3783	.3745	.3707	.3669	.3632	.3594	.3557	.3520	.3483
.4	.3446	.3409	.3372	.3336	.3300	.3264	.3228	.3192	.3156	.3121
.5	.3085	.3050	.3015	.2981	.2946	.2912	.2877	.2843	.2810	.2776
.6	.2743	.2709	.2676	.2643	.2611	.2578	.2546	.2514	.2483	.2451
.7	.2420	.2389	.2358	.2327	.2296	.2266	.2236	.2206	.2177	.2148
.8	.2119	.2090	.2061	.2033	.2005	.1977	.1949	.1922	.1894	.1867
.9	.1841	.1814	.1788	.1762	.1736	.1711	.1685	.1660	.1635	.1611
1.0	.1587	.1562	.1539	.1515	.1492	.1469	.1446	.1423	.1401	.1379
1.1	.1357	.1335	.1314	.1292	.1271	.1251	.1230	.1210	.1190	.1170
1.2	.1151	.1131	.1112	.1093	.1075	.1056	.1038	.1020	.1003	.0985
1.3	.0968	.0951	.0934	.0918	.0901	.0885	.0869	.0853	.0838	.0823
1.4	.0808	.0793	.0778	.0764	.0749	.0735	.0721	.0708	.0694	.0681
1.5	.0668	.0655	.0643	.0630	.0648	.0606	.0594	.0582	.0571	.0559
1.6	.0548	.0537	.0526	.0516	.0505	.0495	.0485	.0475	.0465	.0455
1.7	.0446	.0436	.0427	.0418	.0409	.0401	.0392	.0384	.0375	.0367
1.8	.0359	.0351	.0344	.0336	.0329	.0322	.0314	.0307	.0301	.0294
1.9	.0287	.0281	.0274	.0268	.0262	.0256	.0250	.0244	.0239	.0233
2.0	.0228	.0222	.0217	.0212	.0207	.0202	.0197	.0192	.0188	.0183
2.1	.0179	.0174	.0170	.0166	.0162	.0158	.0154	.0150	.0146	.0143
2.2	.0139	.0136	.0132	.0129	.0125	.0122	.0119	.0116	.0113	.0110
2.3	.0107	.0104	.0102	.0099	.0096	.0094	.0091	.0089	.0087	.0084
2.4	.0082	.0080	.0078	.0075	.0073	.0071	.0069	.0068	.0066	.0064
2.5	.0062	.0060	.0059	.0057	.0055	.0054	.0052	.0051	.0049	.0048
2.6	.0047	.0045	.0044	.0043	.0041	.0040	.0039	.0038	.0037	.0036
2.7	.0035	.0034	.0033	.0032	.0031	.0030	.0029	.0028	.0027	.0026
2.8	.0026	.0025	.0024	.0023	.0023	.0022	.0021	.0021	.0020	.0019
2.9	.0019	.0018	.0018	.0017	.0016	.0016	.0015	.0015	.0014	.0014
3.0	.0013	.0013	.0013	.0012	.0012	.0011	.0011	.0011	.0010	.0010
3.1	.0010	.0009	.0009	.0009	.0008	.0008	.0008	.0008	.0007	.0007
3.2	.0007	.0007	.0006	.0006	.0006	.0006	.0006	.0005	.0005	.0005
3.3	.0005	.0005	.0005	.0004	.0004	.0004	.0004	.0004	.0004	.0003
3.4	.0003	.0003	.0003	.0003	.0003	.0003	.0003	.0003	.0003	.0002
3.6	.0002	.0002	.0001	.0001	.0001	.0001	.0001	.0001	.0001	.0001
3.9	.0000									

Present Value of Tax Allowances Related to Depreciation

This appendix discusses the computation of the present value of tax allowances that arise in the case of the two most commonly used methods of depreciation accounting—the reducing balance and straight line depreciation methods. In addition, related percentages of investment and initial allowances are taken into account.

Let us first consider the present value P' of tax allowances related to the reducing balance method of depreciation:

$$P' = pC(U + S + d) + pdCm/(1 + i) + pdCm(1 - d)/(1 + i)^2 + \cdots$$
$$+ pdCm(1 - d)^{n-1}/(1 + i)^n + p(W - V)/(1 + i)^n \qquad (1)$$

where

p = percentage rate of tax
C = initial capital cost
U = percentage investment allowance
S = percentage initial allowance
d = percentage rate of depreciation
m = $(1 - S - d)$
i = interest rate
n = life of the asset in years
W = written-down value at end of year n
V = the lower of the resale value at end of year n and C.

The first, second, third, and next-to-last terms of expression (1) represent tax allowances in years 1, 2, 3, and n, respectively. Thus, tax relief is assumed to arise at annual intervals from the purchase of the asset.

At the time of the purchase of the asset (the start of the first year), a firm is allowed as an expense for tax purposes $(U + S + d)\%$ of the capital cost C. Each dollar of depreciation saves the firm tax at the rate p. Thus, the tax saved in the first year is $pC(U + S + d)$. The written-down value of the asset for tax purposes is then the capital cost C less the initial and annual allowance or $C(1 - S - d) = Cm$. At the end of the first year, the firm is allowed for its annual tax depreciation the percentage d of the written-down value Cm. Consequently, the tax saving is $pdCm$. The written-down value considered for tax purposes at the end of the second year becomes $Cm(1 - d)$, at the end of the third year $Cm(1 - d)^2$, and at the end of the nth year $Cm(1 - d)^{n-1}$.

We therefore have:

$$P' = pC[(U + S + d) + pwf(i=k\%, n=n) \cdot dm/(1 - d)] + p(W - V)/(1 + i)^n \quad (2)$$

where $k = (i + d)/(1 - d)$ or $(1 - d)/(1 + i) = 1/(1 + k)$.

The balance allowance or charge $(W - V)$ is the difference between $W = Cm(1 - d)^n$ and V. Consequently, the present value of the balancing allowance or charge is:

$$p\{Cm(1 - d)^n - V\}/(1 + i)^n = pCm(1 - d)^n/(1 + i)^n - pV/(1 + i)^n = pCm/(1 + k)^n - pV/(1 + i)^n.$$

Substituting this expression for $p(W - V)/(1 + i)^n$ in expression (2) and allowing for an average delay of q years between capital expenditure and receipt of tax relief from capital allowances, results in:

$$P' = [pC/(1 + i)^q] \cdot [(U + S + d) + \{pwf(k, n) + sppwf(k, n)(1 - d)/d\}dm/(1 - d) \\ - V/C(1 + i)^n]. \quad (3)$$

Expression (3) represents the present value of tax savings resulting from the use of the reducing balance depreciation method. The terms $pwf(k, n)$ and $sppwf(k, n)$ are defined in Appendix 1.

Following the same line of reasoning, we arrive at expression (4) which represents the present value of tax savings resulting from the use of the straight-line depreciation method.

$$P'' = [pC/(1 + i)^q] \cdot \{(U + S + d) + d \cdot pwf(i, n) \\ + [(1 - S - nd) - V/C]sppwf(i, n)\} \quad (4)$$

where all symbols are as defined before.

Note that expressions (3) and (4) allow for delays between capital expenditure and receipt of tax relief from capital allowances through the variable q. These delays frequently occur, and may amount to one or two years. With high values of the interest rate i, the effect of such delays should not be ignored. Naturally, if delays do not occur, we simply fill out $q = 0$ or $1/(1 + i)^{q=0} = 1$ in the above expressions.

The variable U or the percentage investment allowance is the right to set against corporate taxes a given proportion of the initial cost of an asset. Governments who use investment allowances as incentives do not require companies to depreciate the asset by this amount for the purpose of computing other future tax-allowable depreciation charges. Naturally, the variable U is set equal to zero in expressions (3) and (4) if investment allowances do not exist.

The variable S or the percentage initial allowance is a special allowance permitting an asset to be depreciated for tax purposes by an exceptionally large amount in the first year compared to subsequent years. It is evident that the percentage initial allowance reduces the amount of future tax-allowable depreciation.

The variable V relates to balancing allowances or charges. That is, when an asset is disposed of by a firm at a price below its written-down tax value, then a tax allowance is made in respect of the difference. However, a balancing charge is made on the difference between selling price and the written-down value, if the selling price is higher than this value. Expressions (3) and (4) assume that the balancing charge is restricted to the difference between net initial cost and written-down value if the selling price exceeds the initial cost. This is the practice of most governments.

The variable d (or the percentage rate of depreciation) represents the annual allowances or the annual amounts by which an asset may be depreciated for tax purposes. These amounts are computed on initial capital cost less initial allowance, if applicable. Expressions (3) and (4) contain annual depreciation for tax purposes on the basis of an asset's written-down value at the end of the preceding year (that is, the reducing balance method) and on the basis of straight-line depreciation, respectively.

Index

About the Author

HENRI L. BEENHAKKER is a principal economist at the World Bank and Adjunct Professor, School of Advanced International Studies, Johns Hopkins University. With professional experience in economics, finance, and engineering, he has assisted major industrial and governmental organizations here and abroad in their long-range planning. Dr. Beenhakker has served as Chairman, Department of Industrial Management, University of Iowa, and was also employed by Stanford Research Institute. He is the author of four textbooks and more than 35 articles published in leading business and economics journals.

ISBN 1-56720-028-1

9 781567 200287

EAN

90000>

HARDCOVER BAR CODE